VITAL RECORDS

OF

BELFAST

MAINE

TO THE YEAR 1892

VOLUME I — BIRTHS

EDITOR
ALFRED JOHNSON, A.M., LITT.D.

COMMITTEE ON PUBLICATION
HENRY SEWALL WEBSTER, A.M.   ALFRED JOHNSON, A.M., LITT.D.

Southern Historical Press, Inc.
Greenville, South Carolina

This volume was reproduced
from a personal copy located in
the Publishers private library

All rights reserved. No part of this publication may be reproduced,
stored in a retrieval system, transmitted in any form, posted
on the web in any form or by any means without the
prior written permission of the publisher.

Please direct all correspondence and book orders to:
SOUTHERN HISTORICAL PRESS, Inc.
1071 Park West Blvd.
Greenville, SC 29611

Published 1917 by:
  Maine Historical Society
ISBN #978-1-63914-642-0
Printed in the United States of America

THE SHIRE TOWN OF BELFAST was first settled in 1770 by persons from Londonderry, N. H., and was incorporated June 22, 1773. The settlement was broken up by the British in 1779, and was re-established in 1784.

In 1845 a portion of the town, with a part of Prospect, was incorporated as Searsport.

In 1853 the city charter was adopted.

Population by Census:

1776 (Prov.), 229;
1790 (U.S.), 245;
1800 (U.S.), 674;
1810 (U.S.), 1274;
1820 (U.S.), 2026;
1830 (U.S.), 1377;
1840 (U.S.), 4194;
1850 (U.S.), 5052;
1860 (U.S.), 5520;
1870 (U.S.), 5278;
1880 (U.S.), 5308;
1890 (U.S.), 5294;
1900 (U.S.), 4615;
1910 (U.S.), 4618.

EXPLANATIONS

1. The fact that a birth, marriage, or death is recorded in Belfast does not prove that it occurred in this town; but when places other than Belfast and Maine are named in the original records, they are given in the printed copy.

2. In all items from town records the original spelling is followed, and no attempt is made to correct errors appearing in the records.

3. The various spellings of a name should be examined, as items about the same family or individual may be found under different spellings.

4. A baptism is not printed, if it occurs within one year after the recorded date of birth of a child of the same name and parents or if it is clear that the child baptized is identical with the child of the birth record; but variations found in the baptismal record are added to the birth record.

5. The birth of a married woman is recorded under her maiden name, if it is known. But if the maiden name cannot be determined, the entry appears under the husband's name, with a dash enclosed in brackets, i.e., [———], to signify that the maiden name is unknown. If it is not known whether the surname is that of a married or unmarried woman, ? m. is placed in brackets after the Christian name.

6. Marriages and intentions of marriage are printed under the names of both parties. When both the marriage and intention of marriage are recorded, only the marriage record is printed; and where a marriage appears without the intention being recorded, it is designated with an asterisk.

7. Additional information which does not appear in the original text of an item, i.e., any explanation, query, inference, or difference shown in other entries of the record, is bracketed. Parentheses are used to show variations in the spelling of a name in the same entry, to indicate the maiden name of a wife, to enclose an imperfect portion of the original text, and to separate clauses in the original text.

ABBREVIATIONS

a. — age
abt. — about
b. — born
bp. — baptized
bur. — buried
ch. — child
chn. — children
C.R.1. — church record, Unitarian Church
C.R.2. — church record, Congregational Church
C.R.3. — church record, Methodist Episcopal Church
C.R.4. — church record, Baptist Church
Co. — county
CO.R. — county record
d. — daughter; day; died
Dea. — deacon
dec'd — deceased
dup. — duplicate entry
Ens. — Ensign
G.R.1. — gravestone record, Grove Cemetery
G.R.2. — gravestone record, North Belfast Cemetery
G.R.3. — gravestone record, City Point Cemetery
G.R.4. — gravestone record, West Belfast Cemetery
G.R.5. — gravestone record, East Side Cemetery
G.R.6. — gravestone record, Gordon Cemetery, Searsport
G.R.7. — gravestone record, Evergreen Cemetery
G.R.8. — gravestone record, West Belfast Cemetery, Centre Belmont road
G.R.9. — gravestone record, private burial ground on Redman Road, West Belfast
G.R.10. — gravestone record, private burial ground on Elijah Knowlton's farm, West Belfast
G.R.11. — gravestone record, private burial ground on east side of Redman Road, West Belfast
G.R.12. — gravestone record, private burial ground on Samuel Bateman's farm, West Belfast
G.R.13. — gravestone record, South Belfast Cemetery

G.R.14. — gravestone record, Russ Cemetery, City Point
h. — husband
hrs. — hours
inf. — infant
int. — publishment of intention of marriage
Jr. — junior
Lt. — Lieutenant
m. — married; month
min. — minutes
P.R.1. — private record, from a Johnson family Bible, now in the possession of Alfred Johnson of Brookline, Mass., and Belfast
P.R.2. — private record, from the Edward Wight family Bible, now in the possession of James C. Durham of Belfast
P.R.3. — private record, from the Joseph Wight family Bible, now in the possession of James C. Durham of Belfast
P.R.4. — private record, from the Franklin H. Durham family Bible, now in the possession of James C. Durham of Belfast
P.R.5. — private record, from the family Bible of John W. Ferguson of Belfast, now in his possession
P.R.6. — private record, from the Jonathan Durham family Bible, now in the possession of Miss Mildred Black of Belfast
P.R.7. — private record, from a Ferguson family record, now in the possession of Miss Jane W. Ferguson of Belfast
P.R.8. — private record, from the John S. Osborn family Bible, now in the possession of Capt. George T. Osborne of Belfast
P.R.9. — private record, from the Alonzo Osborn family Bible, now in the possession of Capt. George T. Osborne of Belfast
P.R.10. — private record, from the John Ryan family Bible, now in the possession of Mrs. George F. Ryan of Belfast
P.R.11. — private record, from a Patterson family Bible, now in the possession of Mrs. George W. Pattershall of Belfast
P.R.12. — private record, from a Pattershall family Bible, now in the possession of Melvin Pattershall of Belfast
P.R.13. — private record, from an Otis family Bible, now in the possession of Miss Martha Jane Otis of Belfast

P.R.14. — private record, from an Otis-Nickerson family Bible, now in the possession of Miss Martha Jane Otis of Belfast

P.R.15. — private record, from a Nickerson family Bible, now in the possession of Miss Martha Jane Otis of Belfast

P.R.16. — private record, from the Jonathan Ferguson family record, now in the possession of Miss Jane W. Ferguson of Belfast

P.R.17. — private record, from the Moses Wason Ferguson family record, now in the possession of Miss Jane W. Ferguson of Belfast

P.R.18. — private record, from the William Thaxter Colburn family Bible, now in the possession of Miss Charlotte Colburn of Belfast

P.R.19. — private record, from the Colburn-Spring family record, now in the possession of Miss Charlotte Colburn of Belfast

P.R.20. — private record, from the Samuel Spring family record, now in the possession of Miss Charlotte Colburn of Belfast

P.R.21. — private record, from the George A. Miller family Bible, now in the possession of Mrs. Henry C. Marden of Belfast

P.R.22. — private record, from the Nehemiah Abbott family Bible, now in the possession of Mrs. Fannie Horn of Belfast

P.R.23. — private record, from the family Bible of Edgar S. McDonald of Belfast, now in his possession

P.R.24. — private record, from a Brown family record, now in the possession of Miss Emma Wording of Belfast

P.R.25. — private record, from the Calvin Hervey family Bible, now in the possession of Mrs. Calvin Hervey of Belfast

P.R.26. — private record, from the Charles B. Hazeltine family Bible, now in the possession of Mrs. Charles B. Hazeltine of Belfast

P.R.27. — private record, from a Smalley family Bible, now in the possession of Alexander D. Smalley of Belfast

P.R.28. — private record, from the family Bible of Alexander D. Smalley of Belfast, now in his possession

P.R.29. — private record, from a Holt family Bible, now in the possession of Mrs. Eleanor Orcutt Dyer of Belfast

P.R.30. — private record, from the George Dyer family Bible, now in the possession of Mrs. Eleanor Orcutt Dyer of Belfast

P.R.31. — private record, from the William Holt family Bible, now in the possession of William P. Holt of Belfast

P.R.32. — private record, from the Richard Holt family Bible, now in the possession of Mrs. C. F. Wyman of Belfast

P.R.33. — private record, from the Miles S. Staples family Bible, now in the possession of Basil Herbert Staples Newell of Belfast

P.R.34. — private record, from the Rufus P. Hassell family Bible, now in the possession of Mrs. Fred P. Nason of Belfast

P.R.35. — private record, from the family Bible of Otis K. Ryder of Belfast, now in his possession

P.R.36. — private record, from the David Robinson family Bible, now in the possession of Benjamin Robinson of Belfast

P.R.37. — private record, from the family Bible of Benjamin Robinson of Belfast, now in his possession

P.R.38. — private record, from the Warren E. Marsh family Bible, now in the possession of Mrs. Warren E. Marsh of Belfast

P.R.39. — private record, from the James Bucklin family Bible, now in the possession of Leon O. Bucklin of Belfast

P.R.40. — private record, from the Enoch C. Hilton family Bible, now in the possession of Mrs. Enoch C. Hilton of Belfast

P.R.41. — private record, from the William O. Cunningham family Bible, now in the possession of Harvey S. Cunningham of Belfast

P.R.42. — private record, from the family Bible of Harvey S. Cunningham of Belfast, now in his possession

P.R.43. — private record, from the John Hassell family Bible, now in the possession of Mrs. John Hassell Jackson of Belfast

P.R.44. — private record, from the Russ family Bible, now in the possession of Ralph D. Shute of Belfast

P.R.45. — private record, from the Alonzo Shute family Bible, now in the possession of Ralph D. Shute of Belfast

P.R.46. — private record, from the Joseph McKeen family Bible, now in the possession of Mrs. George E. Havener of Belfast

P.R.47. — private record, from a Shuman family Bible, now in the possession of Elijah S. Shuman of Belfast

P.R.48. — private record, from the Elijah M. Shuman family Bible, now in the possession of Mrs. Otis K. Ryder of Belfast

P.R.49. — private record, from the Benjamin P. Ryder family Bible, now in the possession of Otis K. Ryder of Belfast

P.R.50. — private record, from the William F. Triggs family Bible, now in the possession of Mrs. William F. Triggs of Belfast

P.R.51. — private record, from the David Burgess family record, now in the possession of Mrs. Lydia Ann Burgess of Belfast

P.R.52. — private record, from the Horace S. Perkins family Bible, now in the possession of Mrs. Horace S. Perkins of Belfast

P.R.53. — private record, from the Benjamin T. Black family Bible, now in the possession of Miss Mildred Black of Belfast

P.R.54. — private record, from the Henry J. Chaples family Bible, now in the possession of Miss Florence D. Chaples of Belfast

P.R.55. — private record, from the family Bible of Dr. Augustine O. Stoddard of Belfast, now in his possession

P.R.56. — private record, from the Samuel W. Miller family record, now in the possession of Mrs. James F. McKeen of Belfast

P.R.57. — private record, from a Patterson family Bible, now in the possession of Charles B. Eaton of Belfast

P.R.58. — private record, from a Chaples family Bible, now in the possession of Miss Sarah Chaples of Belfast

P.R.59. — private record, from the Samuel W. Miller family Bible, now in the possession of Mrs. Annabelle (Miller) Underwood of Belfast

P.R.60. — private record, from the John Nelson Stewart family Bible, now in the possession of Mrs. John Nelson Stewart of Belfast

P.R.61. — private record, from the Eben P. Bramhall family record, now in the possession of Mrs. Eli Cook of Belfast

P.R.62. — private record, from the George W. Speed family Bible, now in the possession of Mrs. Thomas D. Barr of Belfast

P.R.63. — private record, from the Simeon A. Heath family Bible, now in the possession of Mrs. Spencer W. Mathews of Belfast

P.R.64. — private record, from the Spencer W. Mathews family Bible, now in the possession of Mrs. Spencer W. Mathews of Belfast

P.R.65. — private record, from the Edward J. Morison family Bible, now in the possession of Mrs. Spencer W. Mathews of Belfast

P.R.66. — private record, from the Lewis A. Knowlton family Bible, now in the possession of Mrs. Lewis A. Knowlton of Belfast

P.R.67. — private record, from the Charles Pendleton family Bible, now in the possession of Mrs. Lewis A. Knowlton of Belfast

P R.68. — private record, from the Isaac Conant family Bible, now in the possession of Bancroft H. Conant of Belfast

P.R.69. — private record, from the William B. Conant family Bible, now in the possession of Bancroft H. Conant of Belfast

P.R.70. — private record, from the Bible of Isaac A. Conant, now in the possession of Mrs. Ralph H. Howes of Belfast

P.R.71. — private record, from the James Calderwood family Bible, now in the possession of Mrs. Alvin Blodgett of Belfast

P.R.72. — private record, from the James Aborn family Bible, now in the possession of John G. Aborn of Belfast

P.R.73. — private record, from the John Flowers family Bible, now in the possession of Mrs. Eveline H. Gilmore of Belfast

P.R.74. — private record, from the Cyrus Patterson family Bible, now in the possession of Mrs. Henry D. Clark of Belfast

P.R.75. — private record, from the Timothy Chase family Bible, now in the possession of Miss E. Maude Barker of Belfast

P.R.76. — private record, from the David Barker family Bible, now in the possession of Miss E. Maude Barker of Belfast

P.R.77. — private record, from an Allard family Bible, now in the possession of Miss E. Maude Barker of Belfast

P.R.78. — private record, from the Parker-Drinkwater family Bible, now in the possession of T. Frank Parker of Belfast

P.R.79. — private record, from the Lemuel R. Palmer family Bible, now in the possession of Miss Lucy Palmer of Belfast

P.R.80. — private record, from the Capt. Reuben H. Burgess family Bible, now in the possession of Mrs. Lydia Ann Burgess of Belfast

P.R.81. — private record, from the Ebenezer Newell Jr. family Bible, now in the possession of Basil Herbert Staples Newell of Belfast

P.R.82. — private record, from the family Bible of Israel W. Parker of Belfast, now in his possession

P.R.83. — private record, from the Josiah Sanborn family record, now in the possession of Eben M. Sanborn of Belfast

P.R.84. — private record, from the family record of Eben M. Sanborn of Belfast, now in his possession

P.R.85. — private record, from the Dr. Richard Moody family Bible, now in the possession of James H. Howes of Belfast

P.R.86. — private record, from the James H. Howes family Bible, now in the possession of James H. Howes of Belfast

P.R.87. — private record, from the Joseph S. Noyes family Bible, now in the possession of Mrs. William B. Swan of Belfast

P.R.88. — private record, from the Asa Faunce family Bible, now in the possession of Mrs. William B. Swan of Belfast

P.R.89. — private record, from the Sanford H. Mathews family Bible, now in the possession of Mrs. Sanford H. Mathews of Belfast

P.R.90. — private record, from the Rev. William Frothingham family record, now in the possession of Miss Emily Miller of Belfast

P.R.91. — private record, from the Thomas W. Lothrop family Bible, now in the possession of Miss Lois Lothrop of Belfast

P.R.92. — private record, from the Ansel Lothrop family Bible, now in the possession of Miss Lois Lothrop of Belfast

P.R.93. — private record, from the family Bible of Jefferson F. Wilson of Belfast, now in his possession

P.R.94. — private record, from the John Wilson family Bible, now in the possession of Jefferson F. Wilson of Belfast

P.R.95. — private record, from the Wilson-Mahoney family Bible, now in the possession of Mrs. Ida A. Mahoney of Belfast

P.R.96. — private record, from the Capt. Mark Welch family Bible, now in the possession of Capt. William F. Welch of Belfast

P.R.97. — private record, from the Robert H. Coombs family Bible, now in the possession of Charles R. Coombs of Belfast

P.R.98. — private record, from the Robert Coombs family Bible, now in the possession of W. Jordan Coombs of Belfast

P.R.99. — private record, from the George W. Cottrell family Bible, now in the possession of R. Emery Cottrell of Belfast

P.R.100. — private record, from the Bullen-West family Bible, now in the possession of Mrs. William Beckwith of Belfast

P.R.101. — private record, from the William H. Knowlton family Bible, now in the possession of Marcellus R. Knowlton of Belfast

P.R.102. — private record, from the family record of Sanford Howard of Belfast, now in his possession

P.R.103. — private record, from the Asa F. Riggs family Bible, now in the possession of Mrs. Jacob K. Dennett of Belfast

P.R.104. — private record, from the Henry C. Gray family Bible, now in the possession of Mrs. Henry C. Gray of Belfast

P.R.105. — private record, from the Joseph Dennett family Bible, now in the possession of Mrs. Joseph Gilmore of Belfast

P.R.106. — private record, from a copy of the David Gilmore family record, now in the possession of Mrs. Joseph Gilmore of Belfast

P.R.107. — private record, from the Thomas Marshall family Bible, now in the possession of William R. Marshall of Winchester, Mass.

P.R.108. — private record, from a copy of a Lancaster family record, now in the possession of Mrs. Hartson C. Pitcher of Belfast

P.R.109. — private record, from the George I. Mudgett family Bible, now in the possession of Mrs. Jennie Mudgett of Belfast

P.R.110. — private record, from the Benjamin Cunningham family Bible, now in the possession of George W. Davis of Belfast

P.R.111. — private record, from the Thomas A. Beckwith family Bible, now in the possession of Alonzo Beckwith of Belfast

P.R.112. — private record, from the John Peirce family Bible, now in the possession of the heirs of Mrs. Frank Peirce of Belfast

P.R.113. — private record, from the Willard P. Harriman family Bible, now in the possession of Miss Abbie Stoddard of Belfast

P.R.114. — private record, from the Stephen G. Bicknell family Bible, now in the possession of Mrs. Alice B. Macdonald of Belfast

P.R.115. — private record, from the Henry Dunbar family Bible, now in the possession of Mrs. Henry Dunbar of Belfast

P.R.116. — private record, from the Henry A. Starrett family record, now in the possession of Mrs. Annie Craig of Belfast

P.R.117. — private record, from a Gammans family Bible, now in the possession of Miss Maud Gammans of Belfast

P.R.118. — private record, from the Phineas P. Quimby family Bible, now in the possession of Mrs. Augusta Frederick of Belfast

P.R.119. — private record, from the John Tufts Patterson family Bible, now in the possession of Mrs. Aurelia P. Goud of Caribou

P.R.120. — private record, from the James Woodbury Frederick family Bible, now in the possession of Mrs. Augusta Frederick of Belfast

P.R.121. — private record, from the Nathaniel Bradbury family Bible, now in the possession of Charles W. Frederick of Belfast

P.R.122. — private record, from the William Frederick family Bible, now in the possession of Jabez Frederick of Brookline, Mass.

P.R.123. — private record, from the manuscript day book of Dr. Nahum Parker Munroe, now in the possession of Alfred Johnson of Brookline, Mass., and Belfast

P.R.124. — private record, from the Levi Lindley Robbins family record, now in the possession of Mrs. Frank Wallace Chase of Newtonville, Mass.

P.R.125. — private record, from the Samuel L. Sweetser family Bible, now in the possession of Miss Grace Walton of Belfast

P.R.126. — private record, from the John Walton family Bible, now in the possession of Miss Grace Walton of Belfast

P.R.127. — private record, from the Joseph Kaler Bennett family Bible, now in the possession of Mrs. Marcella Kaler Bennett of Belfast

P.R.128. — private record, from the Joseph H. Kaler family Bible, now in the possession of Mrs. Marcella Kaler Bennett of Belfast

P.R.129. — private record, from the Joshua Eustis Partridge family record, now in the possession of Miss Sue M. Partridge of Belfast

P.R.130. — private record, from the Robert R. Swett family Bible, now in the possession of Mrs. Lizzie M. Cunningham of Belfast

P.R.131. — private record, from the James H. Cunningham family Bible, now in the possession of Mrs. Lizzie M. Cunningham of Belfast

P.R.132. — private record, from the John Maddocks family record, now in the possession of Mrs. George F. Ryan of Belfast

P.R.133. — private record, from the Christopher Y. Cottrell family record, now in the possession of his son, Christopher Y. Cottrell of Belfast

P.R.134. — private record, from the Christopher Y. Cottrell family Bible, now in the possession of his son, Christopher Y. Cottrell of Belfast

P.R.135. — private record, from the William T. Rogers family Bible, now in the possession of Byron M. Rogers of Belfast

P.R.136. — private record, from the Martin Rogers family record, now in the possession of Byron M. Rogers of Belfast

P.R.137. — private record, from the William C. Tuttle family Bible, now in the possession of Mrs. Georgia Varney of Belfast

P.R.138. — private record, from the James McCrillis family record, now in the possession of Mrs. George C. Trussell of Belfast

P.R.139. — private record, from the Elijah Torrey family Bible, now in the possession of Mrs. James S. Harriman of Belfast

P.R.140. — private record, from the Nathaniel Wells family Bible, now in the possession of George G. Wells of Belfast

P.R.141. — private record, from the William Durham family Bible, now in the possession of Mrs. George G. Wells of Belfast

P.R.142. — private record, from the William Poor family Bible, now in the possession of Clarence Poor of Belfast

P.R.143. — private record, from the William Osgood Poor family Bible, now in the possession of Clarence O. Poor of Belfast

P.R.144. — private record, from the family record of Asa A. Howes of Belfast, now in his possession

P.R.145. — private record, from the Walter B. Rankin family record, now in the possession of Mrs. Elmer Sherman of Belfast

P.R.146. — private record, from the Sherburne Sleeper family Bible, now in the possession of J. Llewellyn Sleeper of Belfast

P.R.147. — private record, from the Daniel Faunce family Bible, now in the possession of Mrs. Hartwell L. Woodcock of Belfast

P.R.148. — private record, from the Robert White family Bible, now in the possession of Mrs. Hartwell L. Woodcock of Belfast

P.R.149. — private record, from the Joshua Bramhall family record, now in the possession of Mrs. Caroline E. Aldus of Belfast

P.R.150. — private record, from the Benjamin Banks family Bible, now in the possession of William A. Banks of Belfast

P.R.151. — private record, from the William M. Woods family Bible, now in the possession of Mrs. Alice Shales Mason of Belfast

P.R.152. — private record, from the Lendal T. Shales family Bible, now in the possession of Mrs. Lendal T. Shales of Belfast

P.R.153. — private record, from the family record of Elisha H. Haney of Belfast, now in the possession of Mrs. Cleora Read of Belfast

P.R.154. — private record, from the William Twombly family Bible, now in the possession of Mrs. Mary Twombly of Belfast

P.R.155. — private record, from the Bohan P. Field family Bible, now in the possession of Ben D. Field of Belfast

P.R.156. — private record, from the John S. Caldwell family register, now in the possession of Mrs. Amos Clement of Belfast

P.R.157. — private record, from the family Bible of Amos Clement of Belfast, now in his possession

P.R.158. — private record, from the Joseph Perkins family Bible, now in the possession of Capt. James H. Perkins of Belfast

P.R.159. — private record, from the Samuel G. Thurlow family record, now in the possession of Mrs. Eliza Harmon of Brewer

P.R.160. — private record, from the Augustus Perry family Bible, now in the possession of Miss Julia Perry of Belfast

P.R.161. — private record, from the Alexander Shibles family Bible, now in the possession of Ralph H. Mosher of Belfast

P.R.162. — private record, from the Fisher A. Pitcher family Bible, now in the possession of Thomas P. Mathews of Liberty

P.R.163. — private record, from the William Ryan family record, now in the possession of Mrs. George F. Ryan of Belfast

p.r.164. — private record, from the Samuel Maddocks family record, now in the possession of Mrs. George F. Ryan of Belfast

p.r.165. — private record, from the Horatio Palmer Thompson family record, now in the possession of Albert Wooster Thompson of Denver, Colo.

p.r.166. — private record, from the Charles Read family record, now in the possession of George Read of Belfast

p.r.167. — private record, from the Alden Marriner family Bible, now in the possession of Mrs. Ada M. Bowman of Belfast

p.r.168. — private record, from the John Burgess family Bible, now in the possession of Mrs. Albert C. Burgess of Belfast

p.r.169. — private record, from the Ezekiel Burgess family Bible, now in the possession of Albert C. Burgess of Belfast

p.r.170. — private record, from the Hiram Chase family Bible, now in the possession of Miss Frances Chase of Belfast

p.r.171. — private record, from the Daniel Sullivan family Bible, now in the possession of John H. Sullivan of Searsport

p.r.172. — private record, from the Calvin Pitcher family Bible, now in the possession of Ellis Pitcher of South Weymouth, Mass.

p.r.173. — private record, from the Martin Stone family Bible, now in the possession of Mrs. Edith S. Walden of Belfast

p.r.174. — private record, from the Henry Lunt Lord family Bible, now in the possession of Maurice W. Lord of Belfast

p.r.175. — private record, from a family record, now in the possession of Mrs. Ada C. Daniels of Newton, Mass.

q.v. — which see; whom see

rec. — recorded

s. — son

Sr. — senior

w. — week; wife

wid. — widow

widr. — widower

y. — year

BELFAST BIRTHS

BELFAST BIRTHS

To the year 1892

ABBOT (see Abbott), Elizabeth, ch. Otho and Lucy, Apr. 1, 1829.
Isaac Coombs, ch. Otho and Lucy, Feb. 28, 1816.
Lucy Ann, ch. Otho and Lucy, Apr. 1, 1824.
William Frederick, ch. Otho and Lucy, Apr. 11, 1822.

ABBOTT (see Abbot), Annie G., w. ——— West, May 15, 1853, G.R.1. [d. Nehemiah and Caroline W. (Belcher), P.R.22.]
C. B., ———, 1851, G.R.1. [Clifford B., s. Nehemiah and Caroline W. (Belcher), Mar. 23, P.R.22.]
Caroline B. (see Carrie B.).
Caroline W. [———], w. Nehemiah, Oct. 18, 1812, G.R.1. [Caroline W. (Belcher), P.R.22.]
Carrie B., Apr. 10, 1837, G.R.1. [Caroline B., d. Nehemiah and Caroline W. (Belcher), in Calais, P.R.22.]
Clifford B. (see C. B.).
Desire G., ch. Ransom and Livonia S., ———, 1865, G.R.1.
Emma F., w. L. F. McDonald, ———, 1841, G.R.1. [w. Lucius F. McDonald, d. Nehemiah and Caroline W. (Belcher), Nov. 17, P.R.22.]
George M., ch. Ransom and Livonia S., ———, 1853, G.R.1.
Henry F., s. Nehemiah and Caroline W. (Belcher), May 14, 1855, P.R.22.
Howard, s. Nehemiah and Caroline W. (Belcher), June 23, 1839, in Calais, P.R.22.
Livonia S. [———], w. Ransom, ———, 1829, G.R.1.
Mary Fuller, inf. Isaac C. and Mary, bp. Oct. 16, 1853, C.R.2.
Nehemiah, h. Caroline W., Mar. 29, 1804, G.R.1. [h. Caroline W. (Belcher), P.R.22.]
Ransom, h. Livonia S., ———, 1820, G.R.1.
———, s. William, July 8, 1848, P.R.123.

ABORN, Alice L., d. James and Sarah J. (Brown), Sept. 5, 1862, in Knox, P.R.72.
Bertrand L., h. Anabell Kenney, s. James and Sarah J. (Brown), Nov. 19, 1867, in Knox, P.R.72.

ABORN, Eugenia L., w. Elbridge Tufts, w. Henry H. Cobbett, d. James and Charlotte M. (Brown), Aug. 6, 1842, in Knox, P.R.72.
Hattie G., d. James and Sarah J. (Brown), Mar. 27, 1865, in Knox, P.R.72.
James, h. Charlotte M. (Brown), h. Sarah J. (Brown), ——, 1808, in Knox, P.R.72.
James C., s. James and Sarah J. (Brown), Apr. 17, 1860, in Knox, P.R.72.
John G., h. Ida E. (White), s. James and Sarah J. (Brown), Aug. 26, 1850, in Knox, P.R.72.
Julia F., w. Charles W. Grant, w. Charles F. Collins, d. James and Sarah J. (Brown), Sept. 13, 1852, in Knox, P.R.72.
Lizzie P., d. James and Sarah J. (Brown), Aug. 28, 1855, in Knox, P.R.72.
Mattie W., d. James and Sarah J. (Brown), July 13, 1857, in Knox, P.R.72.
Maud Elizabeth, Apr. 12, 1875, P.R.72.
Stella J., w. W. P. Kenney, d. James and Sarah J. (Brown), Oct. 12, 1870, in Knox, P.R.72.

ADAMS, Abigail Frances Ladd, ch. Joshua and Abigail, July 19, 1827.
Alfred Frederic, h. Isabella F. (Osborne), Jan. 22, 1828, P.R.9.
Alfred Frederic, ch. Alfred Frederic and Isabella F. (Osborne), Feb. 3, 1868, P.R.9.
Betsey, ch. Joel and Amy, Dec. 29, 1819.
Edward Payson, ch. Alfred Frederic and Isabella F. (Osborne), Apr. 8, 1859, P.R.9.
Ella Isaphine, ch. Alfred Frederic and Isabella F. (Osborne), Oct. 24, 1866, P.R.9.
George Moulton, ch. Alfred Frederic and Isabella F. (Osborne), May 20, 1870, P.R.9.
Isabella Tilden, ch. Alfred Frederic and Isabella F. (Osborne), Jan. 23, 1864, P.R.9.
Jane Johnson, ch. Joshua and Abigail, Oct. 5, 1816.
John Quincy, ch. Joshua and Abigail, Sept. 13, 1825.
Louise Dana, ch. Alfred Frederic and Isabella F. (Osborne), June 21, 1865, P.R.9.
Lucy Moulton, ch. Alfred Frederic and Isabella F. (Osborne), Apr. 18, 1860, P.R.9.
Lydia, ch. Joel and Amy [dup. *crossed out adds* (Burges)], Feb. 10, 1822.
Mabel, ch. Alfred Frederic and Isabella F. (Osborne), Sept. 12, 1872, P.R.9.

ADAMS, May, ch. Alfred Frederic and Isabella F. (Osborne), May 15, 1869, P.R.9.
Nathaniel Johnson, ch. Joshua and Abigail, May 15, 1821.
Polly Weymouth, ch. Joshua and Abigail, Apr. 8, 1823.
Rebecca, ch. Joshua and Abigail, Oct. 15, 1818.
Samuel, ch. Alfred Frederic and Isabella F. (Osborne), June 20, 1862, P.R.9.

ALBEE, ———, s. Henry B. and Annie B., Apr. 22, 1887.

ALDEN, Darius Oliver, ch. Apolos and Priscilla, Mar. 5, 1808.
Edith Fannie, ch. Walter B. and Julia E., Sept. 13, 1856.
Emily Harriet, ch. Hiram O. and Emily B., June 29, 1830.
Hiram O., ch. Hiram O. and Emily B., ———, 1834.
Sarah Jane, ch. Apolos and Priscilla, Oct. 5, 1812.
Walter Bingham, ch. Hiram O. and Emily B., Apr. 4, 1827.
William Otis, ch. Apolos and Priscilla, Apr. 3, 1810.

ALDUS, ———, s. Thomas, May 6, 1847, P.R.123.

ALEXANDER, David M., h. Eliza P., May 15, 1828, G.R.1.
Eliza P. [———], w. David M., Feb. 6, 1834, G.R.1.
John, s. John and Marget, bp. July 16, 1797, C.R.2.
William, s. John and Marget, bp. Nov. 3, 1799, C.R.2.

ALLARD, Abigail, w. Silvanus Clark, d. Job and Susanna (Durgin), Oct. 1, 1794, P.R.77.
David Sr., h. Lydia (Berry), ———, 1743, P.R.77.
David, h. Mary Leavitt, s. Job and Susanna (Durgin), Oct. 28, 1792, P.R.77.
Hiram, s. Job and Susanna (Durgin), July 17, 1805, P.R.77.
Isaac, h. Wealthy Comes, s. Job and Susanna (Durgin), June 30, 1799, P.R.77.
Isaac Jr., h. Mary Eleanor (Chase), ——— [? in Northport], P.R.75.
Jacob, h. Sally Thurston, s. Job and Susanna (Durgin), Dec. 4, 1796, P.R.77.
Job, h. Susanna (Durgin), s. David Sr. and Lydia (Berry), Feb. —, 1777, P.R.77.
Stephen, h. Lydia (Randol), s. Job and Susanna (Durgin), Oct. 17, 1802, P.R.77.

ALLEY, Caroline Chandler, ch. Ephraim and Sarah K., Oct. 3, 1825.
John Wesley, ch. Ephraim and Sarah K., Feb. 1, 1827.
Joshua Franklin, ch. Ephraim and Sarah K., Mar. 9, 1824.
Sarah Ann, ch. Ephraim and Sarah K., Sept. 20, 1828.

AMES (see Eames), Drucilla, [twin] ch. Jacob and Miriam (second w.), Feb. 24, 1803.
Emeline A., ch. David G. and Eliza, Jan. 11, 1828.
Eunice A., w. Capt. E. D. Ryder, Dec. 31, 1834, G.R.1.
George H., ch. David G. and Eliza, Sept. 13, 1824.
Henry W., h. Viola M. (Wellman), Nov. 13, 1846, G.R.1.
Jenney, ch. Jacob and Jenney, Mar. 22, 1790.
Jenney, ch. Jacob and Jenney, Feb. 27, 1792.
Johanna, [twin] ch. Jacob and Miriam (second w.), Feb. 24, 1803.
John, ch. Jacob and Jenney, July 16, 1786.
Maria E., ch. David G. and Eliza, Feb. 9, 1826.
Samuel, ch. Jacob and Jenney, Nov. 25, 1788.
Sarah L., ch. David G. and Eliza, Oct. 27, 1831.

ANDERSON, Hannah Ann, ch. Hugh J. and Martha Jane, July 25, 1834. [July 25, 1833, G.R.1.]
Horace, ch. Hugh J. and Martha Jane, June 9, 1839.
Hugh Johnston, h. Martha J. (Dummer), May 10, 1801, G.R.1.
John Francis, ch. Hugh J. and Martha Jane, Dec. 4, 1832. [Gen., G.R.1.]
Joseph Dummer, ch. Hugh J. and Martha Jane, Oct. 4, 1837.
Thomas Davee, ch. Hugh J. and Martha Jane, Mar. 6, 1842.
William Henry, ch. Hugh J. and Martha Jane, Oct. 17, 1835.

ANGIER, Charles Frederick, ch. John and Lavinia, Aug. 12, 1809.
Ezekiel Whitman, ch. Oakes and Helen McLeod Mitchell, Mar. 27, 1843.
George Christopher, ch. John and Lavinia, Mar. 10, 1812.
Harriet Lavinia (Angir), ch. John and Lavinia, Apr. 12, 1806.
Harriot Lavinia (Anger), ch. John and Lavinia, Mar. 26, 1814.
John Francis Howard, ch. John and Lavinia, Nov. 22, 1807.
Lavinia Hathaway, ch. Oakes and Helen McLeod Mitchell, Nov. 11, 1844.
Oakes, ch. John and Lavinia, July 26, 1816.

ANNIS, ———, ch. John, Sept. 7, 1848, P.R.123.

APPLIN, James, Nov. 6, 1841, G.R.3.

ARCHIBALD, Faustena [———], w. Henry O., Aug. 31, 1863, G.R.1.

ARNOLD, Justina [? m.], Oct. 25, 1818, G.R.1.
Mary Abbie, w. Joshua Eustis Partridge, Apr. 18, 1833, in Orland, P.R.129.

ATKINSON, Amos [h. Anna (Knowlton)], Mar. 3, 1755 [in Newbury, Mass.], P.R.1.
Nancy [w. Alfred Johnson Jr.], July 22, 1797 [in Newbury, Mass.], P.R.1.

AVERY, Albert, ch. Willian and w., Jan. 9, 1828.
Elizabeth Frances, ch. Willian and w., June 4, 1822.
Franklin, ch. Willian and w., Aug. 4, 1832.
Henry, ch. Willian and w., Sept. 13, 1826.
Willian L., ch. Willian and w., Oct. 9, 1824.

AYER (see Eayrs).

BADGER, Rebeca, ch. James and Anna, Oct. 19, 1803.

BAGLEY, Alonzo Justin, ch. Charles and Catharine, Oct. 2, 1838.
Ann Sarah, ch. Charles and Catharine, Sept. 28, 1844.
Dwight Preston, ch. Jeremiah and Harriet A., Oct. 3, 1839.
John Herschell, ch. Charles and Catharine, Mar. 27, 1842.
Melissa, ch. Charles and Catharine, Oct. 16, 1836.
————, d. Capt. John, Aug. 15, 1848, P.R.123.

BAILEY, Betsey M. [————], w. Wesley J., July 13, 1842, G.R.1.
Frances E., d. Frank M. and Mary E., Mar. 30, 1891, G.R.3.
George A., h. Sarah F., June 22, 1864, G.R.1.
George O., Aug. 27, 1831, G.R.1.
Lois Viola, w. Henry Joseph Chaples, June 17, 1850, in Knox, P.R.54.
Rebecca (see Rebecca Gammans).
Sarah F. [————], w. George A., Nov. 14, 1876, G.R.1.
Wesley J., "Co. G. 26th Me. Regt.," h. Betsey M., Feb. 2, 1839, G.R.1.

BAKER, Georgianna Freeland, inf. Edward and Harriet (Osborn), bp. July 5, 1840, C.R.2.
Harriet Louis, inf. Edward and Harriet (Osborn), bp. Mar. 3, 1839, C.R.2.
John Francis, s. Edward and Harriet S., bp. June 29, 1851, C.R.2.
Sarah Abba, d. Edward and Harriet S., bp. Nov. 15, 1846, C.R.2.

BANKS, Adelia Ann, ch. Sharon E. and Frances, May 16, 1837.

BANKS, Adoniram, ch. Benjamin and Martha, Feb. 7, 1833.
[Adoniram H., h. Frances M. (Shephard), s. Benjamin
and Martha (Cross), Feb. 17, P.R.150.]
Adoniram, s. Benjamin H. and Virginia H. (Jones), Nov. 2,
1874, P.R.150.
Almira E., ch. John and Releif, May 17, 1829.
Annis C., ch. John and Releif, Aug. 3, 1822.
Benjamin, h. Martha (Cross), Jan. 22, 1807, P.R.150.
Benjamin H., ch. Benjamin and Martha, Aug. 18, 1829. [h.
Martha C. (Williams), h. Virginia H. (Jones), s. Benjamin
and Martha (Cross), P.R.150.]
Benjamin H., s. Benjamin H. and Virginia H. (Jones), Sept. 12,
1872, P.R.150.
Charles P., ch. Sharon E. and Frances, Feb. 28, 1842 [sic, see
Julia Isabella].
Franklin J., h. Rhoda Ann [(Hicks)], July 13, 1826, G.R.4.
John Jr., h. Relief [(Campbell)], Mar. 25, 1796, G.R.4.
John, ch. John and Releif, ——— [rec. after ch. b. Sept. 26,
1832]. [This entry crossed out.]
John, ch. Sharon E. and Frances, July 1, 1839.
John F., ch. John and Releif, July 13, 1826.
John W., s. Benjamin H. and Martha C. (Williams), July 16,
1866, P.R.150.
Joseph H., s. Benjamin H. and Martha C. (Williams), July 20,
1861, P.R.150.
Joseph W., ch. Benjamin and Martha, May 9, 1838. [h. Elsie
E. (Brown) of N. Haven, s. Benjamin and Martha
(Cross), P.R.150.]
Josiah H., ch. Benjamin and Martha, Oct. 29, 1844. [h. Eliza
A. (Rice) of Lowell, Mass., s. Benjamin and Martha
(Cross), P.R.150.]
Julia Isabella, ch. Sharon E. and Frances, Nov. 1, 1841 [sic,
see death and Charles P.].
Lewis B., Aug. 8, 1825, G.R.4.
Lucy M., ch. Benjamin and Martha, Nov. 12, 1831. [w.
Thomas H. Clark, d. Benjamin and Martha (Cross),
Nov. 30, 1830, P.R.150.]
Martha A., d. Benjamin H. and Virginia H. (Jones), Feb. 19,
1870, P.R.150.
Mary A., ch. Benjamin and Martha, Aug. 27, 1835. [w. Ben-
j[amin] Hutchinson, d. Benjamin and Martha (Cross),
Aug. 27, 1834, P.R.150.]
Pheobe A., ch. Benjamin and Martha, Feb. 16, 1843. [Phebe
A., w. David H. Nutt, d. Benjamin and Martha (Cross),
P.R.150.]

BANKS, W[illia]m H., ch. John and Releif, Sept. 26, 1832.

BARKER, David, h. Susan Rebeckah (Chase), Sept. 9, 1816, in Exeter, P.R.75. [s. Nathaniel and Sarah (Pease), P.R.76.]
Emma C. [―――], w. Frederick, May 13, 1848, G.R.1.
Frederick [h. Emma C.], Apr. 29, 1839, G.R.1.
Maude Eleanor, d. David and Susan Rebeckah (Chase), Nov. 4, 1862, in Exeter, P.R.75. [Maud Eleanor, P.R.76.]
Nathaniel, h. Sarah (Pease), ―――, in Limerick, P.R.76.
Walter Chase, s. David and Susan Rebeckah (Chase), Aug. 28, 1856, in Exeter, P.R.75.

BARNS, Charles Edwin, ch. William and Sophronia, ――― [*rec. between ch. b.* Aug. 4, 1828 *and ch. b.* Aug. 4, 1833].
Elizabeth Ann, ch. William and Sophronia, Sept. 17, 1821, in Bucksport.
Emma Martins, ch. William and Sophronia, July 10, 1825.
Frederick Barker, ch. William and Sophronia, ――― [*rec. after ch. b.* Aug. 4, 1833].
Geo[rge] Monroe, ch. William and Sophronia, Aug. 4, 1833.
Horace Manly, ch. William and Sophronia, Feb. 27, 1823, in Bucksport.
Mary Lauriet, ch. William and Sophronia, Apr. 8, 1820, in Bucksport.
William Augustus, ch. William and Sophronia, Mar. 11, 1827.
William W., ch. William and Sophronia, Aug. 4, 1828.

BARR, Annie L., d. Tho[ma]s D. and Mary R. (Speed), May 18, 1876, P.R.62.
Ethel G., w. Hall F. Hoxie, d. Tho[ma]s D. and Mary R. (Speed), Apr. 3, 1880, P.R.62.
Tho[ma]s D., h. Mary R. (Speed), Jan. 7, 1849, P.R.62.

BARROWS, Jennie Crary [? m.], ―――, 1861, G.R.6.

BARSTOW, Thomas M., Apr. 9, 1835, G.R.1.

BARTER, ―――, twin daughters Peltiah, Mar. 23, 1850, P.R.123.

BARTLET (see Bartlett), Charlotte French, ch. Thomas and Huldah, July 18, 1824.
Lucy Ann, ch. Thomas and Huldah, Aug. 2, 1816.

BARTLETT (see Bartlet), Thomas G., Capt., May 2, 1847, G.R.1.

BARTON, Rose [―――], w. R. C., ―――, 1864, G.R.1.

BASFORD, Almira, ch. Jonathan and Elizabeth, Oct. 22, 1808. [w. George W. Buckmore, G.R.1.]
Andrew Jackson, Aug. 9, 1833.
Dianna, ch. Jonathan and Elizabeth, May 30, 1805.
Sabrina, ch. Jonathan and Elizabeth, June 30, 1802.

BATCHELDER, Margaret, w. George W. Speed, July 22, 1816, P.R.62.

BATES, Abigail Jane [———], w. Thomas Wilson, ———, 1829, G.R.1.
Rosa, w. Geo[rge] W. Wise, ———, 1839, G.R.1.
Thomas Wilson, h. Abigail Jane, ———, 1825, G.R.1.

BATSON, Mary A., w. William Holt, Mar. 1, 1809, P.R.31.

BEAMAN, Charlotte Wiggin, adopted ch. Edwin (Beman) and Sarah, bp. July 10, 1836, C.R.2. [Charlotte Freeman, b. June 22, 1825, G.R.1.]
Edwin, h. Sarah P., Aug. 27, 1801, G.R.1.
Sarah P. [———], w. Edwin, Apr. 9, 1808, G.R.1.

BEAN, Abigail, ch. Joseph and Mary, Mar. 29, 1819.
Andrew Derby, ch. Josiah and Eunice, Mar. 18, 1813.
Caroline, ch. Lewis 2d and Nancy (second w.), Sept. 14, 1833.
Charles Albion, ch. Lewis 2d and Nancy (second w.), May 17, 1835.
Charles N., h. Caroline C. (Keniston), Apr. 11, 1824, G.R.1.
Daniel B., ch. Lewis 2d and Tamsin, Mar. 31, 1823.
Elizabeth, ch. Lewis and Betsy, Dec. 12, 1814.
Eunice, ch. Josiah and Eunice, Dec. 11, 1816.
Francis Asbury, ch. Josiah and Eunice, Feb. 6, 1820.
Franklin Augustus, ch. Lewis 2d and Nancy (second w.), July 18, 1839.
Frederic, ch. Joseph 2d and Maria Antoinette, Mar. 10, 1847.
George Washington, ch. Joseph and Mary, Aug. 1, 1812.
Harison, ch. Joseph and Mary, Feb. 17, 1821.
Harry Eells, ch. Jeremiah, Nov. 13, 1803.
Helen Maria, ch. Joseph and Mary, Feb. 28, 1828.
Henry Otis, ch. Lewis 2d and Nancy (second w.), Mar. 2, 1837.
James, ch. Josiah and Eunice, Feb. 25, 1815.
John Kinsman, ch. Josiah and Eunice, Dec. 10, 1823.
Joseph, ch. Lewis and Betsy, Sept. 5, 1812.
Joseph Howard, ch. Joseph and Mary, Apr. 28, 1830.
Julia Ann, ch. Joseph and Mary, Dec. 26, 1817.
Lavina, ch. Lewis 2d and Tamsin, July 7, 1821.
Lavina, ch. Lewis 2d and Nancy (second w.), July 8, 1831.

BEAN, Lewis Jr., ch. Lewis and Betsy, Apr. 24, 1818.
Maria Elizabeth, ch. Josiah and Eunice, Oct. 17, 1821.
Mary, ch. Lewis and Betsy, Dec. 16, 1821.
Mary Ann, ch. Lewis 2d and Nancy (second w.), Feb. 15, 1829.
Mary E., w. Charles C. Stephenson, Nov. 12, 1856, G.R.1.
Oliver, h. Sabrina V., Oct. 24, 1793, G.R.1.
Otis R., ch. Lewis 2d and Tamsin, May 18, 1824.
Sabrina V. [———], w. Oliver, Sept. 26, 1802, G.R.1.
Sally, ch. Jeremiah, Nov. 5, 1800.
Sarah Jane, ch. Josiah and Eunice, June 30, 1818.
Susan E., ch. Joseph 2d and Maria Antoinette, Jan. 23, 1845.
Warren Stephenson, ch. Joseph and Mary, Jan. 10, 1826.
William F., ch. Joseph 2d and Maria Antoinette, July 10, 1842.
William H., ch. Lewis 2d and Tamsin, Apr. 26, 1819.

BECKET, Caroline, ch. William and w., Feb. 11, 1808, in Camden.
Eliza, ch. William and w., Nov. 2, 1814, in Orono.
Hannah, ch. William and w., July 22, 1805, in Camden.
Isaac Mayo, ch. William and w., Jan. 30, 1820.
John, ch. William and w., Jan. 6, 1824.
Mary, ch. William and w., June 22, 1812, in Camden.
Sophia, ch. William and w., Feb. 22, 1822. [Sophia Matilda Beckett, w. Thomas Whittier Lothrop, P.R.91.]
Susanna, ch. William and w., Mar. 12, 1810, in Camden.
William Allin, ch. William and w., May 20, 1818. [Beckett, May 20, 1816, G.R.1.]
William R., ch. William and w., July 23, 1806, in Camden.
———, s. Bill, Aug. 16, 1847, P.R.123.

BECKWITH, Alice F., d. Thomas A. and Hannah E. (Patterson), May 3, 1859, P.R.111.
Alonzo F., h. Lizzie M. (Choate) (second w.), s. Thomas A. and Hannah E. (Patterson), Oct. 17, 1841, P.R.111.
Cha[rle]s F., s. Thomas A. and Hannah E. (Patterson), Oct. 17, 1849, P.R.111.
Edwin W., Jan. 5, 1851, G.R.2. [s. Thomas A. and Hannah E. (Patterson), P.R.111.]
Ellen Melissa, d. Thomas A. and Hannah E. (Patterson), Oct. 14, 1845, P.R.111.
Emma J., d. Thomas A. and Hannah E. (Patterson), Mar. 10, 1855, P.R.111.
Frederic E., s. Thomas A. and Hannah E. (Patterson), Aug. 4, 1857, P.R.111.
Geo[rge] O., s. Thomas A. and Hannah E. (Patterson), Nov. 17, 1853, P.R.111.

BECKWITH, Hannah E., Nov. 17, 1817, G.R.2. [Hannah E. (Patterson), w. Thomas A., Nov. 17, 1816, P.R.111.]
Martin W., "Co. H. 8th Me. Inf.," Dec. 30, 1839, G.R.2. [s. Thomas A. and Hannah E. (Patterson), P.R.111.]
Silas S., s. Thomas A. and Hannah E. (Patterson), May 4, 1843, P.R.111.
Thomas A., Dec. 29, 1811, G.R.2. [h. Hannah E. (Patterson), Dec. 29, 1816, P.R.111.]
William H., s. Thomas A. and Hannah E. (Patterson), Oct. 27, 1847, P.R.111.

BELCHER, Caroline W. (see Caroline W. Abbott).

BELDING, Vesta S., w. Calvin Monroe, May 24, 1814, G.R.3.

BENNER, Caroline M. [———] [w. Thomas H.], ———, 1843, G.R.1.
Edmund, ———, 1817, G.R.1.
Edmund J., ———, 1867, G.R.1.
Gilbert A., ———, 1847, G.R.1.
Lizzie B., ———, 1871, G.R.1.
Margaret E., ———, 1882, G.R.1.
Mary A. [? m.], ———, 1809, G.R.1.
Thomas H. [h. Caroline M.], ———, 1845, G.R.1.
Walter E., ———, 1879, G.R.1.

BENNETT, Abba Jane, ch. Abel and Mary, Mar. 22, 1841.
Philena M., ch. Abel and Mary, July 3, 1838.

BENYON, Gertrude E., w. W. Eugene Parker, Dec. 4, 1861, G.R.1.

BERGIN (see Burgin), ———, d. Arthur, Dec. 20, 1848, P.R.123.

BERRY, Lydia, w. David Allard Sr., ———, 1746, P.R.77.

BICKFORD, Mary Adelaide, ch. Ezra and Lydia T., Apr. 25, 1840.
———, s. Ezra, Mar. 22, 1847, P.R.123.

BICKNELL, Abba S., ch. Edmund and Nancy, May 25, 1835.
Alice, w. John T. Macdonald Jr., d. Stephen G. and Sarah W. (Spratt), Apr. 10, 1860, P.R.114.
Arthur Eugene, h. Dorothy (Webb), s. Stephen G. and Sarah W. (Spratt), Feb. 7, 1868, P.R.114.
Axel Hayford, ch. William and Christina, Dec. 26, 1822.

BICKNELL, Edmund [h. Nancy], Sept. —, 1803, in Luningburg, Mass. [*This entry written on paper pasted in book.*]
Henry G. [h. Luella M.], Nov. 10, 1852, G.R.I.
James Hervey, ch. William and Christina, May 8, 1824.
James M., ch. Edmund and Nancy, May 14, 1827.
Luella M. [———] [w. Henry G.], June 8, 1855, G.R.I.
Minnie, d. Stephen G. and Sarah W. (Spratt), July 4, 1863, P.R.114.
Nancy [———] [w. Edmund], Sept. —, 1803, in Luningburg [Mass.]. [*This entry written on paper pasted in book.*]
Stephen G., ch. Edmund and Nancy, Oct. 29, 1828. [h. Sarah W. (Spratt), P.R.114.]

BIGSBEE (see Bixby), Mary S. [? m.], Jan. 16, 1837, G.R.I.

BILLINGS, ———, d. Amos, July 20, 1847, P.R.123.

BIRD (see Burd), David E. [h. Caroline M.], Sept. 23, 1838, G.R.I.
John [h. Mary A.], June 10, 1810, G.R.I.

BISHOP, Sarah Cony, ch. Nathaniel Cony and Sarah, May 27, 1834.

BIXBY (see Bigsbee), Georgiana Gaillard, d. Thomas Daniel and Henrietta Francés (Bullen), Sept. 9, 1853, P.R.100.
Henrietta Louisa, d. Thomas Daniel and Henrietta Frances (Bullen), Sept. 28, 1856, P.R.100.
Thomas Daniel, h. Henrietta Frances (Bullen), Dec. 24, 1820, P.R.100.

BLACK, Alexander G., ch. Franklin H. and Carrie F. [Franklin Hall and Caroline F. (Durning), G.R.I.], Mar. 20, 1888.
Benjamin T., h. Mary Eleanor [(Durham)], Sept. 7, 1824, G.R.I. [h. Mary E. (Durham), in Frankfort, P.R.53.]
Clarissa, d. Henry and Anna, bp. June 27, 1802, C.R.2.
Edith M., d. Benjamin T. and Mary E. (Durham), June 7, 1872, P.R.53.
Franklin H. Jr., ch. Franklin H. and Carrie F., June 26, 1885.
Franklin Hall, "Co. I. 1st Me. Vet. Vols.," h. Caroline F. (Durning), ———, 1822, G.R.I.
Herbert A., May 7, 1864, G.R.I. [h. Annie L. (Chaples), s. Benjamin T. and Mary E. (Durham), P.R.53.]
John O., ———, 1853, G.R.I.
Oren Rice, ch. Franklin H. and Carrie F., Mar. 29, 1889.
Sarah R., w. George W. Lewis, Apr. 10, 1836, G.R.I.

BLACK, Sewall A., h. Abbie (Moore), Sept. 22, 1831, G.R.1.
Susie D., w. Charles A. Doe, July 18, 1868, G.R.1. [Susan D., d. Benjamin T. and Mary E. (Durham), P.R.53.]
William M., ch. Franklin H. and Carrie F., Nov. 4, 1886.

BLAKE, Frank Dennett, s. Oramel B. and Mary Ann (Dennett), Oct. 6, 1875, P.R.105.
George W., s. Oramel B. and Mary Ann (Dennett), Apr. 30, 1873, in Franklin, Mass., P.R.105.
———, ch. Amaziah, June 20, 1848, P.R.123.

BLANCHARD, Alfred, ch. Shepherd and Sarah, June 30, 1809, in Prospect.
Benjamin, ch. Shepherd and Sarah, July 26, 1821.
Clifton, ch. Shepherd and Sarah, July 13, 1827.
Elbridge Gerry, ch. Shepherd and Sarah, Apr. 15, 1814.
John Clifford, ch. Shepherd and Sarah, Dec. 3, 1811.
Lorenzo Loumus, ch. Shepherd and Sarah, Jan. 12, 1829.
Martha Abarine, ch. Shepherd and Sarah, Aug. 15, 1816.
Rosina, w. Cha[rle]s Read, ———, 1817, G.R.1.
Sarah [———], w. Shepherd, Apr. 2, 1793, in Prospect.
Shepherd, h. Sarah, Aug. 12, 1786, in Woolwich.
Shepherd Jr., ch. Shepherd and Sarah, Apr. 15, 1819.
William French, ch. Shepherd and Sarah, July 17, 1824.

BLAZO, Emily A., d. W[illia]m W. and Nellie E., May 18, 1890, G.R.1.

BLODGETT, Elizabeth J. [———] [w. Samuel A.], Nov. 17, 1829, G.R.1.
George A., grand s. James Calderwood, Nov. 15, 1875, P.R.71.
Samuel A. [h. Elizabeth J.], Dec. 9, 1827, G.R.1.
———, s. Sam[ue]l A., Jan. 22, 1849, P.R.123.

BLOOD, Eleanor, w. Timothy Chase, d. Olive, Oct. 6, 1797, in Charlton, Mass., P.R.75.
Olive [———], mother of Eleanor, Aug. 16, 1777, in Charlton, Mass., P.R.75.

BOARDMAN, Emery, Mar. 23, 1849, G.R.1.
Isaac M., May 24, 1821, G.R.1.

BOND, Abigail Garland Pingree, ch. Stephen B. and Eliza, Apr. 19, 1831.
David Pingree, ch. Stephen B. and Eliza, Oct. 13, 1837.
Thomas Perkins Pingree, ch. Stephen B. and Eliza, Nov. 14, 1833.

BOWEN, Elroy R. [h. Alice (Hart)], Mar. 22, 1862, G.R.1.
Selwin, ch. Esli and Esther S., Jan. 15, 1877.

BOYD, Jean, w. David Otis, d. Capt. Samuel of Bristol, Sept. 25, 1773 [? in Bristol], P.R.13.
Mary M., ch. William A. G. and Hannah, June 6, 1845.
Sarah E., ch. William A. G. and Hannah, July 10, 1843.

BOYINGTON (see Boynton).

BOYLE (see Boyles), E. K., h. Annie (Fuller), ——, 1835, G.R.1.
Edwin Fuller, ch. E. K. and Annie F., ——, 1861, G.R.1.

BOYLES (see Boyle), Francis Caroline, ch. Ichabod and Rebecca, Jan. 13, 1828.
Sarah Elisabeth, ch. Ichabod and Rebecca, Aug. 8, 1825.
William Henry, ch. Ichabod and Rebecca, Oct. 11, 1822, in St. George.

BOYNTON, Amos R., Sept. 20, 1816, in Bangor, G.R.1.
Annie C., only ch. Amos R. and Sarah M., Nov. 9, 1847, G.R.1. [Boyington, P.R.123.]

BRACKETT, Addison, ch. Joshua and Catharine, Aug. 21, 1803.
Caroline W., ch. Adison and Pricilla, July 8, 1829.
Catharine, ch. Joshua and Catharine, May 2, 1808.
Deborah G., ch. Adison and Pricilla, Aug. 29, 1827.
Emily, ch. Joshua and Catharine, Mar. 16, 1823.
Eunice, ch. Joshua and Catharine, Nov. 15, 1827.
Fidelia E. [———], w. John S., May 9, 1817, G.R.1.
Frances E., ch. Joshua and Catharine, Jan. 8, 1830.
Geo[rge] Adison, ch. Adison and Pricilla, Sept. 2, 1843.
George E., Jan. 28, 1838, G.R.1.
John, ch. Joshua and Catharine, Jan. 3, 1811.
John S., h. Fidelia E., Jan. 3, 1810, G.R.1.
Joshua, ch. Joshua and Catharine, Nov. 14, 1816.
Lucy Ann, ch. Adison and Pricilla, May 12, 1840.
Martha A., ch. Adison and Pricilla, Sept. 21, 1834. [w. Elijah L. Knowlton, Sept. 20, 1835, G.R.10.]
Mary, ch. Adison and Pricilla, Apr. 8, 1838.
Mary Jane, ch. Joshua and Catharine, Oct. 7, 1820.
Nathaniel, ch. Joshua and Catharine, May 8, 1806.
Rufus E., "Serg't. Co I 26 Me. Vols.," May 10, 1841, G.R.1.
S. Estelle [w. ——— Wilder], d. John and F. E., June 19, 1843, G.R.1.

BRACKETT, Sabrina, ch. Joshua and Catharine, July 29, 1813.
Sabrina, ch. Adison and Pricilla, Feb. 27, 1836.
Sarah Ann, ch. Joshua and Catharine, July 13, 1818.

BRADBURY, Albion Harmon, ch. Nathaniel [Nathaniel H., P.R.121.] and Sophia, Sept. 16, 1822.
Caroline, ch. Nathaniel [Nathaniel H., P.R.121.] and Sophia, Nov. 2, 1825.
Martha Ann, ch. Nathaniel and Sophia, Dec. 25, 1827. [w. James Woodbury Frederick, P.R.120. w. James W. Frederick, d. Nathaniel H. and Sophia, P.R.121.]
Nathaniel H. [h. Sophia M.], Sept. 16, 1795, in York, G.R.1.
Sophia Ann, ch. Nathaniel and Sophia, Feb. 5, 1824. [d. Nath[anie]l H. and Sophia M., G.R.1. Sophia Anna, d. Nathaniel H. and Sophia, P.R.121.]
Sophia M. [———], w. Nathaniel, May 1, 1793, in York, G.R.1.

BRADMAN, Calista N. [? m.], Nov. 15, 1811, G.R.1.
Edwin N. [h. Mary A.], ———, 1827, G.R.1.
Mary A. [———], w. Edwin N., ———, 1831, G.R.1.

BRAGDON, Charles, ch. Elijah and Sally, Aug. 12, 1811, in Swan Plantation.
Elijah, ch. Elijah and Sally, Dec. 12, 1812, in Swan Plantation.

BRAMHALL, Caroline Elizabeth, w. Fred D. Aldus, d. Joshua and Elmina (Hall), Dec. 15, 1844, P.R.149.
Cornelius Edwin, h. Jane Berry, h. Anne P. Simmons, s. Joshua and Elmina (Hall), July 5, 1839, P.R.149.
Eben F., Capt., "Father," July 10, 1848, G.R.1. [s. Eben P. and Nancy C. (Condon), P.R.61. s. Ebenezer, P.R.123.]
Eben P., h. Nancy C. (Condon), July 24, 1818, P.R.61.
Elmina Angelette, w. Louis Harbaugh, d. Joshua and Elmina (Hall), May 4, 1841, P.R.149.
Erastus F., s. Eben P. and Nancy C. (Condon), Oct. 25, 1846, P.R.61.
Ezra Hall, h. Emma Swan, s. Joshua and Elmina (Hall), Mar. 9, 1846, P.R.149.
Harriet L., d. Eben P. and Nancy C. (Condon), Sept. 9, 1850, P.R.61.
Helen Amelia, d. Joshua and Elmina (Hall), June 2, 1847, P.R.149.
Hiram A., s. Eben P. and Nancy C. (Condon), June 11, 1857, P.R.61.
Jane Sarah, w. Augustus Prescott, d. Joshua and Elmina (Hall), Nov. 21, 1842, P.R.149.

BRAMHALL, John B., s. Eben P. and Nancy C. (Condon), June 14, 1845, P.R.61.
Joshua, h. Elmina (Hall), Dec. 8, 1810, P.R.149.
Joshua Francis, s. Joshua and Elmina (Hall), June 20, 1835, P.R.149.
Solon David, h. Laura Burnett, s. Joshua and Elmina (Hall), May 30, 1849, P.R.149.
Susan Ann, w. Axel Lowney, w. John H. Bourne, d. Joshua and Elmina (Hall), Oct. 27, 1836, P.R.149.

BRAY, Charles H., Dec. 17, 1832, G.R.1.

BRIDGES, Mehitable J. Stover [———], w. John J., ———, 1838, G.R.1.

BRIER, Abigail Perce, ch. Robert and Nabey, Oct. 12, 1812.
Addulina Wilson, ch. Robert and Nabey, Mar. 22, 1810. [Adeline W., w. Leonard B. Cobbett, G.R.2.]
Andalusia, ch. Moses W. and Eunice S., Oct. 22, 1838.
Caroline, ch. Robert and Nabey [Abigail, C.R.2.], Apr. 1, 1807.
Charles Edward, ch. Robert and Nabey, Jan. 28, 1822.
Daniel, ch. Robert and Abigail, bp. ——— [rec. between Oct. 6, 1805 and June —, 1817], C.R.2.
Edwin, ch. Franklin and Mary, Sept. 25, 1836.
Edwin, ch. Franklin and Mary, Apr. 19, 1841.
Francis, ch. Robert and Nabey, ——— [rec. between ch. b. Feb. 8, 1805 and ch. b. Apr. 1, 1807].
Francis, ch. Robert and Abigail, bp. ——— [rec. between Oct. 6, 1805 and June —, 1817], C.R.2.
Franklin, ch. Robert and Nabey, Feb. 8, 1805. [[h. Mary] Feb. 5, G.R.2.]
George F., ch. Franklin and Mary, Sept. 29, 1832.
Henry R., ch. Franklin and Mary, July 22, 1839.
Julia, ch. Robert and Nabey, Sept. 4, 1819.
Mariam, ch. Robert and Abigail, bp. ——— [rec. between Oct. 6, 1805 and June —, 1817], C.R.2.
Marianne, ch. Franklin and Mary, June 19, 1844.
Mary [———], w. Franklin, May 25, 1811, G.R.2.
Olive Tomson, ch. Robert and Nabey, Dec. 2, 1816. [w. [James] Havener, G.R.1.]
Robert, ch. Robert and Nabey, Oct. 13, 1814.
Susan Almira, ch. Moses and Maria, Jan. 13, 1845.
Wilson, ch. Moses and Susanna, Apr. 13, 1811.

BRIGGS, John A., Dec. 28, 1833, G.R.1.

BROOKS, Albert, ch. Helon and Deborah, June 12, 1827.
Caroline, ch. Helon and Deborah, ——— [*rec. after ch. b.* Apr. 11, 1829].
Charles, ch. Helon and Deborah, Apr. 11, 1829.
Charles, ch. Gardner and Catherine, Apr. 19, 1843.
Charlotte, ch. Helon and Deborah, ———.
Clarence C., Feb. 2, 1873, G.R.1.
Emily P., w. Joseph H. Kaler, Nov. 25, 1832, in Orrington, P.R.128.
George Henry, ch. Gardner and Catherine, Apr. 10, 1835.
John G., M.D., Feb. 15, 1821, G.R.1.
Lydia, w. Moses Wason Ferguson, Feb. 6, 1806, G.R.3.
Mary E. [? m.], May 19, 1838, G.R.1.
Mary Jane, ch. Helon and Deborah, Aug. 18, 1825.
Samuel Spring, ch. Gardner and Catherine, Oct. 20, 1833.
Sarah Dow, ch. Gardner and Catherine, Mar. 3, 1839.
William Gardner, ch. Gardner and Catherine, Feb. 9, 1831.

BROWN (see Browne), Alden, ch. John G. and Betsy, Dec. 13, 1823.
Alice, w. Robert Patterson Chase, May 21, 18[ ], in Camden, P.R.75.
Angelett O., w. F. M. Lancaster, ———, 1820, G.R.1. [w. Francis Marion Lancaster, Oct. 9, P.R.108.]
Annie M., Nov. 27, 1857, G.R.1.
Arthur I., ch. Edmund P. and Joanna, Jan. 11, 1845.
Arthur M., ch. John G. and Betsy, May 12, 1820. [Arthur McLellan Brown, P.R.24.]
Bertha R., ch. Silas and Emma, ———, 1876, G.R.1. [Bertha Russ Brown, d. Silas and Emma (Rust), June 9, P.R.44.]
Charles P. [h. Caroline M. (Kimball)], Feb. 24, 1815, G.R.1.
Charles W[illia]m, ch. William H. and Delia, Aug. 3, 1842.
Charlote, ch. John G. and Betsy, Jan. 15, 1809. [Charlotte Miller Brown, P.R.24. Charlotte M., w. James Aborn, P.R.72.]
Clara Augusta, d. Silas and Emma (Rust), May 17, 1879, P.R.44.
Dasie C., w. H. E. McDonald, Mar. 4, 1853, G.R.1.
Delia F., ch. William H. and Delia, Aug. 5, 1840.
Edmund P., ch. John G. and Betsy, Oct. 21, 1815. [h. Joanna (Pierce), G.R.4. Edmund Phiney Brown, P.R.24.]
Elisabeth, ch. John Jr. and Ruth, Oct. 16, 1796.
Elizeabeth, ch. John G. and Betsy, Dec. 8, 1812. [Elizabeth, w. A. K. Pierce, G.R.1. Elizabeth, P.R.24.]
Hannah (see Hannah Torrey).

BROWN, Hannah, ch. John Jr. and Ruth, Mar. 13, 1791.
Hannah Angela, ch. Henry A. and Sarah, Aug. 2, 1841.
Harriet A. [———] [w. Moses M.], Dec. 21, 1821, G.R.1.
Harriot, ch. John and Sally, bp. Sept. 28, 1821, C.R.2.
Henry A., ch. Arno M. and Adelaide C., Nov. 24, 1883.
Henry E., Capt., h. Sarah W., June 22, 1816, G.R.13.
Henry Sewel, ch. John and Sally, bp. Aug. 5, 1821, C.R.2.
Hollis Monroe, ch. Aaron and Jane, Apr. 14, 1831.
Ida, w. ——— Carter, d. Capt. Henry E. and Sarah W., Apr. 9, 1849, G.R.13.
Isaac C., ch. Samuel and Jane, Aug. 8, 1805.
Isaac Call, ch. John G. and Betsy, Oct. 20, 1805. [Isaac Cole Brown, P.R.24.]
James, ch. Samuel and Jane, Feb. 15, 1815.
James Alfred, ch. James W. and Susan, Feb. 7, 1827.
James Irish, ch. John G. and Betsy, Apr. 7, 1822.
Janes [sic] Reed, ch. Aaron and Jane, Mar. 1, 1827.
Jerome, Feb. 26, 1860, G.R.1.
John 3d, [twin] ch. John Jr. and Sally (second w.), Dec. 26, 1802.
John M., ch. John G. and Betsy, Oct. 14, 1817. [Joseph McDonough Brown, Oct 1, P.R.24.]
John Walter, ch. William H. and Delia, Sept. —, 1844.
Jonathan, ch. John Jr. and Ruth, July 11, 1792.
Joseph McDonough (see John M.).
Katie, d. Henry E. and Sarah W., Nov. 20, 1856, G.R.13.
Lavina, ch. Samuel and Jane, Nov. 20, 1803.
Lottie, June 6, 1866, G.R.1.
Lucindy, ch. John G. and Betsy, Feb. 27, 1811. [Lucinda Miller Brown, P.R.24.]
Lydia Ann, ch. Samuel and Jane, Feb. 10, 1813.
Martha H., ch. John G. and Betsy, July 12, 1819. [Martha Houston Brown, July 12, 1818, P.R.22.]
Mary, ch. John Jr. and Ruth, Aug. 18, 1794.
Mary Ann, ch. John G. and Betsy, Aug. 17, 1825. [second w. A. K. Pierce, G.R.1. Mary Anne, P.R.24.]
Mary Bertha, d. Silas and Emma (Rust), Mar. 6, 1885, P.R.44.
Mary F. [———], w. William H., Oct. 10, 1823, G.R.1.
Minnie S., Aug. 11, 1847, G.R.1.
Moses M. [h. Harriet A.], Mar. 24, 1813, G.R.1.
Myra A., d. Silas and Emma (Rust), Feb. 8, 1874, P.R.44.
Nancy (see Nancy B. Miller).
Paul, ch. Samuel and Jane, Oct. 17, 1807.
Robert Wire, ch. John G. and Betsy, May 8, 1807. [Robert Wier Brown, P.R.24.]

BROWN, Ruth, ch. John and Sally (second w.), Dec. 9, 1804.
Sally, ch. Daniel and Lucy, June 11, 1802.
Sally, [twin] ch. John Jr. and Sally (second w.), Dec. 26, 1802.
Samuel J[r.], ch. Samuel and Jane, May 17, 1811.
Sarah Jane, ch. John G. and Betsy, Sept. 27, 1827. [second w. James Aborn, P.R.72.]
Sarah W. [———], w. Capt. Henry E., Sept. 14, 1816, G.R.13.
Sewell, ch. John Jr. and Sally (second w.), May 14, 1801.
Silas, h. Emma (Rust), Apr. 6, 1848, P.R.44.
Silas D., ch. Samuel and Jane, Oct. 31, 1809.
William H., h. Mary F., Feb. 21, 1819, G.R.1.
Willis J., ch. Arno M. and Adelaide C., June 12, 1880.
Zenes Reed, ch. Aaron and Jane, Apr. 5, 1829.
———, d. John, Jan. 5, 1847, P.R.123.
———, s. Luther, June 3, 1847, P.R.123.
———, s. Silas, Apr. 30, 1848, P.R.123.
———, s. John M., Sept. 22, 1848, P.R.123.
———, d. John F., Feb. 5, 1850, P.R.123.
———, s. John, Mar. 17, 1850, P.R.123.
———, ch. Silas and Emma, ———, 1873, G.R.1. [ch. Silas and Emma (Rust), Feb. 8, P.R.44.]
———, d. Frederic and Elvira, Dec. 23, 1891.

BROWNE (see Brown), Amy C. [? m.], Dec. 25, 1874, G.R.1.

BRUCE, George William, ch. George W. and Clarissa, Feb. 3, 1810.

BRYANT, Lovina A. [———], w. Isaiah H., Nov. 14, 1838, G.R.2.

BUCKLIN, Herbert L., s. James and Phebe P. (Warren) (Phipps), Mar. 31, 1846, P.R.39.
James, h. Phebe P. (Warren) Phipps, Mar. 27, 1817, in Knox, P.R.39.
Leon O., h. Susie (Wallace), s. James and Phebe P. (Warren) (Phipps), Oct. 7, 1851, P.R.39.
Leona Wallace, d. Leon O. and Susie (Wallace), Apr. 21, 1886, P.R.39.
Mary Blanche, d. Leon O. and Susie (Wallace), Dec. 4, 1876, P.R.39.

BUCKMAN (see Burkmar).

BUCKMAR (see Burkmar).

BULLEN, Cornelius Samuel, ch. Sam[ue]l and w., bp. May 18, 1836, C.R.2. [H. Orinda Elizabeth (Leland), s. Samuel and Margaret (West), b. June 4, 1826, P.R.100.]
Frances Elizabeth. d. Cornelius Samuel and Orinda Elizabeth (Leland), Sept. 1, 1861, P.R.100.
Frances Relief, d. Samuel and Margaret (West), June 8, 1822, P.R.100.
Hannah Adaline Frances, d. Cornelius Samuel and Orinda Elizabeth (Leland), —— [rec. before ch. b. June 30, 1859], P.R.100.
Henrietta Frances, d. Cornelius Samuel and Orinda Elizabeth (Leland), —— [rec. after ch. b. Sept. 1, 1861], P.R.100.
Henrietta Francis, ch. Sam[ue]l and w., bp. May 18, 1836, C.R.2. [Henrietta Frances, w. Thomas Daniel Bixby, d. Samuel and Margaret (West), b. Feb. 11, 1824, P.R.100.]
John Samuel, s. Cornelius Samuel and Orinda Elizabeth (Leland), June 30, 1859, P.R.100.
John West, ch. Sam[ue]l and w., bp. May 18, 1836, C.R.2. [s. Samuel and Margaret (West), b. Feb. 9, 1830, P.R.100.]
Margaret Gilson, ch. Sam[ue]l and w., bp. Oct. 14, 1836, C.R.2. [Margaret Gibson Bullen, w. George Thomson Marsh, d. Samuel and Margaret (West), b. Dec. 29, 1835, P.R.100.]
Samuel, h. Margaret (West), May 11, 1791, P.R.100.
Sarah Elizabeth, ch. Sam[ue]l and w., bp. May 18, 1836, C.R.2. [w. Daniel McCormic Gates, d. Samuel and Margaret (West), b. Apr. 13, 1832, P.R.100.]

BURBAR, Harriet Velma, w. Allen L. Curtis, Mar. 24, 1881, G.R.1.

BURD (see Bird), Charles H., ch. Sam[ue]l S. and Susan, Nov. 18, 1835. [Lt., G.R.1.]
Darius E., ch. Sam[ue]l S. and Susan, Feb. 14, 1837.
George E., ch. Sam[ue]l F. and Rebecca H., Apr. 27, 1857.
Samuel Frances [*sic*], ch. Sam[ue]l S. and Susan, May 8, 1831.
Samuel S. [h. Susan H.], ——, 1792, G.R.1.
Susan H. [——] [w. Samuel S.], ——, 1807, G.R.1.

BURGESS, Albert C., ch. Ezekiel and Nancy [Nancy P. (Morang), P.R.169.], June 24, 1840.
Caroline, ch. David and Catharine [Catherine (Holmes), P.R.51.], Feb. 11, 1828.
Catherine M. [——], w. David M., ——, 1808, G.R.1. [Catherine, d. Joel Holmes and Eleanor, Oct. 28, in Moultonborough, N. H., P.R.51.]

BURGESS, Charles Jefferson, ch. George W. and Elizabeth [George Washington and Elizabeth (McLean), P.R.169.], Dec. 5, 1859.
Daniel E., ———, 1847, G.R.I. [s. David and Catherine (Holmes), May 12, P.R.51.]
David Jr., ch. David and Catharine [Catherine (Holmes), P.R.51.], Mar. 20, 1832.
David M., h. Catherine M., ———, 1801, G.R.I. [h. Catherine (Holmes), Feb. 12, in Penobscot, P.R.51.]
Edith Louise, ch. Capt. Reuben H. and Lydia Ann (Burgess), Sept. 25, 1876, P.R.80.
Elsie S., w. Augustus Clark, ———, 1848, G.R.I.
Emma Jane, ch. George W. and Esther Ann W. (second w.), Apr. 22, 1850, P.R.168.
Ezekiel, h. Nancy P., Jan. 6, 1797, G.R.I. [h. Nancy P. (Morang), P.R.169.]
Frank, ———, 1859, G.R.I.
Geo[rge] W., ch. Ezekiel and Nancy, Nov. 28, 1834. [h. Elizabeth (McLean), s. Ezekiel and Nancy P. (Morang), P.R.169.]
George Washington, ch. George W. and Hester Ann (second w.), Jan. 16, 1844. [ch. George W. and Esther Ann W. (second w.), Jan. 16, 1843, P.R.168.]
Grace E., Nov. 19, 1868, G.R.I. [Grace Evelyn, d. George Washington and Elizabeth (McLean), P.R.169.]
Hariet A., ch. Ezekiel and Nancy, Nov. 26, 1831. [w. Eben D. Towne, d. Ezekiel and Nancy P. (Morang), P.R.169.]
Harriet F., ch. George W. and Harriet [Harriet F., P.R.168.], Mar. 3, 1841.
Hattie E., d. Capt. R. H. and A. L., ———, 1873, G.R.I. [Hattie Edith, ch. Capt. Reuben H. and Lydia Ann (Burgess), Feb. 22, P.R.80.]
Hiram Anson, ch. George W. and Esther Ann W. (second w.), Mar. 7, 1848, P.R.168.
Isaac, ———, 1853, G.R.I.
James Franklin, ch. David and Catharine [Catherine (Holmes), P.R.51.], Aug. 23, 1834.
James Haskall, ch. James and Nancy, Dec. 26, 1843.
James Leslie, ch. Tolman Y. and Martha A., May 12, 1859.
John Franklin, ch. James and Nancy, Jan. 16, 1846.
Lizzie N. [———], w. Capt. Reuben H., ———, 1843, G.R.I.
Lucy E., ch. David and Catharine, Dec. 2, 1837. [d. David and Catherine (Holmes), P.R.51. w. Horace S. Perkins, P.R.52.]

BURGESS, Lydia Ann, ch. David and Catharine, Dec. 1, 1840. [d. David and Catherine (Holmes), P.R.51. w. Capt. Reuben H. Burgess, P.R.80.]
Nancy E., ch. David and Catharine [Catherine (Holmes), P.R.51.], Apr. 20, 1843.
Nancy P. [———], w. Ezekiel, Dec. 15, 1808, G.R.1. [Nancy P. (Morang), P.R.169.]
Reuben H., Capt., h. Lizzie N., ———, 1838, G.R.1. [h. Lydia Ann (Burgess), Mar. 11, in Islesboro, P.R.80.]
Robert, ch. David and Catharine [Catherine (Holmes), P.R.51.], Jan. 2, 1830.
Rosselle H., s. J. W. and L. F., Jan. 8, 1885, G.R.1.
Sarah (see Sarah Wight).
Thomas J., ch. Ezekiel and Nancy [Nancy P. (Morang), P.R.169.], Feb. 26, 1833.
Tho[ma]s Jefferson, ch. George W. and Hester Ann [Esther Ann W., P.R.168.] (second w.), May 7, 1842.
W[illia]m A., ch. Ezekiel and Nancy [Nancy P. (Morang), P.R.169.], Feb. 16, 1837.

BURGIN (see Bergin), Rodney, ch. S. T. Edgecomb and Nettie Burgin, July 4, 1886, in Poor House.

BURKETT, Harriet A. [———], w. George W., Apr. 2, 1841, G.R.1.

BURKMAR, Albert Channy (Buckman), ch. Samuel and Susan [Susan *written above* Jane *crossed out*], July 15, 1820.
Charles Ulmer, ch. Samuel and Susan [Susan *written above* Jane *crossed out*], Jan. 25, 1816.
Edward Jacob (Buckmar), ch. Samuel and Susan [Susan *written above* Jane *crossed out*], Feb. 15, 1823.
Ellen Frances, ch. Henry E. and Emely K., Jan. 31, 1846.
Henry Elsby, ch. Samuel and Susan [Susan *written above* Jane *crossed out*], Mar. 21, 1814.
Julia Ette, ch. Samuel and Susan [Susan *written above* Jane *crossed out*], Aug. 10, 1818.
Juliett Augusta, ch. Henry E. and Emely K., Feb. 19, 1839.
Julius Augustine, ch. Henry E. and Emely K., June 13, 1842.
Lucius Edward (Buckmar), ch. Samuel and Susan [Susan *written above* Jane *crossed out*], Dec. 27, 1825 [*sic, see death*].

BURRELL (see Burrill), James Franklin, s. Mary, bp. June 6, 1831, C.R.2.

BURRILL (see Burrell), Benjamin George, ch. William, bp. June 22, 1834, C.R.2.
Evilena, ch. William, bp. June 22, 1834, C.R.2.

BURRINGTON, Eliza A. D. [———], w. L. M., Feb. 22, 1833, G.R.1.
L. M., Rev., Nov. 7, 1827, G.R.1.

BURT, ———, d. Charles, June 9, 1847, P.R.123.
———, s. Charles, Sept. 7, 1849, P.R.123.

BUTMAN, Adaline, adopted ch. Samuel and Mary, Nov. 20, 1815.
Richard, ch. Samuel and Mary, Sept. 15, 1800, in Beverly, Mass.
Samuel, ch. Samuel and Mary, ———, 1798, in Beverly, Mass.
Thomas, ch. Samuel and Mary, Mar. 18, 1807.
William, ch. Samuel and Mary, June 7, 1802, in Beverly, Mass.

CALDERWOOD, Annie Marie, d. James and Catherine (Rhoades) (second w.), Dec. 19, 1859, P.R.71.
Catherine [———], w. James, Sept. 29, 1822, G.R.1. [Catherine (Rhoades) (second w.), P.R.71.]
Deborah Jane, ch. James and Mary [(Norton) P.R.71.], Mar. 19, 1838.
Edwin, s. James and Catherine (Rhoades) (second w.), Sept. 20, 1853, P.R.71.
George, s. James and Catherine (Rhoades) (second w.), Jan. 20, 1850, P.R.71.
James, h. Catherine, Apr. 10, 1809, G.R.1.
James Jr., s. James and Mary (Norton), Sept. 19, 1840, P.R.71.
James Jr., ch. James and Catharine [Catherine (Rhoades), P.R.71.] (second w.), Jan. 5, 1846.
Luther Emery, s. James and Catherine (Rhoades) (second w.), Mar. 13, 1857, P.R.71.
Mary Elizabeth, d. James and Catherine (Rhoades) (second w.), Sept. 23, 1848, P.R.71.
Ruth E. [———], w. Luther, Jan. 26, 1857, G.R.1.
William, ch. James and Mary, July 15, 1836. [s. James and Mary (Norton), Aug. 8, P.R.71.]

CALDWELL, Abba Marshall, d. Jo[h]n S. and Mary E., bp. May 30, 1851, C.R.2. [Abbie Marshall Caldwell, d. John S. and Mary E. (Simpson) (first w.), b. Dec. 12, 1850, P.R.156.]

CALDWELL, Annie Elizabeth, d. John S. and Mary E., bp. Nov. 5, 1848, C.R.2. [w. Rev. I. B. Mower of Cambridge, d. John S. and Mary E. (Simpson) (first w.), b. Aug. 8, P.R.156.]
Augustine, inf. John S. and Mary E., bp. Nov. 28, 1852, C.R.2. [s. John S. and Mary E. (Simpson) (first w.), b. Oct. 8, P.R.156.]
Emily Heath, d. John S. and Mary E., bp. Nov. 1, 1846, C.R.2. [w. Dr. Geo[rge] F. Hand of Binghamton, N. Y., d. John S. and Mary E. (Simpson) (first w.), b. July 29, P.R.156.]
John S. [h. Mary Elizabeth, h. Sophia R.], Sept. 12, 1812, G.R.1. [h. Mary E. (Simpson), h. Sophia (Rice), Sept. 14, in Ipswich, Mass., P.R.156.]
John Stanwood, ch. John S. and Sophia, bp. Oct. 19, 1862, C.R.2. [s. John S. and Sophia R., b. July 3, G.R.1. s. John S. and Sophia (Rice) (second w.), b. July 3, P.R.156.]
Mary Rice, ch. J. S. and Sophia, bp. May 6, 1860, C.R.2. [w. Amos Clement of Mt. Desert, d. John S. and Sophia (Rice) (second w.), b. Jan. 12, P.R.156. w. Amos Clement of Mt. Desert, b. Jan. 12, P.R.157.]
Sophia R. [———], w. John S., Aug. 23, 1823, G.R.1. [Sophia (Rice) (second w.), in Meriden, Conn., P.R.156.]
Susan Stanwood, ch. John S. and Mary E. [(Simpson) (first w.) P.R.156.], Sept. 29, 1844.

CALEF (see Calf), Abbe Patten, inf. Horatio G. K. and w., bp. July 17, 1836, C.R.2.

CALF (see Calef), Austin, ch. Daniel and Eunice, Sept. 19, 1830.
George, ch. Daniel and Eunice, Jan. 4, 1836.

CAMPBELL, Almira, ch. Annas and Rhody, Aug. 17, 1809.
Annas, ch. Annas and Rhody, Aug. 26, 1814.
Emerline [Emerline *in later handwriting above* Emmeline], ch. Annas and Rhody, Apr. 18, 1812.
Relief [Relief *in later handwriting*], ch. Annas and Rhody, June —, 1801, in Hawk, N. H. [Relief, w. John Banks Jr., June 8, G.R.4.]
Samuel, ch. Annas and Rhody, Mar. 16, 1807.
Silva, ch. Annas and Rhody, Aug. 13, 1804.

CARGILL, Agnes, ch. Henry and Sarah, Apr. 12, 1832.
Charles Augustus, ch. Henry and Sarah, Dec. 31, 1827.
Charles Augustus, ch. Henry and Sarah, Nov. 13, 1829.

CARLE, Fred A., June 20, 1840, G.R.1.
Harold P., Aug. 14, 1883, G.R.1.
John, Oct. 11, 1845, G.R.1.

CARR, Caroline Elizabeth Webster, ch. Thomas H. and Bethiah, May 26, 1828.

CARSON, Elbridge Cutter, ch. Thomas J. and Hannah, Sept. 13, 1842.
Eliza J., ch. Thomas J. and Hannah, Apr. 17, 1839.
Frances D., ch. Thomas J. and Hannah, Aug. 7, 1845.
Holbrock H., ch. Thomas J. and Hannah, Apr. 15, 1836.
Seth S., ch. Thomas J. and Hannah, Oct. 24, 1831.
William A., ch. Thomas J. and Hannah, Mar. 15, 1834.

CARTER, Albert M., May 1, 1835, G.R.1.
Alma E., ch. Enoch B. and Mary A., Mar. 9, 1855.
Annie M., w. Philip T. Eastman, w. Thomas Taylor, d. J. Nelson and Mary, July 23, 1834, in Etna, G.R.1.
Aurelia J. [———], w. Henry Austin, ———, 1833, G.R.1.
Caro E. [———], w. Thomas, Sept. 30, 1829, G.R.1.
Carrie M. [———], w. Prescott D. H., Dec. 8, 1866, G.R.1.
Charles E., ———, 1852, G.R.1.
Clara G. [———], w. M. F., Apr. 19, 1843, G.R.1.
Frederick Gleason, s. Everett S. and Mary J. (Walton), ———, P.R.126.
George R., Capt., h. Harriett N. (Perkins), May 14, 1832, G.R.1.
H. A., ch. Henry E. and Elizabeth, May 24, 1838.
Henry Austin, h. Aurelia J., ———, 1828, G.R.1.
Horatio H., h. Lorinda E. [(McCrillis)], ———, 1822, G.R.1.
Inez, d. Fred G. and Geneva E. (Riggs), Mar. 10, 1884, P.R.103.
Isa Mabel, d. Everett S. and Mary J. (Walton), ———, P.R.126.
James F., ch. Henry E. and Elizabeth, Dec. 26, 1844.
Kate W. [———], w. Alzo M., Mar. 28, 1862, on Presque Isle, G.R.1.
Martha S., ch. Henry E. and Elizabeth, Oct. 24, 1840.
Mary D., ———, 1849, G.R.1.
Mary L., d. Fred G. and Geneva E. (Riggs), Apr. 17, 1882, P.R.103.
Roland L., May 9, 1872, G.R.1.
Sarah A. [———], w. M. F., Jan. 4, 1832, G.R.1.
Thomas, h. Caro E., Jan. 18, 1811, G.R.1.
Vesta C., only ch. W[illia]m W. and Martha, July 21, 1869, G.R.1.

CARTER, Walter P., Sept. 30, 1858, G.R.1.
———, d. Horatio, Apr. 5, 1848, P.R.123.

CASS, Andrew Jackson, ch. Daniel and Mary, Mar. 21, 1829.
Mary Eliza, ch. Daniel and Mary, Oct. 15, 1831.

CASTLE, Margaret H., Aug. 27, 1870, G.R.1. [Margaret Hazeltine Castle, great grand ch. Salathiel Nickerson and Martha Rogers, P.R.15.]
William Prescott, July 15, 1869, P.R.14. [great grand ch. Salathiel Nickerson and Martha Rogers, P.R.15.]

CATES, Amelia S. [———] [w. Jediah C.], Nov. 23, 1838, G.R.1.
Jediah C. [h. Amelia S.], Nov. 25, 1835, G.R.1.

CHADWICK, Annie May [? m.], ———, 1872, G.R.1.
Carrie M., ———, 1878, G.R.1.

CHANDLER, Louis Henry, ch. C. C. and Lauvicy K., Feb. 20, 1812.

CHAPIN, Edwin A., July 22, 1883, G.R.1.
Sarah A. [? m.], Nov. 27, 1832, G.R.1.

CHAPLES, Annie Leila, d. Henry Joseph and Lois Viola (Bailey), May 5, 1877, in Knox, P.R.54.
Charles A., s. ——— and Sarah, June 24, 1854, P.R.58.
Drew Hazeltine Livingston, s. Henry Joseph and Lois Viola (Bailey), July 27, 1884, P.R.54.
Emma F., d. ——— and Sarah, Oct. 21, 1845, P.R.58.
Florence Downs, d. Henry Joseph and Lois Viola (Bailey), June 21, 1889, P.R.54.
George W., s. ——— and Sarah, Mar. 24, 1851, P.R.58.
Henry Joseph, h. Lois Viola (Bailey), Sept. 13, 1848, P.R.54.
  [s. ——— and Sarah, Sept. 13, 1847, P.R.58.]
Sarah [———], w. ———, Mar. 15, 1811, P.R.58.
Sarah S., d. ——— and Sarah, Oct. 6, 1849, P.R.58.
———, d. Henry Joseph and Lois Viola (Bailey), Feb. 10, 1874, P.R.54.

CHAPMAN, Michael Roscoe, ch. Michael S. and Pheobe, Aug. 6, 1843.
———, d. Nathaniel, Aug. 20, 1847, P.R.123.
———, d. Michael, July 12, 1848, P.R.123.

CHASE, Adalaide, w. George A. Quimby, Apr. 8, 1859, P.R.118.
Alden Darwin, h. Nancy Jane (Patterson), s. Timothy and Eleanor (Blood), May 1, 1822, in Waldo, P.R.75.
Edward Francis, Aug. 17, 1858, G.R.1.
Ellen Frances, ch. Hiram and Sarah D. [(Titcomb) P.R.75.], Apr. 8, 1847.
Frances Relief, d. Timothy and Eleanor (Blood), July 29, 1826, in Waldo, P.R.75.
Frederic Patterson, ch. Alden D. and Nancy Jane, July 24, 1846. [Frederick, s. Alden Darwin and Nancy Jane (Patterson), P.R.75.]
Frederick Titcomb, s. Hiram and Sarah D. (Titcomb), Jan. 24, 1857, P.R.75.
George S., Feb. 8, 1825, G.R.1.
Hiram, h. Sarah D. (Titcomb), s. Timothy and Eleanor (Blood), Dec. 4, 1817, in Charlton, Mass., P.R.75.
Mary Eleanor, w. Isaac Allard Jr., d. Timothy and Eleanor (Blood), May 26, 1824, in Waldo, P.R.75.
Philo, Nov. 28, 1829, G.R.1.
Robert Patterson, ch. Alden D. and Nancy Jane, Jan. 27, 1852. [h. Alice (Brown), s. Alden D. and Nancy Jane (Patterson), P.R.75.]
Susan Rebeckah, w. David Barker of Exeter, d. Timothy and Eleanor (Blood), Sept. 25, 1827, P.R.75.
Timothy, h. Eleanor (Blood), Nov. 13, 1793, in Charlton, Mass., P.R.75.
Timothy Jr., s. Timothy and Eleanor (Blood), Feb. 25, 1830, P.R.75.
Timothy, s. Hiram and Sarah D. (Titcomb), Feb. 25, 1849, P.R.75. [Timothy Darwin Chase, P.R.170.]
Timothy Jr. [ch. Timothy and Eleanor (Blood)], Jan. 29, 1833, P.R.75.
William Henry, s. Timothy and Eleanor (Blood), Aug. 4, 1819, in Waldo, P.R.75.

CLARK, Abraham, ch. Ichabod and Polly, ———.
Albert [ch. David and Sarah], ———, 1850, G.R.1.
Albert, ch. A. E. and M. H., ———, 1857, G.R.4.
Albert E., ch. Thomas and Celia, Apr. 15, 1827. [h. Matilda H., ———, 1826, G.R.4.]
Angela L., ch. Capt. Isaac and Jennette, Dec. 12, 1839.
Anna, adopted ch. Alexander, bp. ——— [*rec. between* Oct. 6, 1805 *and* June —, 1817], C.R.2.
Anna, ch. Joseph and Celia, Oct. 3, 1836.

CLARK, Arabella, ch. Capt. Isaac and Jennette, Oct. 22, 1843. [Oct. 18, 1846, G.R.1.]
Augustus, h. Elsie S. (Burgess), ⸺, 1840, G.R.1.
Catharine [ch. David and Sarah], ⸺, 1847, G.R.1.
Charles A., ch. Capt. Isaac and Jennette, Nov. 13, 1836.
Charles O., Aug. 22, 1848, G.R.1. [ch. Capt. Isaac, P.R.123.]
Charles William, ch. Charles and w., Mar. 11, 1826.
Charles William, ch. Charles and w., Jan. 5, 1828.
Celia A., ch. Joseph and Celia, Mar. 7, 1843.
Cummings, adopted ch. Alexander, bp. ⸺ [*rec. between* Oct. 6, 1805 *and* June —, 1817], C.R.2.
David, h. Sarah, ⸺, 1810, G.R.1.
Eliza, ch. Joseph and Celia, Oct. 7, 1841.
Eliza Jane, ch. Charles and w., June 16, 1822.
Elizabeth, ch. Capt. Isaac and Jennette, Dec. 2, 1840. [Lizzie, Dec. 2, 1841, G.R.1.]
Halley, ch. Abraham and Anna, May 19, 1798.
Hannah, ch. Elisha and Sally, Apr. 27, 1793.
Isaac, Capt., h. Jennette [(Morrill)], Oct. 26, 1800, G.R.1.
Jacob, ch. Ichabod and Polly, July ⸺.
James H., "Co. I 14 Me. Vol.," h. Georgia S. (Pitcher), Feb. 5, 1837, G.R.1.
James M., ch. Thomas and Celia, Apr. 30, 1829.
James Sherborn, ch. John and Mary, Oct. 16, 1826.
John, ch. Alexander and Elizabeth, July 4, 1842.
John, ch. Ichabod and Polly, ⸺.
Joseph, ch. Abraham and Anna, July 13, 1806.
Joseph, ch. Ichabod and Polly, ⸺.
Lizzie (see Elizabeth).
Louisa Page, ch. John and Mary, Sept. 29, 1820.
Lucinda, ch. Elisha and Sally, Jan. 1, 1789.
Margaret A., ch. Alexander and Elizabeth, Dec. 2, 1839.
Mary Ann, ch. Alexander and Elizabeth, Oct. 20, 1844.
Mary Anna, d. Elizabeth, bp. Feb. 10, 1847, C.R.2.
Mary E., ch. Capt. Isaac and Jennette, Feb. 6, 1831. [Feb. 6, 1832, G.R.1.]
Mary E., ch. A. E. and M. H., ⸺, 1855, G.R.4.
Mary Eleanor, ch. John and Mary, Apr. —, 1824.
Matilda H. [⸺], w. Albert E., ⸺, 1822, G.R.4.
Nancy, ch. Ichabod and Polly, ⸺.
Robert, ch. Alexander and Elizabeth, Oct. 2, 1837.
Sally, ch. Ichabod and Polly, ⸺.
Sarah [⸺], w. David, ⸺, 1816, G.R.1.
Sarah Emily, ch. John and Mary, July 13, 1822.
Sarah Jane, ch. Alexander and Elizabeth, Nov. 24, 1834.

CLARK, Thomas, ch. Abraham and Anna, Apr. 3, 1791.
Thomas K., ch. Capt. Isaac and Jennette, Sept. 21, 1827.
Warren F., ch. Capt. Isaac and Jennette, Dec. 3, 1834.
W[illia]m A., ch. Joseph and Celia, Feb. 27, 1838.
William F., Apr. 9, 1858, G.R.1.

CLARY, Daniel, ch. Daniel and Jenney, Feb. 3, 1803.
Hannah (Clarey), ch. Daniel and Jenney, Dec. 6, 1801.
Jenney (Clarry), ch. Daniel and Jenney, Aug. 31, 1794.
John, ch. Daniel and Jenney, Dec. 28, 1804.
Margret (Clarry), ch. Daniel and Jenney, Sept. 28, 1798.
Maria (Clarry), ch. Daniel and Jenney, July 14, 1808.
William, ch. Daniel and Jenney, May 8, 1796.

CLEMENT (see Clements), Amos, h. Mary Rice (Caldwell), July 30, 1849, in Mt. Desert, P.R.157.
Donald, ch. Amos and Mary R., Jan. 29, 1888. [James Donald Clement, h. Charlotte M. Hayden of Raymond, s. Amos and Mary Rice (Caldwell), P.R.157.]
John Caldwell, ch. Amos and Mary R., Sept. 11, 1883. [h. Jessie T. Fraser of Barre, Vt., s. Amos and Mary Rice (Caldwell), Sept. 10, P.R.157.]

CLEMENTS (see Clement), Abbie J. [————], w. ————, formerly w. W[illia]m O. Cunningham, May 9, 1857, G.R.2.
Addie, w. Sanford Howard, Dec. 1, 1855, P.R.102.

CLIFFORD, Annie L. [————], w. William H., Oct. 26, 1842, G.R.1.
Ferdinand P., Jan. 7, 1867, G.R.1.
William H., "Co. A. 4th Me. Regt.," h. Annie L., June 28, 1840, G.R.1.

CLOUGH, Madora F. [————], Mar. 2, 1864, G.R.1.
Maggie J. [————], Oct. 3, 1863, G.R.1.

COBBETT, Arthur E., s. Henry H. and Eugenia L. (Aborn) (Tufts), ————, 1877, P.R.72.
Charles Frank, ch. William and Ella, Jan. 25, 1887.
Leonard B., ————, 1801, G.R.2.

COCHRAN, Agnes, ch. John 1st and Agnes, Dec. —, 1785.
Annes, [twin] ch. John Jr. and Rebekah, Oct. 28, 1800.
Cordelia, ch. John Jr. and Mary (second w.), Dec. 7, 1808.
Eliza, ch. Robert and Elizabeth, Apr. 28, 1802.
Elizabeth, ch. John Jr. and Mary (second w.), Apr. 11, 1812.

COCHRAN, George, ch. Robert and Elizabeth, Sept. 28, 1799.
Jane, ch. John Jr. and Mary (second w.), Oct. 29, 1806.
John, ch. John and Mary, Mar. 24, 1801. [h. Eunice R. (Morse), G.R.1.]
John, ch. John Jr. and Mary (second w.), July 26, 1810.
Mary, ch. John and Mary, June 16, 1805.
Mary, d. John and Eunice, Nov. 20, 1843, G.R.1.
Polly, ch. Robert and Elizabeth, Sept. 30, 1804.
Rebekah, [twin] ch. John Jr. and Rebekah, Oct. 31, 1800.
Samuel, s. John and Mary, Feb. 23, 1799.

COLBERN (see Colburn), Maria, ch. Ebnezar and Abigal, Feb. 11, 1809.
Nancy, ch. Ebnezar and Abigal, Aug. 13, 1804.

COLBURN (see Colbern), Abigail Jane, ch. Henry and Diana, July 18, 1839.
Albert Thaxter, s. William Thaxter and Olive (Giles), Aug. 11, 1846, P.R.18.
Augustine, s. William Thaxter and Olive (Giles), Mar. 23, 1849, P.R.18.
Charlotte White, d. William Thaxter and Olive (Giles), Sept. 29, 1859, P.R.18.
Fannie, d. William Thaxter and Olive (Giles), Oct. 9, 1855, P.R.18.
Henry [h. Diana (Otis)], July 15, 1800, G.R.1.
Martha Maria, ch. William T. and Olive [William Thaxter and Olive (Giles), P.R.18.], Sept. 20, 1836.
Oakes Angier, ch. Henry and Diana, May 8, 1841.
Samuel Thomas, ch. Henry and Diana, Mar. 13, 1832.
Susan, w. Thomas Marshall, Aug. 30, 1793, in Leominster, Mass., P.R.107.
Susan Maria, w. Albert M. Carter, d. William Thaxter and Olive (Giles), Nov. 20, 1852, P.R.18.
William, h. Betsey (Thaxter), Dec. 13, 1784, P.R.19.
William Henry, ch. Henry and Diana, May 5, 1829.
William James, ch. William T. and Olive, Aug. 28 [28 *in later handwriting*], 1839. [s. William Thaxter and Olive (Giles), Aug. 28, P.R.18.]
William James, ch. William T. and Olive [William Thaxter and Olive (Giles), P.R.18.], Mar. 23, 1844.
William Thaxter, h. Olive (Giles), Oct. 2, 1811, P.R.18. [s. William and Betsey (Thaxter), P.R.19. s. Betsy, Oct. 2, 1812, in Wiscassett, P.R.20.]

COLBY, Miller E., s. Edward H. and Ada S. (Miller), Nov. —, 1879, P.R.21.

COLCORD, Loring H., Nov. 30, 1871, G.R.1.
Lulu M. [————], w. Amos A., Mar. 25, 1871, G.R.1.
Rebecca [? m.], May 31, 1791, G.R.1.

COLEMAN, Martin M., ch. William and Isabel, Nov. 17, 1839. [Martin Murray Coleman, C.R.2.]
Mary Ann, ch. William and Isabel, June 18, 1836, in Lubec.
Robert Alexander, ch. William and Isabel, July 18, 1837.
Sarah E., ch. William and Isabel, Feb. 21, 1846.
Sarah Helen, ch. William and Isabella, bp. May 24, 1848, C.R.2.
William W. (Colman), ch. William and Isabel, Apr. 18, 1844.
William Wilson, ch. William and Isabella, bp. May 24, 1848, C.R.2.

COLLEY, Josephine M. [————] [w. Lemine], Jan. 3, 1828, G.R.1.
Lemine [h. Josephine M.], Apr. 13, 1823, G.R.1.

COLLINS, Anna G. [————], w. Ibrooke, Jan. 30, 1809, G.R.1.
Catherine A. [? m.], ———, 1857, G.R.1.
Charles Clinton, "Co. K. 4th Me Inf.," July 21, 1841, G.R.1.
Hosea, Jan. 24, 1813, G.R.2.
Ibrooke, h. Anna G., Oct. 7, 1805, G.R.1.
Nellie J., ch. Michael J. and Mary (Clark), Oct. 6, 1882.

COLSON, Benjamin, ch. Ephraim Jr. and w., July 20, 1824.
Caroline, ch. Ephraim Jr. and w., Oct. 6, 1826.
Eli, ch. Theophilus and Rhoda, Dec. 22, 1826.
Ephraim, ch. Ephraim Jr. and w., Dec. 10, 1821.
Miles S., ch. Theophilus and Rhoda, Sept. 7, 1823.
Stanto E., ch. Theophilus and Rhoda, Feb. 25, 1825.
Susan, ch. Ephraim Jr. and w., Feb. 4, 1829.

CONANT, Albert, h. Immogene Kalloch, s. Isaac and Nancy (Wentworth), May 21, 1820, P.R.68.
Andrew J., s. Isaac and Nancy (Wentworth), Feb. 11, 1829, P.R.68.
Benj[amin] W., h. Catherine B. (Bailey), s. Isaac and Nancy (Wentworth), Jan. 20, 1823, P.R.68.
Dama H., ———, 1843, G.R.1.
Elisha H., Jan. 22, 1826, G.R.1. [h. Mary Jane (Hawkes), s. Isaac and Nancy (Wentworth), P.R.68.]
Isaac, h. Nancy (Wentworth), Jan. 18, 1793, P.R.68.
Isaac Adelbert, h. Damaetta Havilla (Orcutt), Jan. 9, 1842, P.R.70.

CONANT, Isabella Maria, w. Ralph H. Howes, d. Isaac Adelbert and Damaetta Havilla (Orcutt), July 3, 1864, P.R.70.
Joseph A., h. Julia Ann Johnston, s. Isaac and Nancy (Wentworth), June 5, 1830, P.R.68.
Mary Jane [———] [w. Elisha H.], June 1, 1830, G.R.1.
Nancy, d. Isaac and Nancy (Wentworth), Dec. 22, 1832, P.R.68.
Nellie A., w. Edwin L. Stickney, adopted d. W[illia]m B. and Margaret L. (Handley), Sept. 20, 1857, P.R.69.
Rebecca, d. Isaac and Nancy (Wentworth), May 15, 1836, P.R.68.
Rebecca H., d. Isaac and Nancy (Wentworth), July 31, 1815, P.R.68.
Sarah [? m.], June 13, 1846, P.R.68.
W[illia]m B., h. Margaret (Handley), s. Isaac and Nancy (Wentworth), Aug. 11, 1817, P.R.68.

CONDON, Ada F., Aug. 4, 1862, G.R.1.
Adelbert N., Mar. 2, 1854, G.R.1.
Annie V., d. A. J. and Addie S., May 12, 1876, G.R.1.
Cora, ch. Rufus B. and Helen M., Mar. 28, 1856, G.R.1.
Eddie F., s. A. J. and Addie S., Apr. 24, 1880, G.R.1.
Eliza A. [———], w. Hiram A., Mar. 12, 1848, G.R.13.
Eliza M. Pease [———], w. Thomas, Mar. 14, 1826, G.R.1.
Ella, ch. Rufus B. and Helen M., Aug. 10, 1854, G.R.1.
Hiram A., h. Eliza A., May 18, 1834, G.R.13.
Leona B., d. Hiram A. and Eliza A., Aug. 31, 1888, G.R.13.
Mary J., w. George Howard, Aug. 22, 1844, G.R.1.
Nancy C., w. Eben P. Bramhall, Dec. 5, ——— [? 1818], in Martinicus, P.R.61.
Thomas, Capt., h. Eliza M. Pease, Aug. 12, 1820, G.R.1.
Verranus P., s. Capt. Tho[ma]s and Eliza, Apr. 23, 1849, G.R.1.
Wallie, ch. Rufus B. and Helen M., Apr. 16, 1867, G.R.1.

CONNELL, Daniel O., ———, 1854, G.R.1.

CONNER, Caroline R. [———], w. W[illia]m H., July 2, 1819, G.R.1.
John Augustine, ch. John H. and Lydia, Aug. 26, 1826.
Lucy A. [? m.], May 10, 1849, G.R.1.
Mary Ann, ch. John H. and Lydia, July 26, 1812.
William Harrison, ch. John H. and Lydia, Aug. 5, 1816.

COOK, Ada B., ———, 1872, G.R.1.
Annie A., w. [Fred L.] Mitchell, d. Jacob G. and Roxanna M., ———, 1858, G.R.1.
Jacob G., h. Roxanna M., ———, 1826, G.R.1.

COOK, James, ch. James and Rhoda (second w.), Mar. 9, 1837.
Roxanna M. [———], w. Jacob G., ———, 1824, G.R.I.
William E., ch. James and Rhoda (second w.), Dec. 7, 1839.

COOMBS, Agnes L. [———], w. Charles W., ———, 1865, G.R.I.
Arphaxard, Capt. [h. Harriet Lavina], Feb. 12, 1826, in Islesboro, G.R.I.
Caroline F., d. Robert and Jane P. (Gilkey), June 10, 1844, P.R.98.
Charles H., July 25, 1872, G.R.I.
Charles Henry, ch. Robert and w. [Jane P. (Gilkey), P.R.98.], Apr. 5, 1833.
Charles R., s. Robert H. and Harriet E. (Pendleton), Mar. 20, 1862, P.R.97.
Charles W., h. Agnes L., ———,.1862, G.R.I.
Cora J., d. Robert H. and Harriet E. (Pendleton), Sept. 18, 1852, P.R.97.
Emma F., w. Charles W. Hayes, d. Robert and Jane P. (Gilkey), July 6, 1849, P.R.98.
Frank B., s. Robert H. and Harriet E. (Pendleton), Dec. 12, 1858, P.R.97.
Franklin S., h. Sarah A. Burgess, s. Robert and Jane P. (Gilkey), Jan. 5, 1839, P.R.98.
Geneva A., d. Jordan W. and Julia L. (Riggs), Oct. 7, 1872, P.R.103.
Grace L., d. Jordan W. and Julia L. (Riggs), July 1, 1875, P.R.103.
Grenville A., s. J. B. and Maud M., Aug. 6, 1891, G.R.I.
Harriet Lavina [———] [w. Capt. Arphaxard], Nov. 14, 1827, in Islesboro, G.R.I.
Hollis, s. Robert and Jane P. (Gilkey), Mar. 27, 1837, P.R.98.
Jacob Westly, ch. Luther and Dianah, Aug. 18, 1832.
Jordan W. (see Welcome Jordan Coombs).
Lauriette Estelle, d. Lorenzo, bp. July 4, 1875, C.R.I.
Lorenzo, ch. Robert and w., Nov. 30, 1831. [Lorenzo G., h. Emma (Sleeper), s. Robert and Jane P. (Gilkey), P.R.98.]
Lucretia Mary, ch. Robert and w., June 7, 1830. [w. A. J. Macomber, d. Robert and Jane P. (Gilkey), June 9, P.R.98.]
Lucy Jane, d. Robert and Jane P. (Gilkey), Sept. 5, 1824, P.R.98.
Luther Augustine, ch. Luther and Dianah, May 7, 1829.
Lydia Jane, ch. Robert and w., Mar. 16, 1835. [w. Francis G. Barnes, d. Robert and Jane P. (Gilkey), P.R.98.]

COOMBS, Mary S. [? m.], Aug. 20, 1838, G.R.I.
Philip G., h. Marie Fernald, s. Robert and Jane P. (Gilkey), May 26, 1841, P.R.98.
Preston W., s. Arphaxard and Harriet L., July 14, 1863, G.R.I.
Ralph R., s. Jordan W. and Julia L. (Riggs), Jan. 19, 1886, P.R.103.
Robert, h. Jane P. (Gilkey), June 25, 1799, P.R.98.
Robert Harison [sic, Hudson], ch. Robert and w., July 5, 1828. [h. Harriet E. (Pendleton), July 3, P.R.97. s. Robert and Jane P. (Gilkey), July 3, P.R.98.]
Rosella A., d. Ja[me]s and Mary S., Nov. 24, 1859, G.R.I.
Royal C., July 28, 1883, G.R.I. [Royal G., s. Jordan W. and Julia L. (Riggs), P.R.103.]
Royal N., s. Robert and Jane P. (Gilkey), Sept. 16, 1842, P.R.98.
Statira, ch. Robert and w., Apr. 13, 1826. [Statira P., w. Abram Jordan, d. Robert and Jane P. (Gilkey), P.R.98.]
Walter Hudson, s. Robert H. and Harriet E. (Pendleton), Mar. 20, 1851, P.R.97.
Welcome Jordan, h. Julia C. (Riggs), s. Robert and Jane P. (Gilkey), Mar. 21, 1848, P.R.98.
William C., h. Mary A. (Merchant), ———, 1834, G.R.I.
Winifred, d. Lorenzo, bp. July 4, 1875, C.R.I.
———, s. Robert, Mar. 21, 1847, P.R.123.
———, d. Capt. Robert, July 6, 1848, P.R.123.
———, inf. Lorenzo, bp. ———, 1876, C.R.I.

COOPER, Maud, w. J. G. Burdin, ———, 1877, G.R.I.

CORBETT (see Cobbett).

COTTRELL, Ada Ellen, d. Capt. C. Y. Jr. and Clara E., Mar. 16, 1871, G.R.I.
Adelle, d. George W. and Amelia J. (Hodgdon), Apr. 27, 1855, P.R.99.
C. Y., h. Mary A. (Lucas), May 14, 1819, in Calais, P.R.133. [Christopher Y., h. Mary Ann (Lucas), May 14, 1818, P.R.134.]
C. Y. Jr., s. C. Y. and Mary A. (Lucas), Nov. 9, 1842, P.R.133. [Christopher Y. Jr., h. Clara E. (Knowlton), s. Christopher Y. and Mary Ann (Lucas), P.R.134.]
Charles Clinton, s. C. Y. and Mary A. (Lucas), July 30, 1865, P.R.133. [s. Christopher Y. and Mary Ann (Lucas), P.R.134.]
Chester W., s. George W. and Amelia J. (Hodgdon), Nov. 30, 1859, P.R.99.
Christopher Y. (see C. Y.).

COTTRELL, Edgar S., June 10, 1855, G.R.1.
Emery, s. George W. and Amelia J. (Hodgdon), Dec. 25, 1862, P.R.99.
George P., h. Sadie (Bakeman), s. George W. and Amelia J. (Hodgdon), July 28, 1856, P.R.99.
George W., h. Amelia J. (Hodgdon), Apr. 29, 1831, P.R.99.
Hattie D., d. C. Y. and Mary A. (Lucas), Nov. 19, 1855, P.R.133. [d. Christopher Y. and Mary Ann (Lucas), Nov. 19, 1856, P.R.134.]
Helen M. [———] [w. Judson E.], Sept. 17, 1854, G.R.1.
Ida E. [———], ——, 1859, G.R.1.
J. Y. Jr., ——, 1828, G.R.1.
Josiah C., s. George W. and Amelia J. (Hodgdon), July 13, 1861, P.R.99.
Judson E. [h. Helen M.], Jan. 6, 1858, G.R.1. [h. Nellie (Linekin), s. George W. and Amelia J. (Hodgdon), P.R.99.]
Mary E., d. C. Y. and Mary A. (Lucas), Aug. 30, 1844, P.R.133. [w. Horace T. Dean, G.R.1. Mary Eliza, w. Horace Dean, d. Christopher Y. and Mary Ann (Lucas), P.R.134.]
Phebe G., w. Henry Dunbar, Mar. 14, 1806, P.R.115.
S. R., Capt., Jan. 29, 1829, G.R.1.
Sarah A., d. C. Y. and Mary A. (Lucas), Sept. 16, 1849, P.R.133. [Sarah Abby, w. Valorous Dunton, d. Christopher Y. and Mary Ann (Lucas), P.R.134.]
Susan J., d. C. Y. and Mary A. (Lucas), June 2, 1853, P.R.133. [Susan Jane, w. George H. Braley, d. Christopher Y. and Mary Ann (Lucas), P.R.134.]
Walter M., Nov. 1, 1848, G.R.1.
William R., Sept. 1, 1852, G.R.1.

COUSENS (see Cousins), John H., s. John H. and Emma D., Oct. 24, 1840, in Ellsworth, G.R.1.

COUSINS (see Cousens), John N., ch. John and Diadania, Oct. 15, 1824.
Martha J., ch. John and Diadania, Sept. 7, 1827.
Nathan H., ch. John and Diadania, Nov. 5, 1835.
Sarah E., ch. John and Diadania, July 29, 1826.

COX, Irving Gilmore, ch. Fred G. and Alida M., May 15, 1887.

CRAIG, Authur L., Aug. —, 1834, G.R.1.
Catharine [? m.], June —, 1822, G.R.1.
Elizabeth M. [———], w. James, Nov. —, 1795, G.R.1.
James, h. Elizabeth M., Sept. —, 1787, G.R.1.

CRAIG, John S., Feb. —, 1826, G.R.1.
Robert M., Dec. —, 1827, G.R.1.

CRAM, Almira, ch. Nathan and Elizabeth, June 2, 1805.
Elizabeth, ch. Nathan and Elizabeth, Feb. 28, 1812.
Hannah, ch. Nathan and Elizabeth, July 4, 1807.
Sarah Eleanor, ch. Nathan and Elizabeth, Oct. 20, 1809.

CRARY, Charles C., h. Helen E., Sept. 15, 1828, G.R.6.
Helen E. [———], w. Charles C., May 27, 1834, G.R.6.

CRAWFORD, Alexander, h. Sarah R. (Henderson), Sept. —, 1817, G.R.1.
Charles E., Sept. 17, 1857, G.R.1.
Ellen Frances, d. Alexander and Sarah R. (Henderson), Apr. 9, 1850, G.R.1.
Lida Morse [w. [Melvin J.] Staples], d. Alexander and Sarah R. (Henderson), Mar. 4, 1855, G.R.1.

CRITCHETT, Frank O., June 2, 1858, G.R.1.

CROCKETT, Ida Virginia [? m.], June 15, 1834, G.R.1.

CROOKS, Horatio, ch. William and Jean, Sept. 16, 1801.
John, ch. William and Jean, Aug. 14, 1792.
John, ch. William and Jean, Feb. 6, 1796.
Nancy Gilmor [dup. Crook], ch. William and Jean, Nov. 18, 1793.

CROSBY, Ann Field, ch. William Esq. and Sally, Oct. 11, 1812.
Betsey, ch. Leonard and Mary, Sept. 21, 1814.
Elisha, ch. Leonard and Mary, Feb. 28, 1806.
Fred, July 7, 1844.
George, ch. William Esq. and Sally, Sept. 10, 1805.
Geo[rge] Augustus, ch. James and Mary, Apr. 8, 1845.
Horace, s. William George and Ann M., Dec. 5, 1847, G.R.1.
Jane, ch. William Esq. and Sally, Oct. 5, 1810.
Jane Ross, ch. James and Mary, Sept. 13, 1842.
Mary, ch. William Esq. and Sally, Nov. 20, 1807.
Mary, ch. Leonard and Mary, Sept. 28, 1808.
Sally, ch. Leonard and Mary, Dec. 7, 1803, in Dixmont.
Walter, ch. Leonard and Mary, June 6, 1810.
William George, h. Ann Maria [(Patterson)], Sept. 10, 1805, G.R.1.
W[illia]m Henry, ch. James and Mary, May 14, 1840.
———, s. James, Mar. 11, 1849, P.R.123.

CROSS, Martha, w. Benjamin Banks, Oct. 2, 1807 [? in Morrill], P.R.150.
Sarah [w. Alfred Johnson], June —, 1765 [in Newburyport, Mass.], P.R.1.

CROWELL, John, ——, 1842, G.R.1.
Thomas, ——, 1848, G.R.1.

CROWLEY, Frank E., Aug. 31, 1858, G.R.1.

CROXFORD, Martha Susannah Fuller, ch. Daniel F. and Sophronia, July 13, 1826.
Mary Eliza Folsom, ch. Daniel F. and Sophronia, July 2, 1824.

CUNINGHAM (see Cunningham), Charles [dup. Cunningham], ch. James and Polly, July 25, 1809.
Dulecina, ch. Jacob and Ruth, Dec. 28, 1808.
Frederick, ch. Thomas and Susanna, Jan. 14, 1801.
Jacob, ch. Ebnezar and Abigal, June 17, 1802.
James [dup. Cunningham Jr.], ch. James and Polly, July 21, 1806.
James Oliver, ch. Thomas and Susanna, Aug. 1, 1811.
Louisa, ch. Thomas and Susanna, Oct. 26, 1802.
Mary, ch. Thomas and Susanna, Feb. 14, 1804.
Salathiel Nickeson, ch. James and Polly, Oct. 21, 1807.
William, ch. Ebnezar and Abigal, Sept. 16, 1804.
William Henry Ran., ch. Thomas 2d and Abigail, Dec. 11, 1809.
Yorick Fredrick, ch. Thomas and Susanna, Mar. 17, 1808.

CUNNINGHAM (see Cuningham), A. E., Capt., h. Mary C., "Ju." 15, 1835, G.R.1.
Abigail Jane (see Abigail Jane Patterson).
Albert, ch. James and Sarah, Sept. 20, 1825.
Albert W., ch. Henry Whitman and Sallie R. (Holmes), ——, 1849, G.R.1.
Alex R., ch. James and Sarah, June 19, 1819.
Andros, ch. James and Sarah, Apr. 17, 1829.
Arabella R., w. Elijah Souther Shuman, Oct. 3, 1850, P.R.47.
Augusta Clara, w. Albert Increase Mather, d. Henry Whitman and Sallie R. (Holmes), ——, G.R.1.
B. F., s. Benjamin and Betsey (Stephenson), June 7, 1823, P.R.110.
Benjamin, h. Betsey (Stephenson), Apr. 18, 1790, in Edgecomb, P.R.110.
Edgar M., Jan. 14, 1846, G.R.1.

CUNNINGHAM, Eliza, d. Benjamin and Betsey (Stephenson), Mar. 5, 1819, P.R.110.
Eliza (see Eliza Davis).
Eliza A., ch. James and Philena, Dec. 4, 1830.
Eliza J. [? m.], ——, 1860, G.R.1.
Eliza Jane, ch. Thomas (Cuningham) and Susanna, Jan. 1, 1816.
Ellen V., ch. James and Philena, Dec. 17, 1835.
Emily Jane, ch. Oran and Lucinda, Oct. 29, 1843.
Fannie E., d. E. F. and R. J., Mar. 11, 1850, G.R.1.
Fanny, w. —— Boulter, d. Benjamin and Betsey (Stephenson), Aug. 28, 1825, P.R.110.
Frederick D., ch. Henry Whitman and Sallie R. (Holmes), ——, 1846, G.R.1.
Frederick M., s. William O. and Rachel F. (Smalley), Oct. 12, 1852, P.R.41.
Harvey S., h. Carrie (Shuman), s. William O. and Rachel F. (Smalley), July 2, 1854, P.R.41.
Helen E., w. —— Berry, d. Henry Whitman and Sallie R. (Holmes), ——, 1835, G.R.1.
Henry B., Oct. 21, 1855, G.R.1.
Henry H., ch. Henry Whitman and Sallie R. (Holmes), ——, 1837, G.R.1.
Henry Whitman, h. Sallie R. (Holmes), Sept. 12, 1806, G.R.1.
Hutson Bishop, ch. Samuel 2d and Eliza, July 1, 1821.
James, Aug. 27, 1818, G.R.1.
James H., June 24, 1848, G.R.4. [s. Orrin, P.R.123. h. Lizzie M. (Swett), P.R.131.]
James W., "Co. A. Me. Coast Guards" [ch. William and Mary N.], Mar. 10, 1845, G.R.1.
Jane, d. Benjamin and Betsey (Stephenson), May 29, 1815, P.R.110.
John C., h. Ann, ——, 1808, G.R.1.
Lydia A. Beckett [——], w. Barney, ——, 1821, G.R.1.
Margaret P., ch. James and Philena, Nov. 6, 1838.
Martha A. [——], w. G. W., Sept. 18, 1830, G.R.1.
Martha Jane, ch. Samuel 2d and Eliza, Mar. 17, 1823.
Martin E., ch. Oran and Lucinda, Jan. 14, 1846.
Mary C. [——], w. Capt. A. E., Apr. 23, 1839, G.R.1.
Mary E., ch. James and Philena, May 22, 1832.
Mary Emma, w. Eugene Wood, d. James H. and Lizzie M. (Swett), Oct. 12, 1873, P.R.131.
Mary N. [——], w. William, Jan. 1, 1812, G.R.1.
Oran, ch. Oran and Lucinda, June 17, 1841.

CUNNINGHAM, Orrin H., s. William O. and Rachel F. (Smalley), Aug. 22, 1850, P.R.41.
Polly S., ch. James and Polly, Feb. 22, 1817.
Ralph, triplet s. Harvey S. and Carrie (Shuman), Sept. 29, 1889, P.R.41. [Ralph H., triplet s. Harvey S. and Carrie A. (Shuman), P.R.42.]
Rena, triplet d. Harvey S. and Carrie (Shuman), Sept. 29, 1889, P.R.41. [Rena E., triplet d. Harvey S. and Carrie A. (Shuman), P.R.42.]
Rilla M., ch. Henry Whitman and Sallie R. (Holmes), ———, 1844, G.R.1.
Roscoe W., s. Harvey S. and Carrie (Shuman), Jan. 26, 1885, P.R.41. [William Roscoe, h. Julia B. Brown, s. Harvey S. and Carrie A. (Shuman), P.R.42. Roscoe William, s. Harvey S. and Carrie A. (Shuman), P.R.48.]
Roy, triplet s. Harvey S. and Carrie (Shuman), Sept. 29, 1889, P.R.41. [Roy E., triplet s. Harvey S. and Carrie A. (Shuman), P.R.42.]
Ruth N., ch. Oran and Lucinda, May 18, 1840.
Salathiel N., ch. James and Sarah, Aug. 3, 1827.
Sarah A., w. ——— Brooks, d. Henry Whitman and Sallie R. (Holmes), ———, 1833, G.R.1.
Sarah J., ch. James and Sarah, Oct. 20, 1826.
Thomas, ch. James and Polly, Mar. 24, 1814.
W. O., Feb. 26, 1817, G.R.1. [William O., h. Rachel F. (Smalley), P.R.41.]
Walter E., ch. James H. and Lizzie M., July 27, 1886. [Walter Ernest, h. Isabel Littlefield, s. James H. and Lizzie M. (Swett), P.R.131.]
William, ch. James and Polly, Mar. 2, 1815. [h. Mary N., G.R.1.]
W[illia]m C., s. Benjamin and Betsey (Stephenson), Aug. 4, 1813, P.R.110.
W[illia]m H., s. Benjamin and Betsey (Stephenson), June 24, 1817, P.R.110.
William J., ———, 1852, G.R.1.
William O. (see W. O.).
William Oliver, s. William O. and Rachel F. (Smalley), Dec. 3, 1848, P.R.41.
William Roscoe (see Roscoe W.).
———, s. Jacob W., Aug. 5, 1849, P.R.123.

CURTIS, Edwin D., s. James A. and Mary L. (Patershall), Nov. 27, 1856, P.R.12.
Eugene Watson, ch. James and Eliza A., Dec. 7, 1843.

CURTIS, F. A., ch. James A. and Mary L. (Patershall), Dec. 3, 1859, P.R.12.
Levi L., "1st Me. Regt. Heavy Art.," h. Sarah E., Feb. 26, 1834, G.R.1.
Maurice E., ——, 1875, G.R.1.
Robert P., h. Verena Estella, Nov. 9, 1837, G.R.1.
Russell G., s. James A. and Mary L. (Patershall), June 11, 1868, P.R.12.
Sarah E. [——], w. Levi L., June 2, 1832, G.R.1.
Verena Estella [——], w. Robert P., Aug. 27, 1846, G.R.1.
——, s. Charles G., Nov. 6, 1847, P.R.123.

CUTTER, Caroline McLellan, d. Edw[ard] F. and Mary E., bp. Feb. 13, 1848, C.R.2.
Ellen M. [w. Henry Atherton Starrett], ——, 1838, G.R.1.

DAMON, Annie L. [——], w. J. G., Oct. 27, 1839, G.R.1.

DANFORTH, ——, s. John, Mar. 26, 1848, P.R.123.

DARBY (see Derby), Bertie E., ch. Joseph H. and Martha A. (Patershall), July 15, 1878, P.R.12.
Geo[rge] H., ch. Joseph H. and Martha A. (Patershall), Sept. 20, 1876, P.R.12.
Ida, d. Joseph H. and Martha A., Aug. 11, 1867, G.R.1. [Ida E., ch. Joseph H. and Martha A. (Patershall), P.R.12.]
Lucy, ch. Joseph H. and Martha A. (Patershall), Oct. 6, 1873, P.R.12.
Maud E. [——], w. Ralph F., Aug. 6, 1883, G.R.1.
Millie I., ch. Joseph H. and Martha A. (Patershall), Jan. 22, 1884, P.R.12.
Ralph F., ch. Joseph H. and Martha A. (Patershall), June 29, 1881, P.R.12.
Walter S., ch. Joseph H. and Martha A. (Patershall), Feb. 14, 1870, P.R.12.

DAVIDSON, Abigail, ch. Henry and Sarah, bp. Mar. 1, 1831, C.R.2.
Clarissa Ann, ch. Henry and Sarah, bp. Aug. 22, 1824, C.R.2.
John Quincy Adams, ch. Henry and Jane, bp. Jan. —, 1817, C.R.2.
John S., Aug. 21, 1850, G.R.1.
Louisa, ch. Henry and Sarah, bp. ——, 1825, C.R.2.
Mary, [dup. inf.] ch. Henry and Sarah, bp. Mar. 1, 1831, C.R.2.
Mary Elizabeth, ch. Henry and Jane, bp. Jan. —, 1817, C.R.2.
Robert Dinsmoor, ch. Henry and Jane, bp. Jan. —, 1817, C.R.2.
Robert Dinsmore, ch. Henry and Jane W., July 25, 1810.
Sarah Jane, ch. Henry and Sarah, bp. Sept. 30, 1821, C.R.2.

DAVIS, A. Preston, s. Leander and Eliza (Cunningham), Oct. 2, 1866, P.R.93. P.R.110.
Alfred, ch. Benjamin 2d and Jane (second w.), Feb. 23, 1825.
Asa, ch. Benjamin 2d and Dolly, June 10, 1812.
Asenath Ann, ch. Ansell and Mary, Sept. 22, 1831.
Benjamin, ch. Benjamin 2d and Jane (second w.), July 28, 1821.
Benjamin P., May 3, 1850, G.R.1. [B. Preston Davis, s. Leander and Eliza (Cunningham), P.R.93. Benjamin P., s. Leander and Eliza (Cunningham), P.R.110.]
Betsey Marble, ch. William and Betsey, Oct. 29, 1821.
Charlotte French, ch. Benjamin 2d and Jane (second w.), ———— [rec. after ch. b. Oct. 27, 1829].
Cyrus R., ch. Phineas and Mary, Sept. 1, 1846.
Dolly, ch. Benjamin 2d and Jane (second w.), Sept. 26, 1815.
Elisabeth Jane, ch. James and Ann, Aug. 2, 1839.
Eliza, w. Peter Richardson Holmes, w. Joshua Dennison,————, 1794, P.R.175.
Eliza [————], w. Leander, July 18, 1821, G.R.1. [d. Benjamin Cunningham and Betsey (Stephenson), P.R.93. P.R.110.]
Elizabeth Jane (see Elisabeth Jane).
Emery, ch. James and Ann, Oct. 10, 1837.
Emery, s. E. P. and Annie, Oct. 26, 1889, G.R.1.
Esther, ch. William and Eliza, Nov. 12, 1826.
Esther Tarr, ch. William and Betsey, Apr. 22, 1811.
Frances, ch. Phineas and Mary, Dec. 24, 1839. [Frances A., w. William J. Dennett, Dec. 25, G.R.1.]
Francis, ch. William and Betsey, May 26, 1816.
Franklin Houston, ch. Benjamin 2d and Jane (second w.), ————.
Franklin Houston, ch. Benjamin 2d and Jane (second w.), ————.
Fred S., s. Leander and Eliza (Cunningham), Sept. 19, 1868, P.R.93. [h. Annie, P.R.110.]
George W., s. Leander and Eliza (Cunningham), Apr. 26, 1845, P.R.93. P.R.110.
Harriet Lovina, ch. James and Ann, May 25, 1831.
Henry, ch. Phineas and Mary, Nov. 22, 1836.
James, ch. William and Betsey, Oct. 9, 1817.
Ja[me]s W. Webster, ch. James and Ann, Sept. 16, 1833.
Jesse, Sept. 3, 1859, G.R.1. [s. Leander and Eliza (Cunningham), P.R.93. P.R.110.]
Jones Shaw, ch. Phineas and Mary, Oct. 24, 1825. [[h. Susan A.] G.R.1.]
Joseph E., ch. Phineas and Mary, Sept. 7, 1834.

DAVIS, Leander, h. Eliza, Aug. 23, 1818, G.R.1. [h. Eliza (Cunningham), P.R.93. P.R.110.]
Leander, s. Leander and Eliza (Cunningham), July 14, 1853, P.R.93. P.R.110.
Lizzie F., w. Jefferson F. Wilson, d. Leander and Eliza (Cunningham), July 6, 1847, P.R.93. P.R.110.
Lucy Davis, ch. Phineas and Mary, Feb. 3, 1819.
Lydia R., ch. Benjamin 2d and Jane (second w.), Aug. 21, 1819.
Martha Ann, ch. James and Ann, Oct. 2, 1824.
Mary, ch. William and Betsey, Dec. 5, 1812.
Mary, ch. Phineas and Mary, Apr. 28, 1821.
Mary B., ch. Eleazer and Jane, ——— [rec. before ch. b. June 23, 1823].
Mary Elisabeth, ch. William and Eliza, Feb. 1, 1825.
Mary Jane, ch. Eleazer and Jane, June 23, 1823.
Nancy, ch. Phineas and Mary, Aug. 31, 1831.
Rhoda, ch. Phineas and Mary, Mar. 2, 1823.
Rufus Land, ch. James and Ann, Oct. 26, 1835.
Ruth, ch. Benjamin 2d and Jane (second w.), Mar. 30, 1827.
Ruth Ann, ch. William and Eliza, July 13, 1827.
Ruth W. Bourne, ch. James and Ann, May 26, 1829.
Samuel French, ch. Benjamin 2d and Jane (second w.), Oct. 27, 1829.
Sarah Elisabeth, ch. Phineas and Mary, Mar. 14, 1828.
Susan A. [———], w. Jones S., July 14, 1829, G.R.1.
Susan J., ch. Benjamin 2d and Jane (second w.), Aug. 23, 1817.
William, ch. William and Betsey, May 27, 1814.
William, ch. Benjamin 2d and Jane (second w.), Apr. 23, 1823.
William Bourne, ch. James and Ann, Mar. 21, 1827.
William Thomas, ch. William and Eliza, Apr. 16, 1830.

DAY, George William, ch. George P. and Sarah, Aug. 28, 1825.
Harriet Maria, ch. George P. and Sarah, May 18, 1830.
John Hull, ch. George P. and Sarah, Nov. 28, 1827.
Sarah Elizabeth, ch. George P. and Sarah, May 15, 1823.

DEAN, Andrew Jackson, ch. Andrew and Sarah, Aug. 6, 1834.
Charles Edwin, ch. Andrew and Sarah, Aug. 17, 1840.
Charles R., ch. Horace T. and Mary E., ———, 1870, G.R.1.
Harriet Loisa, ch. Andrew and Sarah, Apr. 13, 1838.
Harriet Matilda, ch. Andrew and Sarah, Nov. 27, 1832.
Horace T., h. Mary E. [(Cottrell)], ———, 1845, G.R.1.
Jesse H., ch. Horace T. and Mary E., ———, 1872, G.R.1.
Laura Ann, ch. Andrew and Sarah, Dec. 29, 1829.

DEAN, Lucy Margaret, second w. David Lancaster, Apr. 2, 1827, P.R.108.
Sarah, ch. Andrew and Sarah, Oct. 2, 1826.

DEARING, Alphonso O., ———, 1850, G.R.4.
Lenora M. [? m.], ———, 1859, G.R.4.

DEMMONS, Mildred A. [? m.], Aug. 12, 1891, G.R.1.

DENNETT, A. Louise, d. Jacob K. and Annie T. (Riggs), Nov. 12, 1889, P.R.103. [Anna Louise, d. Jacob Knight and Annie T., in Bangor, P.R.105.]
Clara Jane, ch. Joseph Jr. and Ann, June 4, 1843. [w. Joseph A. Gilmore, d. Joseph and Ann (Dyer), P.R.105.]
George Williams, ch. Joseph Jr. and Ann [(Dyer) P.R.105.], July 9, 1845.
Jacob Knight, h. Annie T., s. William J. and Fanny, Dec. 1, 1866, P.R.105.
Joseph, Sept. 27, 1815, G.R.1. [h. Ann (Dyer), in Portland, P.R.105.]
Mary Alice, d. William J. and Fanny, Nov. —, 1868, in Ellsworth, P.R.105.
Mary Ann, w. Oramel B. Blake, d. Joseph and Ann (Dyer), Jan. 16, 1839, in Brooksville, P.R.105.
Willard D., s. William J., Jan. 1, 1878, in Tenants Harbor, P.R.105.
William J., h. Fanny, s. Joseph and Ann (Dyer), Feb. 22, 1841, in Castine, P.R.105.

DERBY (see Darby), Mary Ann Soper, ch. Reuben and Mariam, Jan. 25, 1806.
Mary Swett (see Mary S. Frederick).
Samuel, ch. Reuben and Mariam, Dec. 25, 1803.

DICKERSON, Frank W., Maj., "5 U. S. Cavalry," Mar. 26, 1841, G.R.1.
Jerrie, s. J. G. and Jane, Oct. 22, 1850, G.R.1.
Johnnie, s. J. G. and Eliza A., Oct. 3, 1869, G.R.1.
Jonathan G., Judge, Nov. 5, 1811, G.R.1.

DICKEY, Alice G., Dec. 3, 1880, G.R.1.
Cassius R., June 8, 1866, G.R.1.
Homer J., June 16, 1873, G.R.1.

DILLAWAY, Catharine B., ch. Samuel and Nancy (second w.), Aug. 2, 1821.
Eliza, ch. Samuel and Anna, June 7, [18]11, in Northport.

DILLAWAY, Frances Caroline, ch. Samuel and Nancy (second w.), July 29, 1827.
Gilman, ch. Samuel and Anna, June 5, 1806, in Warren [sic, see Silas].
Lovisa C., ch. Samuel and Nancy (second w.), July 21, 1823.
Lucinda, ch. Samuel and Nancy (second w.), Apr. 11, 1817.
Mary A., ch. Samuel and Nancy (second w.), May 10, 1813 [sic, ? 1814, see death].
Sally, ch. Samuel and Anna, Dec. 3, [18]08, in Lincolnville.
Sam[ue]l Jr., ch. Samuel and Nancy (second w.), Mar. 3, 1815.
Silas, ch. Samuel and Anna, Nov. 18, 1805, in Warren [sic, see Gilman].

DINSMORE, B. C., h. Susan A., ———, 1824, G.R.1.
Susan A. [———], w. B. C., ———, 1828, G.R.1.

DODGE, Alfonson, ch. Jeeremy and Betsy, Dec. 7, 1837.
Angelia H. [? m.], Aug. 2, 1841, G.R.13.
Annie Bell, d. Ferdinand and Eliza Ann (Lancaster), July 10, 1856, P.R.108.
Betsey J. [———], w. Jeremy, ———, 1802, G.R.1.
Ellen Gertrude, ch. Jeeremy and Betsy, Mar. 14, 1841.
Eugene, ch. Jeeremy and Betsy, Nov. 25, 1839.
Gustavus, ch. Jeeremy and Betsy, Mar. 8, 1843. [Gustavus C., ———, 1844, G.R.1.]
James H., Jan. 1, 1852, G.R.1.
Jeremy, h. Betsey J., ———, 1806, G.R.1.

DOE, Adolphus W., Dec. 12, 1829, G.R.1.
Charles A., h. Susie D. (Black), July 8, 1863, G.R.1.
Charles H., s. Charles A. and Susan D. (Black), Dec. 22, 1890, in Fort Payne, Ala., P.R.53.

DOLLOFF, John, Mar. 4, 1847, G.R.1.
Vannie, w. William J. Havener, ———, 1879, G.R.1.

DONNELL, Ann Maria (see Maria A. Marriner).

DOUGHERTY, ———, s. Michael (Irish), Apr. 9, 1849, P.R.123.

DOUGLASS, Abigail, ch. James and Abigail, May 11, 1818.
Elizabeth, ch. James and Abigail, Sept. 15, 1815.
James Jr., ch. James and Abigal, June 20, 1814.
Lovisa, ch. James and Abigal, Nov. 27, 1827.
Lovisa Freeman, ch. James and Abigal, Apr. 11, 1823.
Mary, ch. James and Abigal, Jan. 17, 1822.

DOW, Hannah G., ch. Daniel and Mary R., June 20, 1851.
Lorenzo, ——, 1825, G.R.1.
Margaret E., ch. Daniel and Mary R., Sept. 20, 1861.
Sarah, w. Lewis F. Shepard, ——, 1801, in Kensington, N. H. [Apr. 22, G.R.1.]

DOYLE, Alethea Orianna (see Elthoa Oriana).
Charlotte Octavia, ch. John and Charlotte, Nov. 10, 1840.
Elthoa Oriana, ch. John and Charlotte, Oct. 1, 1835.
John Ostinelli, ch. John and Charlotte, Sept. 5, 1837.
William Oliver, ch. John and Charlotte, Oct. 14, 1832.

DRINKWATER, Alonzo J., h. Abbie E. (Marriner), ——, 1835, G.R.1.
David C., Jan. 7, 1828, in Northport, P.R.78.
David M., Apr. 19, 1855, in Northport, P.R.78.
Minnie B. [——], w. Percy M., ——, 1873, G.R.1.
Percy M., h. Minnie B., ——, 1880, G.R.1.
——, d. Mark, Apr. 25, 1848, P.R.123.

DUMMER, Martha J., w. Hugh Johnston Anderson, Oct. 12, 1807, G.R.1.

DUNBAR, Caro[line] Frances, ch. William M. and Elvira, Oct. 16, 1861.
Edward H., h. Elizabeth E. (Dodge), s. Henry Jr. and Sarah J. (Pote), Oct. 7, 1857, P.R.115.
Edward M., July 24, 1885, G.R.1. [s. Edward H. and Elizabeth E. (Dodge), P.R.115.]
Emma A., ch. Henry and Pheobe, May 8, 1845. [w. —— Dexter, d. Henry and Phebe G. (Cottrell), P.R.115.]
Henry, h. Phebe G. (Cottrell), Nov. 24, 1804, P.R.115.
Henry, Mar. 2, 1831, G.R.1. [Henry Jr., h. Sarah J. (Pote), s. Henry and Phebe G. (Cottrell), P.R.115.]
Joshua C., ch. Henry and Pheobe [Phebe G. (Cottrell), P.R.115.], Jan. 25, 1839.
Margaret R. Y., d. Henry and Phebe G. (Cottrell), Aug. 26, 1834, P.R.115.
Phebe Elizabeth, w. Charles E. Crawford, d. Henry Jr. and Sarah J. (Pote), Aug. 29, 1859, P.R.115.
Prudence C., d. Henry and Phebe G. (Cottrell), June 1, 1829, P.R.115.
Sarah V., w. —— Taylor, d. Henry and Phebe G. (Cottrell), Jan. 30, 1833, P.R.115.
Sylvanus G., ch. Henry and Pheobe, Apr. 21, 1843. [Sylvanus G. S., s. Henry and Phebe G. (Cottrell), P.R.115.]

DUNING, ———, s. ——— (Daniels) of Lawrence, Mass., Nov. 15, 1847, P.R.123.

DUNTON, Bertha M., d. R. V. and Sarah A., May 10, 1876, G.R.I.

DURGIN, Susanna, w. Job Allard, Aug. 15, 1767, P.R.77.

DURHAM, Albert, ch. William and Salina [Selina (Hatch), P.R.141.], Apr. 9, 1821.
Anna, ch. John and Elizabeth, Dec. 17, 1795.
Anna, d. John and Elizabeth, bp. July 16, 1797, C.R.2.
Annie Agness, w. Ben Hazeltine, d. Franklin H. and Sarah Ellen (Wight), Aug. 31, 1867, P.R.4.
Anson Edmunds, ch. William and Salina, Dec. 6, 1826. [s. William and Selina (Hatch), Dec. 5, P.R.141.]
Charles, ch. Jonathan and Eunice, Jan. 7, 1823.
Clarinday, ch. Jonathan and Susan (Field), Apr. 2, 1839, P.R.6.
David, ch. John and Elizabeth, Apr. 19, 1783.
David, ch. Tolford and Jean, July 7, 1792.
Edward W., s. William and Selina (Hatch), Aug. 28, 1836, P.R.141.
Elizabeth, ch. John and Elizabeth, Apr. 8, 1785. [w. Alvan Edmunds, G.R.I.]
Emma Lena, d. Franklin H. and Sarah Ellen (Wight), Jan. 28, 1871, P.R.4.
Eunice [———], w. Jonathan, Apr. 29, 1790, G.R.I.
Frank J., s. Frank H. and Sarah E., May 18, 1860, G.R.I. [Joseph Franklin Durham, s. Franklin H. and Sarah Ellen (Wight), P.R.4.]
Franklin Houston, ch. James and Elizabeth, bp. July 10, 1836, C.R.2. [Frank H., b. Mar. 8, 1833, G.R.I. Franklin H., s. James and Betsey, b. Mar. 8, 1833, P.R.4.]
Frederic J., ch. James and Betsey (second w.), Mar. 16, 1835. [James Frederick, ch. James and Elizabeth, C.R.2. Fred J., G.R.I.]
George Anson, ch. Jonathan and Eunice, Mar. 20, 1820.
George Sidney, ch. William and Salina [Selina (Hatch), P.R.141.], Aug. 27, 1810.
Georgiana D., ch. Jonathan and Susan (Field), Aug. 2, 1846, P.R.6.
Harriet, ch. William and Salina [Selina (Hatch), P.R.141.], Apr. 28, 1812.
Harriet Cross, ch. Jonathan and Susan (Field), Sept. 14, 1841, P.R.6.

DURHAM, Isabella Barnet [dup. w. Charles Treadwell], ch.
John and Elizabeth, Dec. 12, 1801. [Isabella Bernard
Durham, C.R.2.]
James, ch. Tolford and Jean, June 6, 1785.
James, ch. John and Elizabeth, June 22, 1787.
James Clinton, s. Franklin H. and Sarah Ellen (Wight), Nov.
17, 1861, P.R.4.
James Frederick (see Frederic J.).
James Monroe, ch. Jonathan and Eunice, Apr. 29, 1821.
Jean, ch. Tolford and Jean, Sept. 23, 1787. [Jane, w. James
McCrillis, P.R.138.]
John, ch. John and Elizabeth, Sept. 29, 1781.
John, ch. Tolford and Jean, Mar. 8, 1783.
John Sargent, ch. Jonathan and Eunice, June 22, 1824.
Jonathan, ch. John and Elizabeth, Apr. 26, 1790.
Jonathan, ch. Tolford and Jean, May 9, 1802. [h. Susan
(Field), P.R.6.]
Jonathan Barnet, ch. Jonathan and Eunice, Mar. 11, 1827.
Joseph Franklin (see Frank J.).
Joseph Jenny, ch. W[illia]m 2d and Emily, Sept. 30, 1832.
Joshua, ch. Tolford and Jean, Jan. 12, 1799. [Joshua Tolford
Durham, ch. Tolford and Jane, C.R.2.]
Joshua Eveleth, ch. William and Salina [Selina (Hatch),
P.R.141.], Feb. 17, 1823.
Margret, ch. Tolford and Jean, July 8, 1794.
Maria Amanda, ch. James and Elizabeth, bp. July 10, 1836,
C.R.2.
Mary, ch. Tolford and Jean, Aug. 20, 1778.
Mary, ch. Tolford and Jean, Apr. 7, 1790.
Mary, ch. John and Elizabeth, Feb. 4, 1793.
Mary Anna, ch. Jonathan and Eunice, Oct. 7, 1818.
Mary Eleanor, ch. Jonathan and w., bp. Nov. 15, 1835, C.R.2.
[w. Benjamin T. Black, b. May 1, 1834, G.R.1. P.R.53.
d. Jonathan and Susan (Field), b. May 1, 1834, P.R.6.]
Mary Elizabeth, ch. James and Betsey (second w.), Feb. 4,
1828.
Mary Elizabeth, ch. James and Elizabeth, bp. July 10, 1836,
C.R.2.
Mary Jane, ch. William and Salina [Selina (Hatch), P.R.141.],
Jan. 8, 1817.
Minna [———], w. William H., ———, 1878, G.R.1.
Nancy Ann, ch. James and Nancy, Jan. 29, 1812.
Narcissa, ch. William and Salina [Selina (Hatch), P.R.141.],
Dec. 7, 1814.

DURHAM, Ralph, s. William and Selina (Hatch), Feb. 3, 1830, P.R.141.
Sally, ch. Tolford and Jean, Dec. 13, 1796. [Sarah, ch. Tolford and Jane, C.R.2.]
Sally Jane, ch. James and Betsey (second w.), Nov. 12, 1819.
Sarah (see Sally).
Sarah, ch. John and Elizabeth, Apr. 22, 1804.
Sarah Burgess, d. Franklin H. and Sarah Ellen (Wight), July 27, 1873, P.R.4.
Sarah Elizabeth, ch. Jonathan and Eunice, Jan. 16, 1826.
Sarah Emeline, ch. Jonathan and w., bp. Nov. 28, 1838, C.R.2. [ch. Jonathan and Susan (Field), b. Jan. 22, 1837, P.R.6.]
Susan Jane, ch. Jonathan and w., bp. Nov. 15, 1835, C.R.2. [ch. Jonathan and Susan (Field), b. Jan. 23, 1831, P.R.6.]
Tolford, ch. James and Betsey (second w.), Apr. 26, 1824.
William, ch. Tolford and Jean, Oct. 29, 1780.
William, ch. John and Elizabeth, Dec. 9, 1798.
William, ch. Jonathan and Eunice, May 31, 1831.
William Nelson, ch. William and Salina, Dec. 30, 1818. [s. William and Selina (Hatch), Dec. 31, P.R.141.]
Willis Allen, s. Franklin H. and Sarah Ellen (Wight), Nov. 21, 1863, P.R.4.

DURNING, Caroline F., w. Franklin Hall Black, ———, 1856, G.R.1.

DUSENBURY, Charles, Nov. 9, 1830, G.R.1.

DUTCH, ———, s. Sam[ue]l, Feb. 26, 1848, P.R.123.

DUTTON, William H., h. Sarah E. [(Torrey)], Jan. 4, 1817, G.R.1.

DWELLEY, Frederick A., h. Hannah W. Snowden, ———, 1833, G.R.1.
Hannah W. Snowden [———], w. Frederick A., ———, 1841, G.R.1.

DYER, Allen Orcutt, s. George and Eleanor J. (Orcutt), Aug. 10, 1870, P.R.30.
Ann, w. Joseph Dennett, Dec. 13, 1815, in Brooksville, P.R.105.
Anna [———], w. James S., July 31, 1850, G.R.1.
Charles Wesley, inf., bp. June 30, 1861, C.R.3.
David W., h. Sarah A. (Shute), Nov. 29, 1815, G.R.1.
Eleanor Ray [———], w. George W., July 5, 1813, P.R.30.
Eliza A., w. Simeon Staples, May 14, 1819, G.R.1.

DYER, Frederick H., Jan. 6, 1875, G.R.1.
Fredric H., ――, 1845, G.R.1.
George, h. Eleanor Jane (Orcutt), Feb. 9, 1837, P.R.30.
George W., h. Eleanor Ray, Mar. 1, 1809, P.R.30.
Harry B., July 27, 1880, G.R.1.
James S., h. Anna, Oct. 17, 1846, G.R.1.
John A., ch. Capt. ―――― and Lacy [sic, ? Lucy], Aug. 11, 1842.
Mary E., ch. Capt. ―――― and Lacy [sic, ? Lucy], Dec. 20, 1840.
Russell G., Nov. 19, 1845, G.R.1.
Sarah Ellen, ch. David W. and Sarah A., Oct. 19, 1840.
W[illia]m P., ch. Capt. ―――― and Lacy [sic, ? Lucy], May 2, 1844.
――――, d. David, June 5, 1847, P.R.123.

EAMES (see Ames), Abigail [――――], w. Lt. Frank P., Nov. 4, 1829.
Frank P., Lt., h. Abigail, July 24, 1825, G.R.1.

EASTMAN, Frank W., s. Philip and Annie M., July 13, 1861, G.R.1.
Philip T., s. Philip and Charlotte B., Feb. 15, 1838, G.R.1.

EATON, Louisa W., w. Charles Pendleton, Aug. 6, 1807, P.R.67.

EAYRS, Joseph, h. Kezia (McKeen), Jan. 5, 1760.

EDGECOMB (see Edgecombe), Percy S., ――, 1858, G.R.1.
Rodney Burgin (see Rodney Burgin).
Sylvanus T. 2d, ch. Herbert W. and Rebecca N., Nov. 16, 1890.

EDGECOMBE (see Edgecomb), Herbert W., Dec. 29, 1855, G.R.1.
Sylvanus T., July 19, 1826, G.R.1.

EDMUNDS, Alvan, h. Elizabeth (Durham), July 21, 1780, G.R.1.
Asa, h. Eunice (Hawley), Aug. 19, 1757, G.R.1.
Charles Chapman, ch. Alvan and Elizabeth, Oct. 27, 1817. [h.Mary Ann, G.R.1.]
Eunice Elizabeth, ch. Alvan and Elizabeth, July 9, 1810. [w. Norman E. Roberts, G.R.1.]
George Anson, ch. Alvan and Elizabeth, Apr. 3, 1807. [Apr. 3, 1809, G.R.1.]
Mary Ann [――――], w. Charles Chapman, Aug. 22, 1818, G.R.1.
Norman N., ch. Charles C. and Marianna, Oct. 22, 1840.

EDWARDS, Abba Elizabeth, ch. Samuel and Ruth, Nov. 28, 1845.
Charles Augustine, ch. Samuel and Ruth, Aug. 15, 1836.
Elizabeth, ch. John and Sabrina, Nov. 22, 1819.
Frederick Hodsdon, ch. Samuel and Ruth, July 9, 1841.
Geo[rge] W., ch. John and Sabrina, Feb. 6, 1836.
Harriet S., ch. John and Sabrina, Jan. 4, 1824.
Jessee, ch. John and Sabrina, Sept. 24, 1822.
John F., ch. John and Sabrina, Jan. 14, 1827.
Julia Elah, ch. Ebenezer and Julia Ann, Mar. 2, 1845.
Mary Emma, ch. Ebenezer and Julia Ann, Mar. 26, 1842.
W[illia]m F., ch. John and Sabrina, Apr. 17, 1845.

EELLS (see Ellis, Ells), Albert Henry, ch. Henry B. and w., May 7, 1819.
Albion Orr, ch. Robert L. and Eunice K., Oct. 30, 1823.
Benj[amin] Franklin, ch. Benjamin and Jane, Nov. 2, 1819.
Bezaleel, ch. Nathaniel and Polly, Oct. 13, 1805.
Charles Josselyn, ch. Benjamin and Jane, May 13, 1813.
Edgar Augustas, ch. Henry B. and w., May 20, 1825.
Eleanor Jane, ch. Benjamin and Jane, Jan. 23, 1811.
Evalina Abby, ch. Henry B. and w., May 20, 1814.
Hannah, ch. Nathaniel and Polly, Jan. 24, 1808.
Harriot Augusta, ch. Henry B. and w., Dec. 18, 1822.
Lorenzo Melvin, ch. Robert L. and Eunice K., Oct. 12, 1818.
Lydia, ch. Samuel and Lydia, June 26, 1799.
Nathaniel Augustas, ch. Henry B. and w., Mar. 30, 1827.
Nathaniel Williams, ch. Robert L. and Eunice K., Oct. 5, 1828.
Polly Terry, ch. Nathaniel and Polly, Jan. 26, 1799.
Pricilla Palmer, ch. Samuel and Lydia, May 7, 1796.
Robert Lenthall, ch. Nathaniel and Polly, June 18, 1794, in Hanover.
Ruth, ch. Nathaniel and Polly, July 9, 1810.
Sally Maria, ch. Benjamin and Jane, Mar. 25, 1817.
Samuel, ch. Benjamin and Jane, May 10, 1815.
Sarah Burnham, ch. Henry B. and w., Mar. 14, 1830.
William, ch. Nathaniel and Polly, Feb. 19, 1801.
William, ch. Nathaniel and Polly, June 13, 1803.
Zebedee, ch. Nathaniel and Polly, Oct. 14, 1796.

ELENWOOD (see Ellenwood, Ellingwood), Christopher Columbus, ch. Benjamin and Nancy, Dec. 11, 1807.
John Starks, ch. Benjamin and Nancy, July 16, 1809.

ELLENWOOD (see Elenwood, Ellingwood), Benjamin, ch. Benjamin (Elenwood) and Nancy, May 14, 1813.

ELLENWOOD, Nancy Elizabeth, ch. Benjamin (Elenwood) and Nancy, Jan. 1, 1812.

ELLINGWOOD (see Elenwood, Ellenwood), Arthur C., Dec. 4, 1846, G.R.1.
Sarah, w. Miles S. Staples, June 1, 1829, in Winterport, P.R.33.

ELLIS (see Eells, Ells), Alfred G., h. Annie W., Sept. 24, 1847, G.R.1.
Annie W. [———], w. Alfred G., Apr. 23, 1848, G.R.1. [Ann Maria, d. John Wilson and Eliza Ann, P.R.94. d. John Wilson Jr., Apr. 24, P.R.123.]
Ch[arle]s Manning, ch. T., bp. Oct. 1, 1858, C.R.2. [b. ———, 1854, G.R.1.]
Dulcina Almeda, ch. Winslow and Emily, Sept. 13, 1842.
Elizabeth [———], w. Edwin R., ———, 1817, G.R.1.
Emma Ruth, ch. Winslow and Emily, Oct. 12, 1838.
Henry Winslow, ch. Winslow and Emily, May 22, 1844.
Mary Ann (see Mary A. Harriman).
Merinda M., w. George C. Lane, Mar. 8, 1857, G.R.1.
Sarah Leonora, ch. Winslow and Emily, Oct. 12, 1840.
———, s. Enoch, Jan. 18, 1847, P.R.123.
———, d. Winslow, Feb. 3, 1847, P.R.123.

ELLS (see Eells, Ellis), Rachel D. [———], w. Van R., ———, 1840, G.R.1.
Van R., h. Rachel D., ———, 1843, G.R.1.

ELMS, Sarah, w. George S. Pitcher, Feb. 7, 1808, G.R.1.

ELWELL, Lucy, first w. Humphrey Lancaster, May 20, 1784, P.R.108.
Robert S., Mar. 4, 1881, G.R.1.

EMERSON (see Emmerson), Ann Maria, ch. Gillet and Jane, Dec. 10, 1840.
Calvin, h. Sarah (Woods), July 18, 1812.
Frank Walter, ch. Calvin and Sarah (Woods), Nov. 26, 1857.
George C., ch. Gillet and Jane, June 7, 1843.
Harriet Eliza, ch. Gillet and Jane, Dec. 15, 1845.
Henry Otis, ch. Calvin and Sarah (Woods), Jan. 26, 1851.
Merinda Jane, ch. Calvin and Sarah (Woods), Sept. 26, 1845.
Moses W., ch. Calvin and Sarah (Woods), July 13, 1839, in Waldo.
Wilson Colcord, ch. Calvin and Sarah (Woods), Feb. 3, 1847.

EMERTON, Augusta Jael, w. William Franklin Triggs, Nov. 24, 1845, in Bucksport, P.R.50.

EMERY, Abigail, ch. Jonas and Mahitible (second w.), July 20, 1826.
Ann, ch. Dennis and Jane (Turnbull), June 2, 1819.
Charles A., s. John H. and Nancy M., May 13, 1864, G.R.1.
Dennis, h. Jane (Turnbull), Apr. 14, 1791, in Thomaston.
Eliza R. [———] [w. Robert T.], Apr. 12, 1839, G.R.1.
Elizabeth, ch. Dennis and Jane (Turnbull), Sept. 22, 1827.
Francis Jane, ch. Jonas and Mahitible (second w.), Jan. 19, 1830.
George, ch. Jonas and Abigail, Dec. 7, 1818, in Thomaston.
Hariet Lois (Emey), ch. Dennis and Jane (Turnbull), Mar. 3, 1832.
Isabella, ch. Dennis and Jane (Turnbull), Nov. 16, 1839.
James, ch. Robert and Martha, Dec. 14, 1820.
John Haraden, ch. Dennis and Jane (Turnbull), Aug. 10, 1829. [h. Nancy M., G.R.1.]
Keziah, ch. Dennis and Jane (Turnbull), June 26, 1825.
Lucy, ch. Jonas and Mahitible (second w.), Dec. 9, 1824.
Lydia J., ch. Dennis and Jane (Turnbull), Jan. 26, 1821.
Nancy, ch. Jonas and Abigail, Nov. 4, 1817, in Thomaston.
Nancy M. [———], w. John H., Aug. 18, 1840, G.R.1.
Nathaniel, ch. Jonas and Mahitible (second w.), Nov. 15, 1822, in Thomaston.
Ralph Maxwell, ch. Dennis and Jane (Turnbull), Oct. 16, 1837.
Robert Jr., ch. Robert and Martha, June 30, 1822.
Rob[er]t T., ch. Dennis and Jane (Turnbull), May 9, 1823. [[h. Eliza R.] G.R.1.]
Rufus Hopkins, ch. Robert and Martha, Apr. 29, 1829.
Sally, ch. Jonas and Mahitible (second w.), Apr. 13, 1828.
Sarah, ch. Jonas and Mahitible (second w.), Apr. 9, 1821, in Thomaston.
Thomas, ch. Robert and Martha, Dec. 27, 1825.
Thomas Bartlett, ch. Robert and Martha, Jan. 9, 1827.
W[illia]m Crosby, ch. Jonas and Mahitible (second w.), Oct. 15, 1831.

EMMERSON (see Emerson), Sarah E., ch. Josiah and Philena (formerly w. James Cunningham), June 10, 1846.

EMMONS, Annie L., Sept. 30, 1871, G.R.2.
Georgie P., May 13, 1877, G.R.2.
John A., Nov. 18, 1868, G.R.2.
Luther H., Apr. 20, 1847, G.R.2.
Orrie E., Sept. 18, 1875, G.R.2.

ESTES, Harry H., s. S. A. and Emma F., ———, 1889, G.R.1.
Stephen A., ———, 1847, G.R.1.

EUSTIS, Charles S., ch. Solon and Lovey, Oct. 31, 1847.
James, ch. Solon and Lovey, Mar. 28, 1853.
Mary, ch. Solon and Lovey, Aug. 30, 1849. [Huestis, P.R.123.]

EVANS, Mary Osgood, w. Isaac C. Abbott, Mar. 3, 1809, in Fryeburg, G.R.1.

FAHY, Andrew S., Oct. 3, 1862, G.R.1.

FALES, Zibiah P., w. Josiah Sanborn, Aug. 9, 1812, P.R.83.

FARINGTON, Sally, w. W[illia]m Poor, Jan. 8, 1785, in Andover, Mass., P.R.142.

FARLEY, ———, d. ———, Oct. 22, 1847, P.R.123.

FARNHAM, Hannah W. [? m.], Sept. 3, 1825, G.R.1.
Mary, w. Isaac W. Smalley, Feb. 16, 1819, in Boothbay, P.R.27.

FARRAR (see Farrow), Benj[amin] W. of Belmont, s. John and Hannah, Jan. 31, 1814, P.R.44.
Edward of Belmont, s. John and Hannah, Sept. —, 1792, P.R.44.
Elizabeth of Belmont, d. John and Hannah, Jan. 8, 1798, P.R.44.
Foster of Belmont, s. John and Hannah, Apr. 29, 1809, P.R.44.
Hannah [———], w. John of Belmont, June 6, 1771, P.R.44.
James W. of Belmont, s. John and Hannah, Jan. 15, 1807, P.R.44.
Jane of Belmont, d. John and Hannah, Dec. 27, 1802, P.R.44.
Jane W. of Belmont, d. John and Hannah, Aug. 4, 1811, P.R.44.
John of Belmont, h. Hannah, Apr. 11, 1756, P.R.44.
John of Belmont, s. John and Hannah, Jan. 16, 1800, P.R.44.
Margaret of Belmont, d. John and Hannah, Apr. —, 1794, P.R.44.
Mary W. of Belmont, w. William Russ, d. John and Hannah, Mar. 23, 1804, P.R.44.
Sarah, w. Capt. Watson Hinds, Feb. 23, 1819, G.R.1.
William of Belmont, s. John and Hannah, Apr. —, 1796, P.R.44.

FARRINGTON (see Farington).

FARROW (see Farrar), Georgianna, ch. Thomas and Deborah, Jan. 1, 1837.
Mary Ellen, ch. Thomas and Deborah, Dec. 10, 1840.

FARROW, Thomas J. L., s. Capt. William and Jerusha D., ———, 1845, G.R.1.
———, s. Capt. W[illia]m, Apr. 18, 1848, P.R.123.
———, s. Thomas, Aug. 14, 1849, P.R.123.

FAUNCE, Abba Haraden, w. William B. Swan, d. Asa and Sarah A. (Haraden), Nov. 22, 1839, P.R.88.
Alice W., r. Hartwell L. Woodcock (b. Searsmont), twin d. Dani l and Mary Ann (White), Nov. 6, 1853, P.R.147.
Asa, h. Sarah (Haraden), Mar. 12, 1813, G.R.1. [h. Sarah A. (Haraden), P.R.88.]
Daniel, h. Mary Ann (White), Apr. 22, 1817, in Waterville, P.R.147.
Ella W., twin d. Daniel and Mary A., Nov. 6, 1853, G.R.1. [twin d. Daniel and Mary Ann (White), P.R.147.]
Mary E., Nov. 4, 1853, G.R.1. [Mary Estelle, ch. Asa and Sarah A. (Haraden), P.R.88.]
William Asa, ch. Asa and Sarah A. (Haraden), Dec. 20, 1843, P.R.88.
———, s. Daniel and Mary A., Sept. 16, 1842, G.R.1. [s. Daniel and Mary Ann (White), P.R.147.]
———, s. Daniel and Mary A., Dec. 9, 1849, G.R.1. [s. Daniel and Mary Ann (White), P.R.147.]

FELCH, Isabella N., ch. Isaac N. and Isabella, Sept. 8, 1842.
William A., ch. Isaac N. and Isabella, Sept. 30, 1845.

FELLOWES (see Fellows), Mary Elizabeth, ch. Ephraim and Mary, Sept. —, 1827.

FELLOWS (see Fellowes), Clark G., Aug. 23, 1870, G.R.1.

FERGUSON (see Furguson), Ada Evelina, ch. George B. and Evelina C., ———, 1861, G.R.3.
Albert Barnet, ch. Moses W. and Lydia, Sept. 2, 1829. [Albert Barnett Ferguson, ch. Moses Wason and Lydia (Brooks), P.R.17.]
Alfred Monroe, ch. John W. and Lucelia Avesta (Monroe), Feb. 4, 1872, P.R.5.
Betty, ch. John 2d and Jane (More), May 19, 1767 [in Pelham, N. H.], P.R.7.
Charles Franklin, ch. Moses Wason and Lydia (Brooks), Dec. 2, 1849, P.R.17. [Furgerson, P.R.123.]
David, ch. John 2d and Jane (More), Nov. 3, 1761 [in Pelham, N. H.], P.R.7.

FERGUSON, George, ch. John 2d and Jane (More), Oct. 13, 1765 [in Pelham, N. H.], P.R.7.
George Brooks, ch. Moses W. and Lydia [Moses Wason and Lydia (Brooks), P.R.17.], Apr. 27, 1831.
Gertrude, ch. John W. and Lucelia Avesta (Monroe), Nov. 3, 1873, P.R.5.
Hannah Elizabeth, ch. Moses W. and Lydia [Moses Wason and Lydia (Brooks), P.R.17.], Apr. 15, 1833.
James, ch. John 2d and Jane (More), July 28, 1759 [in Pelham, N. H.], P.R.7.
Jane Wason (Fergurson), ch. Moses W. and Lydia [Moses Wason and Lydia (Brooks), P.R.17.], Jan. 27, 1835.
John 3d, ch. John 2d and Jane (More), Aug. 11, 1757 [in Pelham, N. H.], P.R.7.
John Warren, h. Lucelia Avesta (Monroe), Nov. 12, 1843, G.R.1. P.R.5. [ch. Moses Wason and Lydia (Brooks), P.R.17.]
Jonas B., Nov. 5, 1838, G.R.2. [Jonas Brooks Ferguson, ch. Moses Wason and Lydia (Brooks), P.R.17.]
Jonathan, ch. John 2d and Jane (More), Mar. 19, 1769 [in Pelham, N. H.], P.R.7.
Lena Brooks, ch. George B. and Evelina C., ———, 1874, G.R.3.
Louisa Hemenway, ch. John W. and Lucelia Avesta (Monroe), Sept. 22, 1876, P.R.5.
Lydia Sophia, ch. Moses Wason and Lydia (Brooks), Sept. 24, 1846, P.R.17.
Sarah, ch. John 2d and Jane (More), Jan. 27, 1764 [in Pelham, N. H.], P.R.7.

FERNALD, Cordelia [———], w. L. O., Feb. 2, 1832, G.R.13.

FIELD, Abba Ellen, d. Bohan P. and Lucy H., bp. Apr. 30, 1852, C.R.2. [d. Bohan P. Esq., b. Dec. 8, 1849, P.R.123. Abby Ellen, d. Bohan Prentiss Jr. and Lucy (Haraden), b. Dec. 8, 1849, P.R.155.]
Abby Miriam, d. Henry Cummins and Asenath (Harriman), May 1, 1843, P.R.155.
Abigail Eleanor, ch. Bohan P. and Abigal [Abigail (Davis), P.R.155.], Mar. 2, 1812.
Alma Claghorn, ch. William Prentiss and Sarah (Ingraham), Nov. 20, 1839, P.R.155.
Annie T. [———], w. B. F., ———, 1831, G.R.1.
Annie Veazie, d. Benjamin Franklin and Caroline Williams (Tobey) (first w.), May 1, 1861, P.R.155.

FIELD, Benj[amin] Davis, s. Benjamin Franklin and Caroline Williams (Tobey) (first w.), Dec. 1, 1862, P.R.155.
Benjamin Franklin, ch. Bohan P. and Abigal, Oct. 10, 1820. [h. Caroline Williams (Tobey), h. Annie (Tobey), s. Bohan P. and Abigail (Davis), P.R.155.]
Bertha C. [———], w. Cha[rle]s H., Mar. 14, 1857, G.R.1.
Bohan Prentis, ch. Bohan P. and Abigal, Sept. 11, 1815. [Bohan Prentiss Field, h. Lucy (Haraden), s. Bohan P. and Abigail (Davis), P.R.155.]
Bohan William Henry, s. Henry Cummins and Asenath (Harriman), Dec. 22, 1839, P.R.155.
Caroline Williams, d. Benjamin Franklin and Annie (Tobey), (second w.) Jan. 10, 1871, P.R.155.
Charles, s. Henry Cummins and Asenath (Harriman), ———, P.R.155.
Charles Davis, ch. Bohan P. and Abigal, Aug. 5, 1814. [h. Elvira (Osgood), s. Bohan P. and Abigail (Davis), P.R.155.]
Charles Haraden, s. B. P. and Lucy H., bp. Sept. 7, 1856, C.R.2. [s. Bohan Prentiss Jr. and Lucy (Haraden), b. Nov. 25, 1855, P.R.155.]
Ebenezer Wright, ch. Bohan P. and Abigal [Abigail (Davis), P.R.155.], Sept. 23, 1813.
Edward Mann, ch. Bohan P. and Abigal, July 27, 1822. [h. Sarah Russ McRuer, s. Bohan P. and Abigail (Davis), P.R.155.]
Francis Gridley, ch. Elisha and Susan, Jan. 20, 1809.
Frank Lee, s. Benjamin Franklin and Caroline Williams (Tobey) (first w.), Aug. 26, 1859, P.R.155.
Franklin, s. Henry Cummins and Asenath (Harriman), July 11, 1845, P.R.155.
George Edward, s. Henry Cummins and Asenath (Harriman), Aug. 6, 1841, P.R.155.
George Prentiss, s. Bohan Prentiss Jr. and Lucy (Haraden), Oct. 17, 1844, P.R.155.
George Warren, ch. Bohan P. and Abigal [Abigail (Davis), P.R.155.], Dec. 9, 1818.
Henry Cummings, ch. Bohan P. and Abigal, Sept. 14, 1809. [Henry Cummins Field, h. Asenath (Harriman), s. Bohan P. and Abigail (Davis), P.R.155.]
Herbert Tobey, s. Benjamin Franklin and Annie (Tobey) (second w.), Mar. 25, 1868, P.R.155.
Mary Osgood, d. Charles Davis and Elvira (Osgood), Apr. 15, 1844, P.R.155.
Sarah Elizabeth, d. William Prentiss and Sarah (Ingraham), Dec. 22, 1836, P.R.155.

FIELD, Susan, w. Jonathan Durham, Mar. 5, 1810, P.R.6.
William Ingraham, s. William Prentiss and Sarah (Ingraham), Nov. 8, 1835, P.R.155.
William Prentiss, ch. Bohan P. and Abigal, Jan. 31, 1811. [h. Sarah (Ingraham), s. Bohan P. and Abigail (Davis), P.R.155.]

FITCH, Catharine, d. Ferris and Sarah S., bp. Feb. 19, 1832, C.R.2.

FLANDERS, Alfonso L., Aug. 14, 1853, G.R.13.
Annie L. [―――], w. F. W., ―――, 1853, G.R.1.
Elisha M., Nov. 10, 1846, G.R.13.
George O., h. Sarah J., May 10, 1857, G.R.2.
Hezekiah, Apr. 24, 1806, G.R.13.
Mary B. [? m.], Nov. 13, 1813, G.R.13.
Sarah J. [―――], w. George O., Feb. 25, 1859, G.R.2.

FLETCHER, John M., Mar. 23, 1846, G.R.1.

FLOWERS, Albert, s. John and Mary (McCorrison), Mar. 9, 1845, P.R.73.
Ann Maria, ch. Capt. William and Lydia, Aug. 14, 1842.
Edward Kimball, ch. Capt. William and Lydia, Nov. 17, 1838.
Emma A., ch. Capt. John and Mary [(McCorrison) P.R.73.], Apr. 3, 1838.
Emma Josephine, ch. Capt. William and Lydia, Nov. 23, 1844.
Esther [―――], w. Samuel G., ―――, 1820, G.R.1.
Eveline H. (see Harriet E.).
Frances, d. John and Mary (McCorrison), June 23, 1847, P.R.73.
Frederic W[illia]m, ch. Capt. William and Lydia, Nov. 15, 1836.
Frederick William, s. Capt. William and w., bp. Oct. 31, 1839, C.R.2.
George A., ch. Capt. John and Mary, Apr. 7, 1836. [h. Lydia J. Rich, s. John and Mary (McCorrison), P.R.73.]
Harriet E., ch. Capt. John and Mary, Mar. 18, 1834. [Eveline H., w. Charles T. Gilmore, d. John and Mary (McCorrison), P.R.73.]
Isabel, w. Edward J. Deegan, w. W[illia]m H. Hooper, d. John and Mary (McCorrison), May 9, 1850, P.R.73.
John F., ch. Capt. John and Mary, May 29, 1843. [John Francis, s. John and Mary (McCorrison), P.R.73.]

FLOWERS, Mary A., ch. Capt. John and Mary, Feb. 24, 1841.
[Mary Ann, w. Emerson Robbins, d. John and Mary
(McCorrison), P.R.73.]
Samuel G. [h. Esther], ———, 1820, G.R.1.

FOLLETT, Charles Willis, May 28, 1857, G.R.1.
Franklin A., h. Jennette F., ———, 1843, G.R.1.
Jennette F. [———], w. Franklin A., ———, 1846, G.R.1.
Percy R., Aug. 15, 1872, G.R.1.

FOLSOM, William Otis, May 22, 1836, G.R.1.

FORBES, Sophia W. [———], w. Henry H., Aug. 17, 1822,
G.R.1.
———, d. Henry H., Feb. 23, 1848, P.R.123.

FOSTER, Abigal, ch. Nathen B. and Susand, Sept. 21, 1809.
Mary, ch. Nathen B. and Susand, Jan. 5, 1805.
Susand, ch. Nathen B. and Susand, Aug. 13, 1803.
William, ch. Nathen B. and Susand, Feb. 11, 1807.

FREDERICK (see Fredrick), Charles Woodbury, h. Emma
Lena (Peirce), s. James Woodbury and Martha Ann
(Bradbury), Aug. 5, 1857, P.R.120.
Charlotte French, ch. William (Fredrick) and Mary S. [William and Mary Swett (Derby), P.R.122.], Mar. 2, 1837.
Frank B., Jan. 10, 1872, G.R.1.
Franklin Bartlett, ch. William (Fredrick) and Mary S., Sept. 6,
1834. [Frank B., G.R.1. Frank Bartlett Frederick, s.
William and Mary Swett (Derby), P.R.122.]
George W., Oct. 12, 1865, G.R.1.
Georgiana [———], Apr. 29, 1835, G.R.1.
Harmon Bradbury, s. James Woodbury and Martha Ann
(Bradbury), Feb. 25, 1853, P.R.120. P.R.121.
James Woodbury, ch. William (Fredrick) and Mary S., Feb. 6,
1826. [h. Martha Ann (Bradbury), h. Augusta S. (Quimby), P.R.120. s. William and Mary Swett (Derby),
P.R.122.]
Mary Elizabeth, ch. William (Fredrick) and Mary S. [William
and Mary Swett (Derby), P.R.122.], Sept. 14, 1821.
Mary Elizabeth, ch. William (Fredrick) and Mary S. [William
and Mary Swett (Derby), P.R.122.], Feb. 3, 1832.
Mary S. [———], w. William, Nov. 19, 1798, G.R.1. [Mary
Swett (Derby), w. William, in York, P.R.122.]
William, Apr. 11, 1796, G.R.1. [h. Mary Swett (Derby), in
Gloucester, Mass., P.R.122.]

FREDERICK, William Crooker, ch. William (Fredrick) and Mary S., Oct. 26, 1829. [s. William and Mary Swett (Derby), Oct. 28, P.R.122.]

FREDRICK (see Frederick), Cornelia Olive, ch. William and Mary S., Oct. 20, 1839. [Frederick, d. William and Mary Swett (Derby), P.R.122.]
Jabez, ch. William and Mary S., Feb. 22, 1820. [Jabez Frederick, s. William and Mary Swett (Derby), P.R.122.]
James Woodbury (Frederic), ch. William and Mary S., Jan. 11, 1824. [Frederick, s. William and Mary Swett (Derby), P.R.122.]

FREEMAN, Charlotte (see Charlotte Wiggin Beaman).

FRENCH, Abraham, ch. Nathaniel, bp. June 14, 1797, C.R.2.
Charlotta, ch. Eliphelet and Abigal, Apr. 11, 1804.
Eliphalet, ch. Nathaniel, bp. June 14, 1797, C.R.2.
Elizabeth, ch. Nathaniel, bp. June 14, 1797, C.R.2.
Hannah, ch. Nathaniel, bp. June 14, 1797, C.R.2.
Jacob, ch. Nathaniel, bp. June 14, 1797, C.R.2.
Josiah, ch. Nathaniel, bp. June 14, 1797, C.R.2.
Levina, ch. Eliphelet and Abigal, Apr. 10, 1801.
Nanna, ch. Nathaniel, bp. June 14, 1797, C.R.2.
Nathaniel, ch. Nathaniel, bp. June 14, 1797, C.R.2.
Nathaniel, ch. Eliphelet and Abigal, Sept. 26, 1806.
Phebe, ch. Eliphelet and Abigal, June 2, 1809.
Rebeccah, ch. Nathaniel, bp. June 14, 1797, C.R.2.
Sarah, ch. Nathaniel, bp. June 14, 1797, C.R.2.
———, d. Benj[amin] Jr., July 19, 1847, P.R.123.
———, s. Benj[amin], Sept. 17, 1849, P.R.123.

FRISBEE, Flora B. [? m.], Jan. 11, 1882, G.R.1.

FROST, Amanda M., ch. Nathaniel and Sarah, Aug. 25, 1834.
Benjamin A., Apr. 8, 1881, G.R.1.
Benjamin H., ch. John and Elizabeth F., Jan. 8, 1832.
Caroline A., ch. John and Elizabeth F., Oct. 29, 1829.
Charles A., ch. Nathaniel and Sarah, Sept. 21, 1832.
Ellen Frances, ch. Nathaniel and Sarah, Mar. 7, 1840.
Hosea Ballou, ch. John and Elizabeth F., Apr. 19, 1840.
James H. K., ch. John and Elizabeth, Jan. 16, 1834.
John Tyler, ch. John and Elizabeth, Dec. 16, 1835.
Margaret A. [———], ———, 1843, G.R.1.
Margaret H., ch. John and Elizabeth F., Dec. 16, 1843.
Moses W., ———, 1835, G.R.1.

FROST, Nathan[ie]l Jr., ch. Nathaniel and Sarah, Feb. 7, 1836.
William, ch. John and Elizabeth, May 19, 1838.

FROTHINGHAM, Caroline, d. Rev. William and Lois (Barrett) (first w.), Sept. 5, 1806, P.R.90.
Caroline M., ch. William and Lydia, May 10, 1830. [w. Samuel Miller, d. Rev. W[illia]m, G.R.1. Caroline Mellen Frothingham, d. Rev. William and Lydia (Prentiss) (second w.), P.R.90.]
Elizabeth, d. Rev. William and Lois (Barrett) (first w.), Nov. 7, 1813, P.R.90.
Ellen P., d. William and Lydia, Aug. 30, 1828. [Ellen Prentiss Frothingham, d. Rev. William and Lydia (Prentiss) (second w.), P.R.90.]
George Prentiss, s. William and Lydia, Jan. 14, 1824, G.R.1. [s. Rev. William and Lydia (Prentiss) (second w.), Jan. 14, 1823, P.R.90.]
George Prentiss, s. William and Lydia, Nov. 17, 1825, G.R.1. [s. Rev. William and Lydia (Prentiss) (second w.), P.R.90.]
Harriet, d. Rev. W[illia]m, Sept. 6, 1810, G.R.1. [d. Rev. William and Lois (Barrett) (first w.), P.R.90.]
W[illia]m, Rev., Mar. 14, 1777, G.R.1. [h. Lois (Barrett), h. Lydia (Prentiss), in Cambridge, P.R.90.]
William, s. Rev. William and Lois (Barrett) (first w.), Dec. 25, 1808, P.R.90.

FRYE, Annie Elizabeth [? m.], July 23, 1829, G.R.1.
Celia J., w. W[illia]m M. Woods, Aug. 31, 1826, G.R.1. P.R.151.
Henry W., Apr. 21, 1868, G.R.1.
J. Lovell, Feb. 23, 1815, G.R.1.
Joanna P. [———], w. John C., Sept. 4, 1832, G.R.1.
John C. [h. Joanna P.], June 10, 1820, G.R.1.
Jonathan, h. Mercy, July 21, 1788, in Pembroke, N. H., G.R.1.
Mercy [———], w. Jonathan, Mar. 17, 1795, in Durham, G.R.1.
Wakefield Gale, Dec. 20, 1826, G.R.1.
———, s. Baker, Oct. 19, 1849, P.R.123.

FULLER, Annie, w. E. K. Boyle, ———, 1836, G.R.1.
Sarah A. [———], w. S. M., Nov. 10, 1817, in Augusta, G.R.1.
Silas M., Feb. 24, 1819, in Castine, G.R.1.

FURBER, Ellen Francis, ch. James P. and Mary B., July 23, 1843.
George Decator, ch. William and Polly, Sept. 16, 181[torn, ? 5].
James Patterson, ch. William and Polly, June 16, 1811.

FURBER, Ma[r]ianm, ch. James P. and Mary B., Nov. 4, 1845.
Thomas Martin, ch. William and Polly, Apr. 17, 1808.
William Gray, ch. William and Polly, July 21, 18[*torn, rec. after ch. b.* June 16, 1811].

FURGUSON (see Ferguson), Hannah (Ferguson), ch. Jonathan and Jane, May 28, 1806. [Ferguson, ch. Jonathan and Jane (Wason), P.R.16.]
Jane (Forguson), ch. Jonathan and Jane, Apr. 17, 1804. [Ferguson, ch. Jonathan and Jane (Wason), Aug. 17, P.R.16. Ferguson, w. John Tufts Patterson, Aug. 17, P.R.119.]
Jonathan (Ferguson), ch. Jonathan and Jane, Sept. 8, 1809. [Ferguson, ch. Jonathan and Jane (Wason), P.R.16.]
Moses (Forguson), ch. Jonathan and Jane, Jan. 7, 1802. [Moses Wason Ferguson, Jan. 7, 1803, G.R.3. Moses Wason Ferguson, ch. Jonathan and Jane (Wason), Jan. 7, 1803, P.R.16.]

GAMMANS (see Gammon), Albert, ch. James and Rebecca, Nov. 26, 1833. [h. Martha Jane (Littlefield), s. James and Rebecca (Bailey), P.R.117.]
Franklin B., s. James and Rebecca, Oct. 31, 1839, G.R.3. [Franklin Blackstone Gammans, s. James and Rebecca (Bailey), Oct. 3, P.R.117.]
George Bailey, ch. James and Rebecca [(Bailey) P.R.117.], Mar. 22, 1828.
Huldah M. [————], w. James, Dec. 11, 1815, G.R.3. [Huldah (Maxfield), second w. James, P.R.117.]
James, June 5, 1767, in Pembroke, Mass., G.R.3. [James Sr., Aug. —, in Pembroke, N. H., P.R.117.]
James, Nov. 23, 1795, G.R.3. [h. Rebecca (Bailey), h. Huldah (Maxfield), s. James Sr., in Lincolnville, P.R.117.]
James Jr., ch. James and Rebecca [(Bailey) P.R.117.], Sept. 6, 1824, in Woolwich.
James Albert, s. Albert and Martha Jane (Littlefield), Feb. 16, 1868, P.R.117.
Laura [w. Sherburne A. Sleeper], May 27, 1841, G.R.1. [Laura Jane, d. James and Rebecca (Bailey), May 24, P.R.117.]
Maria Patten, ch. James and Rebecca, Feb. 14, 1832. [w. W[illia]m B. Swan, G.R.1. d. James and Rebecca (Bailey), Feb. 11, P.R.117.]
Mary Abbott, d. James and Huldah (Maxfield) (second w.), July 8, 1849, P.R.117. [d. Capt. James, June 8, P.R.123.]
Maud, d. Albert and Martha Jane (Littlefield), Jan. 18, 1866, P.R.117.

GAMMANS, Rebecca [———], w. James, Nov. 5, 1798, G.R.3.
[Rebecca (Bailey), first w. James, in Wiscassett, P.R.117.]
Rebecca, ch. James and Rebecca, June 15, 1826, in Woolwich.
[w. John B. Wadlin, G.R.3. d. James and Rebecca (Bailey), P.R.117.]
Sarah Elizabeth, ch. James and Rebecca [(Bailey) P.R.117.], July 2, 1836.
Silas Pierce, ch. James and Rebecca [(Bailey) P.R.117.], Feb. 9, 1830.

GAMMON (see Gammans), George [h. Patience], Feb. 14, 1794, in Halifax, N. S., G.R.2.
Hattie M. [? m.], Apr. 17, 1875, G.R.1.
Patience [———], w. George, Apr. 4, 1795, in Portletore, G.R.2.

GANNETT, Caleb, ch. Luther and Olive (Washburn), June 19, 1818, in E. Bridgwater.
Caleb Henry, ch. Luther and Olive (Washburn), Dec. 18, 1825.
Elisa Ann, ch. Luther and Olive (Washburn), Apr. 11, 1811, in E. Bridgwater.
George, ch. Luther and Olive (Washburn), Apr. 15, 1815, in E. Bridgwater.
Geo[r]ge, ch. Luther and Olive (Washburn), Oct. 29, 1819, in E. Bridgwater.
George, ch. Luther, bp. July 7, 1833, C.R.2.
Luther, h. Olive (Washburn), Sept. 22, 1784, in E. Bridgwater.
Luther, ch. Luther and Olive (Washburn), Jan. 26, 1814, in E. Bridgwater.
Olive Washburn, ch. Luther and Olive (Washburn), Jan. 15, 1822.
Olive Washburn, ch. Luther, bp. July 7, 1833, C.R.2.

GANNON, Bartlett, ———, 1844, G.R.1.
Catharine [———], w. John, ———, 1808, G.R.1.
John, h. Catharine, ———, 1812, G.R.1.
Michael, ———, 1840, G.R.1.

GARDINER (see Gardner), ———, d. Thomas W., Sept. 9, 1849, P.R.123.

GARDNER (see Gardiner), Bradford P., June 23, 1850, G.R.1.
Roxana [? m.], ———, 1816, G.R.1.
William, ———, 1813, G.R.1.
William H., Sergt. Maj., "4th Me. Regt.," ———, 1843, G.R.1.
———, w. Thomas W., June 6, 1847, P.R.123.

GARLAND, Henry M., Dec. 5, 1838, G.R.1.
Mary J. [? m.], July 1, 1842, G.R.1.
———, d. Ephraim, Jan. 24, 1849, P.R.123.

GATES, Daniel McCormic, h. Sarah Elizabeth (Bullen), May 28, 1828, P.R.100.
Edith Luella, d. Daniel McCormic and Sarah Elizabeth (Bullen), Oct. 18, 1855, P.R.100.
Frank Nash, s. Daniel McCormic and Sarah Elizabeth (Bullen), July 26, 1857, P.R.100.
Ida Belle, d. Daniel McCormic and Sarah Elizabeth (Bullen), Oct. 26, 1867, P.R.100.
Samuel Foster, s. Daniel McCormic and Sarah Elizabeth (Bullen), Jan. 20, 1853, P.R.100.

GAY, Richard S., h. Mary A., Oct. 3, 1834, G.R.2.

GENTNER, Evelyn L., ———, 1842, G.R.1.
Henry M., Aug. 23, 1883, G.R.1.
Henry P., ———, 1806, G.R.1.
Sarah S. [———], ———, 1820, G.R.1.
Williette S. [————], July 25, 1859, G.R.1.

GIBSON, Margaret, w. Stetson West, Oct. 24, 1769, P.R.100.

GILBERT, Evalena, ch. Sewall and Lucy, Nov. 2, 1828.
Evealena, d. Sewall and Lucy, bp. Apr. 8, 1832, C.R.2.
Sarah, d. Sewall and Lucy, bp. Apr. 8, 1832, C.R.2.

GILBRETH, Caroline F., ch. Samuel and Emily, Mar. 22, 1843.
David Taggart, ch. Samuel and Emily, May 3, 1836.
Elisabeth Barnes, ch. Samuel and Emily, Dec. 27, 1827.
Emely Taggart, ch. Samuel and Emily, June 4, 1838.
Esther, ch. Samuel and Emily, Feb. 27, 1832.
Frances A., ch. Samuel and Emily, July 28, 1845.
Harriet Haskell, ch. Samuel and Emily, Dec. 9, 1823.
James, ch. Samuel and Emily, Oct. 24, 1821.
Martha Ann, ch. Samuel and Emily, Oct. 19, 1825.
Mary E. [———], w. Francis A., Dec. 12, 1853, G.R.2.
Samuel Gordon, ch. Samuel and Emily, Mar. 8, 1830.
Sarah Josephine, ch. Sam[ue]l G. and Sarah E., Feb. 25, 1859.
———, d. James, Apr. 28, 1848, P.R.123.

GILCHRIST, Emma F., ch. Capt. James and Abigail, Sept. 24, 1837.
Harriet E., ch. Capt. James and Abigail, May 10, 1845.
James A., ch. Capt. James and Abigail, June 3, 1841.
Margaret E., ch. Capt. James and Abigail, June 10, 1843.

GILES, Chandler, ch. Paul and Betey, Apr. 7, 1803.
Charles, ch. Paul and Betey, Dec. 14, 1817.
Florence, ch. Charles and Eunice B., Feb. 11, 1853.
Hannah, ch. Paul and Betey, Dec. 15, 1809.
Mary, ch. Paul and Betey, July 16, 1812.
Olive, ch. Paul and Betey, June 16, 1814. [w. William Thaxter Colburn, P.R.18.]
Plummer, ch. Paul and Betey, May 10, 1807.
Suckey, ch. Paul and Betey, Apr. 1, 1805.

GILKEY, Anna Cushing, twin ch. Capt. Philip and Deborah (second w.), Oct. 20, 1823, in Islesboro.
Isaac, ch. Capt. Philip and Jane, Oct. 3, 1811, in Islesboro.
Jane Pendleton, ch. Capt. Philip and Jane, Apr. 9, 1807, in Islesboro. [w. Robert Coombs, P.R.98.]
Judith Pendleton, ch. Capt. Philip and Jane, Apr. 29, 1817, in Islesboro.
Lincoln, ch. Capt. Philip and Deborah (second w.), July 3, 1825, in Islesboro.
Lydia, ch. Capt. Philip and Jane, Apr. 15, 1815, in Islesboro.
Mary Butman, ch. Capt. Philip and Deborah (second w.), May 27, 1829.
Philip, ch. Capt. Philip and Jane, Oct. 14, 1809, in Islesboro.
Robert Cushing, ch. Capt. Philip and Deborah (second w.), Nov. 13, 1827.
Royal, ch. Capt. Philip and Jane, May 24, 1821, in Islesboro.
Welcome, twin ch. Capt. Philip and Deborah (second w.), Oct. 20, 1823, in Islesboro.

GILLAM, Samuel B., h. Ellen L., May 28, 1824, G.R.1.

GILLMORE (see Gilmer, Gilmor, Gilmore), Agness, d. John and Margret, Nov. 1, 1785.
Charles Thomas, ch. James and Martha, Sept. 10, 1832.
Frederick Augustas, ch. James and Martha, Oct. 14, 1834. [Gilmore, G.R.1.]
Lucy Piper, ch. John and Sally, Mar. 10, 1830.

GILMAN, Alfonzo Fairfield, twin ch. Capt. John Taylor and Pamelia, Feb. 3, 1840.
Alonzo Morton, twin ch. Capt. John Taylor and Pamelia, Feb. 3, 1840.
Eliza S., ch. Capt. John Taylor and Pamelia, Oct. 23, 1831.
Harriet L., ch. Capt. John Taylor and Pamelia, June 17, 1842.
Henry D., ch. Capt. John Taylor and Pamelia, Feb. 11, 1838.

GILMAN, John Taylor Jr., ch. Capt. John Taylor and Pamelia, Mar. 2, 1833.
Juliett M., ch. Capt. John Taylor and Pamelia, Apr. 21, 1844.
Pamelia A., ch. Capt. John Taylor and Pamelia, Jan. 7, 1830.
Warren D., ch. Capt John Taylor and Pamelia, Mar. 1, 1836.
William Henry, ch. Capt. John Taylor and Pamelia, Mar. 9, 1828.

GILMER (see Gillmore, Gilmor, Gilmore), David, ch. John 2d and Sally, Apr. 25, 1804. [Gilmore, h. Eliza (McKeen), P.R.106.]

GILMOR (see Gillmore, Gilmer, Gilmore), James [dup. Gillmore], ch. John and Margret, Apr. 21, 1793.
John [dup. Gillmore], ch. John and Margret, Feb. 12, 1795.
Jonathan, ch. John and Margret, Sept. 3, 1801. [Gilmore, s. John and Peggy, C.R.2.]
Margaret (see Peggy).
Nancy, ch. John and Margret, Nov. 1, 1788.
Peggy, ch. John and Margret, Dec. 20, 1798. [Margaret Gilmore, d. John and Peggy, C.R.2.]
Polly, ch. John and Margret, Apr. 1, 1797. [Gilmore, d. John and Peggy, C.R.2.]
Robert, ch. John and Margret, Apr. 2, 1804. [Gilmore, s. Dea. John and Peggy, C.R.2.]
Samuel [dup. Gillmore], ch. John and Margret, Jan. 20, 1791.

GILMORE (see Gillmore, Gilmer, Gilmor), Abner Graham, ch. David and Eliza [(McKeen) P.R.106.], Dec. 8, 1828.
Adelaide S. [———], w. F. A., June 2, 1844, G.R.1.
Albert F., ———, 1825, G.R.1.
Albion N., July 2, 1829, G.R.6.
Anna (Gilmor), ch. James and Asenath, May 5, 1797.
Anna Eliza, d. Joseph A. and Clara Jane (Dennett), Aug. 4, 1868, P.R.105.
Betey (Gilmor), ch. James and Asenath, Feb. 19, 1803.
David Porter, ch. David and Eliza, ——— [rec. after ch. b. Feb. —, 1839]. [s. David and Eliza (McKeen), Mar. 7, 1841, P.R.106.]
Edgar F., s. David and Eliza (McKeen), Feb. 7, 1846, P.R.106.
Elisabeth C., ch. John 3d and Susan N., June 13, 1829.
Eliza [———], w. David, May 25, 1807, G.R.1. [Eliza (McKeen), May 25, 1817, P.R.106.]

GILMORE, Eliza Ellen, ch. David and Eliza, ——— [*rec. before ch. b.* Feb. —, 1839]. [d. David and Eliza (McKeen), Dec. 18, 1836, P.R.106.]
Elizabeth C. (see Elisabeth C.).
Florence, w. ——— Mutchler, Nov. 29, 1877, G.R.1.
James, Feb. 18, 1809, G.R.1.
John Simpson, ch. David and Eliza, ———. [s. David and Eliza (McKeen), Apr. 25, 1834, P.R.106.]
Joseph Eayrs, ch. David and Eliza, Feb. —, 1839. [Joseph A., Feb. 18, G.R.1. Joseph A., s. David and Eliza (McKeen), Feb. 18, P.R.106.]
Juliette A., d. David and Eliza (McKeen), Aug. 29, 1843, P.R.106.
Lucy Ann, inf. Martin, bp. Mar. 4, 1827, C.R.2.
Margaret H., ch. John 3d and Susan N., Sept. 25, 1827.
Martha J. [———], w. James, Aug. 7, 1812, G.R.1.
Martin (Gilmor), ch. James and Asenath, Aug. 2, 1799.
Nancy (Gilmor), ch. James and Asenath, May 15, 1791.
Nathaniel (Gilmer), ch. James and Asenath, Feb. 10, 1794.
Sally Jane, ch. David and Eliza, ——— [*rec. after ch. b.* Dec. 8, 1828]. [Sarah J., d. David and Eliza (McKeen), Nov. 9, 1830, P.R.106.]
Sarah Elizabeth, d. Martin, bp. Nov. 2, 1828, C.R.2.
Willard S., ———, 1866, G.R.1.
———, d. Alfred, Oct. 8, 1849, P.R.123.

GILSON, Edward, ch. Peter and Aphia, Oct. 17, 1827.
Eunica M., ch. Peter and Aphia, Nov. 7, 1838.
Mary Jane, ch. Peter and Aphia, Dec. 31, 1833.
Peter Jr., ch. Peter and Aphia, Feb. 3, 1838.
William H., ch. Peter and Aphia, Jan. 22, 1830.

GINN, Charles F. [h. Susan E.], Jan. 9, 1847, G.R.1.
Susan E. [———] [w. Charles F.], May 16, 1846, G.R.1.

GLIDDEN, Allen, ch. Robert and Mercy, Apr. 17, 1838.
Anna Louise [ch. Barker B. and Julia E. (Parker)], Oct. 22, 1855, P.R.78.
Charlotte, ch. Robert and Mercy, May 20, 1827.
Francis A. (Gliddin), ch. Robert and Mercy, June 3, 1829.
Jonathan H., ch. Robert and Mercy, June 24, 1832.
Nancy W., ch. Robert and Mercy, Nov. 7, 1835.
Willis Everard [ch. Barker B. and Julia E. (Parker)], Oct. 17, 1852, P.R.78.

GODDERD, Asahel, ch. Asahel and Anna, Mar. 5, 1804.
Emory (Godard), ch. Asahel and Anna, Apr. 2, 1807.

GODDERD, Eunice (Godard), ch. Asahel and Anna, Apr. 24, 1805.
Henry, ch. Asahel and Anna, Dec. 16, 1802.

GOODWIN, Charles Edwin, ch. Charles and Martha H., Jan. 3, 1830.

GORDEN (see Gordon), John, ch. Joseph and Dotheny, May 7, 1807.
Nancy, ch. Joseph and Dotheny, Feb. 5, 1803.
Polly, ch. Joseph and Dotheny, Feb. 7, 1799.

GORDON (see Gorden), Addie Stimpson, ch. Jason and Ann S., Oct. 13, 1878.
Ann Sarah [———], w. Jason, May 14, 1839, G.R.1.
Annie B., w. Charles F. Shaw, ———, 1864, G.R.1.
Jason, h. Ann Sarah, May 15, 1833, G.R.1.
Martha Elizabeth, d. Ames and w., bp. Sept. 6, 1835, C.R.2.
Nellie Farris, ch. Jason and Ann S., Apr. 21, 1876.

GORMAN, ———, ch. Henry (Irish), Dec. 22, 1849, P.R.123.

GOULD, Abigail, ch. John M. and Abigail, June 22, 1834.
Lucy E., ch. John M. and Abigail, May 31, 1836.
Ralph Wadlin, June 14, 1884, G.R.1.

GOYENS, Eliza [———], w. John S., Aug. 21, 1838, G.R.13.
John S., h. Eliza, July 3, 1837, G.R.13.

GRADY, Genie, s. Thomas C. and Addie H., Sept. 7, 1883, G.R.1.
Irene [? m.], ———, 1826, G.R.1.
Linford, ———, 1854, G.R.1.
Marcellus, ———, 1849, G.R.1.
Thomas, ———, 1822, G.R.1.

GRANT, Effie M., w. Charles R. Harrison, June 27, 1857, G.R.1.
Ellen J. [———], w. Adoniram J., July 1, 1842, G.R.13.
Katherine M. [———], w. Horace A., June 20, 1881, G.R.1.

GRAY, Abbie [———], w. Ezra P., Jan. 12, 1806, G.R.8.
Alpheus H., June 15, 1828, G.R.8.
Daniel, ch. John and Sarah, Sept. 1, 1826.
Ezra P., h. Abbie, Oct. 1, 1805, G.R.8.
Flora Bell, d. Henry Cushman and Margarett Frances (Ryder), July 2, 1865, P.R.104.
Frank R., ———, 1858, G.R.1.

GRAY, Gertrude, d. L. and H. L., May 20, 1882, G.R.8.
Henry C., Dec. 19, 1831, G.R.1. [Henry Cushman Gray, h. Margarett Frances (Ryder), in Penobscot, P.R.104.]
Katie C., d. Walter and Joannah, Mar. 15, 1860, G.R.1.
Lewis Fitz, s. Henry Cushman and Margarett Frances (Ryder), Sept. 5, 1862, P.R.104.
Lizzie C. Carter [―――], w. Harvey H., ―――, 1871, G.R.1.
Luette [―――], w. H. L., Feb. 28, 1855, G.R.8.
Mary Crockett [? m.], July 3, 1833, G.R.1.
Munroe, s. Ezra P. and Abbie, Nov. 12, 1838, G.R.8.
Parker Ezra, s. Henry Cushman and Margarett Frances (Ryder), Aug. 5, 1858, P.R.104.
Russell Henry, s. Henry Cushman and Margarett Frances (Ryder), Mar. 31, 1860, P.R.104.

GREELEY (see Greely), Jane, ch. Phillip and Dorothy, Dec. 24, 1808.
Lindovina, ch. Phillip and Dorothy, Dec. 26, 1805.
William George, ch. William 2d and Margaret, Aug. 22, 1838.

GREELY (see Greeley), George Gilmore, ch. John and Mary, Feb. 24, 1817.
John Tilton, ch. John and Mary, Dec. 25, 1812.
Martha Ann, ch. John and Mary, May 30, 1819.

GREENE, ―――, s. Henry, July 26, 1848, P.R.123.

GREER, Francis O., Oct. 16, 1828, G.R.1.
Mary [? m.], Jan. 6, 1836, G.R.1.

GRIFFIN, Abigail [―――], w. Dudley, Oct. 24, 1794, G.R.1.
David, [twin] ch. William and Hannah, Nov. 8, 1798.
Ebenezer, ch. Ebenezer and Lydia, bp. ――― [*rec. between* Oct. 6, 1805 *and* June ―, 1817], C.R.2.
Elisha, ch. Ebenezer and Lydia, bp. ――― [*rec. between* Oct. 6, 1805 *and* June ―, 1817], C.R.2.
George Moulton, ch. William and Hannah, Mar. 13, 1803.
James, ch. William and Hannah, Sept. 26, 1800.
Otis, ch. Ebenezer and Lydia, bp. ――― [*rec. between* Oct. 6, 1805 *and* June ―, 1817], C.R.2.
Peleg Pendleton, ch. Ebenezer and Lydia, bp. ――― [*rec. between* Oct. 6, 1805 *and* June ―, 1817], C.R.2.
Phineas, ch. Ebenezer and Lydia, bp. ――― [*rec. between* Oct. 6, 1805 *and* June ―, 1817], C.R.2.
Robert, [twin] ch. William and Hannah, Nov. 8, 1798.
Thomas, ch. Ebenezer and Lydia, bp. ――― [*rec. between* Oct. 6, 1805 *and* June ―, 1817], C.R.2.

GRIFFIN, Thomas, ch. Lydia, bp. ——— [*rec. between* Oct. 6, 1805 *and* June —, 1817], C.R.2.
William, ch. William and Hannah, July 13, 1796.

GRINDLE, ———, d. Addison, Jan. 9, 1847, P.R.123.

GRINNELL, Sarah M., w. Martin Rogers, Sept. 5, 1792, P.R.136.

GUPTEL, James, ch. Lemuel and Nancy, Aug. 20, 1808.

GURNEY, Richard A., ———, 1836, G.R.2.

HADLEY, Aaron, ch. Aaron and Polly, Apr. 25, 1811.
Anna, ch. Aaron and Polly, May 24, 1797.
Anna, ch. Aaron C. and Mary, bp. ——— [*rec. between* Oct. 6, 1805 *and* June —, 1817], C.R.2.
Eliza, ch. Aaron and Polly, June 29, 1805.
Elizabeth, ch. Aaron and Polly, Jan. 16, 1801.
Fred N., ch. Orville P. and Urania G., Sept. 25, 1876.
Harrot, ch. Aaron and Polly, Mar. 9, 1807.
Mary, ch. Aaron and Polly, July 30, 1803.
Mary, ch. Aaron C. and Mary, bp. ——— [*rec. between* Oct. 6, 1805 *and* June —, 1817], C.R.2.
Porrot, ch. Aaron and Polly, Apr. 22, 1809.
Samul, ch. Aaron and Polly, Feb. 27, 1813.
William, ch. Aaron and Polly, Nov. 16, 1798.
William, ch. Aaron C. and Mary, bp. ——— [*rec. between* Oct. 6, 1805 *and* June —, 1817], C.R.2.

HAIN (see Haynes), Ellen M. [? m.], Mar. 10, 1868, G.R.1.

HALL, Abner B., ch. Ziba and Unice, May 25, 1812.
Albert, ch. Ezra and Jane, Jan. 8, 1834.
Albert, ch. Josiah Jr. and Louisa, Jan. 7, 1844.
Ambrose A. [h. Lavinia C.], May 17, 1827, G.R.3.
Andrew D., ch. Ziba and Unice, Oct. 16, 1814.
Annie B., ch. Albert and Lucy R., Oct. 14, 1876. [w. Wallace W. Shaw, G.R.1.]
Augusta [*sic*, ? Augustine], ch. John G. and Bashaba, Aug. 16, 1842.
Brian, ch. Ziba and Unice, May 28, 1810.
Cordelia, ch. Charles and Lowis, Aug. 20, 1808.
Cyrus [h. Martha (Weeks)], Apr. 27, 1787, G.R.1.
Cyrus James, ch. Cyrus and Martha, Oct. 9, 1833. [———, 1834, G.R.1.]
Daniel B., ch. Josiah and Sarah, July 17, 1817.

HALL, David, ch. Ezra and Jane, Aug. 20, 1845.
Elisha Henry, ch. Frye and Eliza, bp. June 6, 1831, C.R.2.
Eliza Jane, w. Richard Moody, M.D., Aug. 18, 1815, in Camden, P.R.85.
Elizabeth Y., ch. Josiah and Sarah, June 22, 1810.
Elmina, w. Joshua Bramhall, Mar. 19, 1813, in Ma[r]tinicus, P.R.149.
Emily Rosine, ch. Bryan F. and Cynthia, Aug. 14, 1846.
Eunice Elisabeth, ch. Bryan F. and Cynthia, Jan. 15, 1834.
George Chancey, ch. Frye and Eliza, bp. June 6, 1831, C.R.2.
Hervey King, ch. Frye and w., bp. Sept. 17, 1839, C.R.2.
Huldah, ch. Allen and Maria, Feb. 1, 1800.
Irene Augusta, ch. Bryan F. and Cynthia, Feb. 17, 1843.
Isa E., ch. Albert and Lucy R., Apr. 10, 1879.
Isaac Andrew, ch. Bryan F. and Cynthia, July 10, 1838.
James G., ch. Josiah and Sarah, Dec. 8, 1806.
James Weeks, ch. Cyrus and Martha, Nov. 24, 1822.
Jeremiah, ch. Jeremiah and Nancy, Mar. 28, 1811.
John F., ch. John G. and Bashaba, Mar. 10, 1832.
John Farnham, ch. Frye and Eliza, bp. June 6, 1831, C.R.2.
John G., ch. Josiah and Sarah, Oct. 2, 1808.
Josephine, ch. Cyrus and Martha, July 31, 1843.
Josiah Jr., ch. Josiah and Sarah, Dec. 31, 1811.
Josiah, ch. John G. and Bashaba, Oct. 31, 1839.
Julia Amelia, ch. Frye and w., bp. Sept. 17, 1839, C.R.2.
Lavinia C. [w. Ambrose A.], Apr. 11, 1832, G.R.3.
Margaret Emeline, ch. Washington and Harriet, July 21, 1843.
Mariah, ch. Charles, Nov. 7, 1811.
Martha Ann, ch. Cyrus and Martha, Apr. 3, 1827. [Apr. 3, 1826, G.R.1.]
Mary F., ch. John G. and Bashaba, Jan. 1, 1845.
Mary White, ch. Bryan F. and Cynthia, Sept. 28, 1840.
Melvill, ch. Josiah Jr. and Louisa, Jan. 28, 1843.
Moses, ch. Jeremiah and Nancy, Apr. 15, 1809.
Nabby, ch. Allen and Maria, Mar. 1, 1802.
Nancy, ch. Jeremiah and Nancy, Jan. 6, 1807.
Ruth, ch. Jeremiah and Nancy, Nov. 9, 1805.
Samuel P., ch. Josiah and Sarah, Dec. 17, 1814.
Sarah Boardman, ch. Frye and Eliza, bp. June 6, 1831, C.R.2.
Sarah E., ch. Josiah and Sarah, July 3, 1820.
Sarah E., ch. John G. and Bashaba, Feb. 15, 1834.
Sarah Jane, ch. Ezra and Jane, Oct. 20, 1837.
Susan G., ch. Jeremiah and Nancy, Mar. 16, 1804.
Susan P., ch. Josiah and Sarah, July 9, 1805.
W[illia]m Abner, ch. Bryan F. and Cynthia, Mar. 25, 1836.

HALL, William Henry, ch. Cyrus and Martha, Nov. 19, 1824.
William James, ch. John G. and Bashaba, Nov. 19, 1836.
William Millson, youngest ch. Eliza, bp. Oct. 18, 1852, C.R.2.
——, s. Josiah Jr., Apr. 10, 1847, P.R.123.
——, s. Washington, May 15, 1849, P.R.123.

HALLOWELL, Gracie D., Aug. 19, 1867, G.R.1.
John H., h. Nancy F., June 4, 1828, G.R.1.
Nancy F. [——], w. John H., Jan. 19, 1827, G.R.1.

HAMILTON, Betey, ch. Solomon and Elizabeth, July 30, 1808.
Daniel, ch. Solomon and Elizabeth, Dec. 5, 1804.
Daniel, ch. Solomon and Elizabeth, May 25, 1806.
Phebe, ch. Solomon and Elizabeth, Nov. 13, 1802.
Solomon, ch. Solomon and Elizabeth, Dec. 25, 1800.

HANEY, Annie [——], w. James, ——, 1845, G.R.1.
Charles, s. Patrick and Johanna, Mar. 25, 1880, G.R.1.
Charles W., July 26, 1841, G.R.1.
Cleora Rosa, d. Elisha H. and Lucy A. (Condon), June 22, 1881, P.R.153.
Ellen, ——, 1859, G.R.1.
Inez L., ch. Charles W. and Philura, Apr. 10, 1876.
James, h. Ellon A., Aug. —, 1841, G.R.1.
Lena M., ch. Charles W. and Philura, June 12, 1871.
Nellie Francis, ch. Charles W. and Philura, June 13, 1866.
Waitie Maud, d. Elisha H. and Lucy A. (Condon), Apr. 1, 1877, P.R.153.

HANFORD, Edwin [h. Lucy], ——, 1775, G.R.1.
Lucy [——] [w. Edwin], ——, 1781, G.R.1.
Susannah R., w. Lemuel R. Palmer, June 17, 1812, P.R.79.

HANSCOM, Elizabeth Parsons [? m.], Aug. 20, 1848, in E. Machias, G.R.1.

HANSON, Albert [s. James B. and Bethiah T.], Nov. 20, 1819, G.R.1.
Atwood James, ch. James B. and Bethia [Bethiah T., G.R.1.], Jan, 21, 1823.
Augustus, ch. James B. and Bethia, Oct. 7, 1826. [Augustus R. [s. James B. and Bethiah T.], G.R.1.]
Bethiah T. [——] [w. James B.], Sept. 5, 1797, G.R.1.
Ephriam Loring, ch. Samuel B. and Lucy, Oct. 5, 1826.
Francis [sic] Caroline, ch. James B. and Bethia, Aug. 16, 1828. [Frances C., w. Joseph Osgood, [d. James B. and Bethiah T.] G.R.1.]

HANSON, Franklin S., ch. James B. and Bethia [Bethiah T., G.R.1.], Dec. 20, 1824.
James B. [h. Bethiah T.], Aug. 4, 1792, G.R.1.
Lucy Maria, ch. Samuel B. and Lucy Maria, Sept. 26, 1836.
Mary Laticia, ch. Samuel B. and Lucy Maria, Sept. 13, 1828.
Robert Calvert, ch. Samuel B. and Lucy Maria, June 26, 1834.
Rosilla M., ch. James B. and Bethia, Jan. 4, 1832.
Samuel Clarence, ch. Samuel B. and Lucy Maria, June 27, 1831.
Thomas Clarendon, ch. Samuel B. and Lucy Maria, Feb. 18, 1840.

HARADEN, Caroline Saville (Heraden), ch. John and Hannah, Nov. 10, 1820. [Caroline Saidie Haraden, w. Enoch Crowell Hilton, Aug. 9, P.R.40.]
Charles Frederick, ch. Daniel and Julia M., Nov. 26, 1850.
Daniel, ch. John and Hannah, Mar. 28, 1811.
Jane, ch. John and Hannah, Aug. —, 1826. [w. Joseph S. Noyes, Aug. 29, P.R.87.]
John French, ch. John and Hannah, May 18, 1825.
John William, ch. Daniel and Julia M., Dec. 8, 1848.
Josephine Shipley (Haradin), ch. Daniel and Lucy Ann, May 1, 1837.
Lucy, ch. John and Hannah, Oct. 28, 1817. [w. Bohan P. Field, G.R.1.]
Sarah Ann, ch. John and Hannah, Mar. 18, 1814. [w. Asa Faunce, G.R.1. P.R.88.]
Susanna Burnham, ch. John and Hannah, Oct. 4, 1808. [w. Phineas P. Quimby, G.R.1. P.R.118.]

HARDY, Edward G., Jan. 26, 1859, G.R.1.
Frances J. [———], w. George, Apr. 19, 1830, G.R.1.
George, h. Frances J., June 11, 1826, G.R.1.

HARMON, Charles Arthur, s. I. H. and Eliza Myra (Thurlow), Apr. 7, 1884, P.R.159.
Herbert Thurlow, s. I. H. and Eliza Myra (Thurlow), Dec. 15, 1879, P.R.159.

HARRIMAN (see Herriman), Alonzo Jesse, h. Mary Jane, Nov. 28, 1830, G.R.1.
Amanda Maria, w. Geo[rge] W. Stoddard, d. Willard P. and Mary A., July 6, 1845, G.R.1. [d. Willard Pope and Mary Ann (Ellis), P.R.113.]
George Frank, s. Willard Pope and Mary Ann (Ellis), Sept. 16, 1852, P.R.113.

HARRIMAN, James Sumner, s. Willard Pope and Mary Ann (Ellis), Nov. 24, 1848, P.R.113. [in Waldo, P.R.123.]
Joseph W., "Co. I. 26 Regt. Me. Vol. 1," Feb. 16, 1843, G.R.1. [Joseph Willard Harriman, s. Willard Pope and Mary Ann (Ellis), P.R.113.]
Mary A. [------], w. Willard P., Aug. 15, 1817, G.R.1. [Mary Ann (Ellis), w. Willard Pope Harriman, P.R.113.]
Mary A., July 7, 1840, G.R.1. [Mary Ann, d. Willard Pope and Mary Ann (Ellis), P.R.113.]
Mary Jane [------], w. Alonzo Jesse, July 8, 1831, G.R.1.
Sarah B., w. [Dr. George Wesley] Stoddard, May 9, 1855, G.R.1. [Sarah Benson Harriman, d. Willard Pope and Mary Ann (Ellis), P.R.113.]
Willard P., h. Mary A., July 1, 1814, G.R.1. [Willard Pope Harriman, h. Mary Ann (Ellis), P.R.113.]

HARRISON, Annie E., ch. C. R. and E. M., Apr. 5, 1882, G.R.1.
Charles R., h. Effie M. (Grant), Aug. 10, 1850, G.R.1.
Elizabeth E., ch. C. R. and E. M., Aug. 3, 1875, G.R.1.
Florence B., ch. C. R. and E. M., Dec. 19, 1886, G.R.1.
Margaret C., d. Charles R. and Effie M. (Grant), July 31, 1877, G.R.1.
Mary [------], w. Thomas, Apr. 25, 1841, in Halifax, N. S., G.R.1.

HART, Alice, w. Elroy R. Bowen, May 11, 1864, G.R.1.
Byron A., ch. William and Caroline, Nov. 1, 1842.
Caroline F., ch. William and Caroline, Oct. 22, 1845.
Lillian M. [------], w. Fred W., June 16, 1870, G.R.2.

HARTSHORN, Addie M., [twin] ch. Henry H. and Sophia W., Aug. 24, 1879.
Almira Abigail, ch. Benj[amin] Jr. and Ann, Feb. 11, 1839.
Benja[min], ch. Benjamin and Nabby, Dec. 31, 1800.
Benj[amin] F. K., ch. Benj[amin] Jr. and Ann, Feb. 6, 1827.
Betsy, ch. Benjamin and Nabby, Dec. 22, 1804.
Celia Elizabeth, ch. Benj[amin] Jr. and Ann, Dec. 18, 1833.
Elmer F., ch. Henry H. and Sophia W., Jan. 20, 1876.
Harriet J., w. Freeman Tufts, ------, 1808, G.R.1.
Henry Harrison, ch. Benj[amin] Jr. and Ann, Dec. 31, 1840.
Isa M., ch. Henry H. and Sophia W., Dec. 16, 1872.
James Sullivan, ch. John and Sally, Dec. 27, 1808.
Margaret, d. Abigail, June 27, 1825.
Margaret D., d. Abigail, bp. July 6, 1833, C.R.2.
Mary Ann, ch. Benj[amin] Jr. and Ann, Oct. 30, 1831.

HARTSHORN, Nabby, ch. Benjamin and Nabby, Feb. 16, 1803.
Nellie V., ch. Henry H. and Sophia W., Mar. 29, 1871.
Nettie V., [twin] ch. Henry H. and Sophia W., Aug. 24, 1879.
Richard Moody, ch. Benj[amin] Jr. and Ann, May 27, 1835 [sic, "Should be [May] 26th 1845"].
Sarah Leach, ch. John and Sally, Feb. 18, 1806.
Thomas, ch. Benj[amin] Jr. and Ann, Mar. 1, 1837.
Welthy, ch. John and Sally, Oct. 27, 1804.
W[illia]m West, ch. Benj[amin] Jr. and Ann, May 20, 1829.

HARWOOD, Henry, Mar. 4, 1822, in Hope, G.R.1.

HASEY, Sarah, first w. George R. Lancaster, Aug. 16, 1826, P.R.108.

HASKELL, Betsy Priscilla Gray, ch. John and Sally, Jan. 15, 1802.

HASSELL, Cora B., w. Ephraim Wood, adopted d. John and Rebecca S. (first w.), Feb. 15, 1862, P.R.43.
Cora E., w. Eldorous Mayo, d. Rufus P. and Harriet (Parker), Aug. 1, 1856, P.R.34.
Ella E., w. Francis J. Hunter, w. Roland Patterson, d. Rufus P. and Harriet (Parker), Jan. 18, 1854, P.R.34.
Esther W. [———], third w. John, Feb. 14, 1847, in Prospect, P.R.43.
John, ch. John and Elizabeth, Oct. 16, 1822. [h. Rebecca, h. Josephine, h. Esther W., P.R.43.]
John Henry, s. John and Josephine (second w.), Mar. 9, 1870, P.R.43.
Joseph, ch. John and Elizabeth, Mar. 23, 1831.
Josephine [———], w. Capt. John, Aug. 25, 1841, G.R.1. [second w. John, in Belmont, P.R.43.]
Mary Eliza, ch. John and Elizabeth, Jan. 23, 1820.
Rebecca [———], first w. John, Mar. 11, 1829, in Belmont, P.R.43.
Rufas, ch. John and Elizabeth, July 16, 1825. [Rufus P., h. Harriet (Parker), P.R.34.]
Sarah C., w. Fred P. Nason, d. Rufus P. and Harriet (Parker), Dec. 5, 1858, P.R.34.
Susan E., w. Alton K. Braley, d. Rufus P. and Harriet (Parker), Mar. 26, 1862, P.R.34.
Susan Rosella, ch. John and Elizabeth, Jan. 31, 1828.

HASSON, ———, ch. Albert W., Nov. 17, ———.

HATCH, Charles Lewis, s. David L. and Sarah Elizabeth (Wilson), Jan. 7, 1853, P.R.94.
Dorcas Angelette, ch. Horatio Nelson and Dorcas, May 13, 1833.
Eunice Kingman, ch. Horatio Nelson and Dorcas, Nov. 22, 1831.
Horatio Nelson Jr., ch. Horatio Nelson and Dorcas, May 9, 1826.
Mary Catherine, ch. Horatio Nelson and Dorcas, Nov. 17, 1828.
Mary E. [――――], Oct. 7, 1805, G.R.1.

HAUGH, Frank, Apr. 15, 1852, G.R.1.
Thomas, July 4, 1854, G.R.1.
――――, d. Charles, Apr. 21, 1847, P.R.123.

HAVEN, ――――, d. ――――, Apr. 5, 1850, P.R.123.

HAVENER, Abbie C., "Sister," Jan. 14, 1839, G.R.1.
Almatia S. [――――], w. Frank O., June 28, 1835, G.R.1.
Charles Matthias, s. Jacob and Nancy, bp. May 5, 1839, C.R.2.
Lizzie, Apr. 16, 1832, G.R.1.
Nancy Southwick, youngest ch. Jacob L., bp. Aug. 22, 1851, C.R.2.

HAWES, Abigail, d. Noyes P. and Abigail, bp. Apr. 3, 1831, C.R.2.

HAWKES, ――――, s. Edward, Apr. 7, 1848, P.R.123.
――――, d. Edward, Jan. 15, 1850, P.R.123.

HAWLEY, Eunice, w. Asa Edmunds, Dec. 17, 1756, G.R.1.

HAYES, Charles Edwin, ch. Charles W. and Emma F., Nov. 1, 1866.
―――― (Hays), s. Michael (Irish), Mar. 30, 1849, P.R.123.

HAYFORD, A[r]vida, ch. Axel and Mary Ann, Oct. 21, 1845.
Francelia, d. Harrison and Julia A., Oct. 22, 1845, G.R.4.
Harrison, July 31, 1824, G.R.4.
Hattie P. [――――], w. Loretto, June 28, 1853, G.R.4.
Julia A. [――――], w. Harrison, Nov. 10, 1823, G.R.4.
Marion E., w. B. R. Mosher, May 1, 1882, G.R.4.
Olive, ch. Axel and Elizabeth, Jan. 12, 1839.
Richard H., s. Loretto and Hattie P., Jan. 29, 1879, G.R.4.
Samuel F. L., ch. Arvida Jr. and Almira E., Nov. 28, 1825.
William Bicknell, ch. Arvida Jr. and Almira E., May 20, 1827.

HAYFORD, ———, d. [Harrison and Julia A.], Mar. 19, 1847, G.R.4.
———, s. Axel, Aug. 2, 1847, P.R.123.
HAYNES (see Hain), Joanna, ch. Samuel and Joanna, Feb. 24, 1829.
Tristam Augustine, ch. Samuel and Joanna, Nov. 9, 1826.
HAZELTINE, Benjamin, h. Annie (Durham), s. Charles B. and Frances L. (Jones), Mar. 24, 1857, in Boston, P.R.26.
Benj[ami]n Prescott, ch. Benjamin and Mary Ann, Dec. 19, 1830.
Caroline, ch. Paul R. and Caroline, May 25, 1830.
Charles Bellows, ch. Benjamin and Mary Ann, Apr. 2, 1828. [h. Frances L. (Jones), P.R.26.]
Charles Prescott, grand ch. Salathiel Nickerson and Martha Rogers, Oct. 13, 1847, P.R.15.
Ellen Nickerson, grand ch. Salathiel Nickerson and Martha Rogers, Aug. 28, 1842, P.R.15.
Fanny, d. Charles B. and Frances L. (Jones), Feb. 2, 1868, in Nice, France, P.R.26.
Grace, Apr. 28, 1855, G.R.1. [d. Charles B. and Frances L. (Jones), P.R.26.]
Harriet H. [———], w. Paul R., July 24, 1811, G.R.1.
Julia Longfellow, ch. Paul R. and Caroline, Feb. 29, 1828.
Lewis Prescott, Sept. 4, 1874, P.R.14. [great grand ch. Salathiel Nickerson and Martha Rogers, P.R.15.]
Louise, d. Charles B., bp. July 4, 1875, C.R.1. [d. Charles B. and Frances L. (Jones), b. Nov. 21, 1873, P.R.26.]
Margaret Ann, ch. Benjamin and Mary Ann, Feb. 19, 1825.
Margaret Florence, grand ch. Salathiel Nickerson and Martha Rogers, Mar. 27, 1846, P.R.15.
Margaret Nickerson, Apr. 17, 1880, P.R.14. [great grand ch. Salathiel Nickerson and Martha Rogers, P.R.15.]
Margaret Sarah, ch. Benjamin and Mary Ann, Feb. 6, 1826.
Mary, w. James H. Howes, d. Charles B. and Frances L. (Jones), July 9, 1861, P.R.26.
Mayo Norris, ch. Benjamin and Mary Ann, Sept. 16, 1833.
HEAGAN, Emery M., Oct. 27, 1880, G.R.1.
True S., Jan. 29, 1851, G.R.1.
HEALY, Althea A. [———] [w. James], Mar. 20, 1859, G.R.1.
HEATH, Edwin W., ———, 1856, G.R.1. [Edwin White Heath, grand s. Simeon A. and Mary (Hinkley), Dec. 5, 1857, P.R.63.]

HEATH, Elmer Hinkley, grand s. Simeon A. and Mary (Hinkley), Apr. 6, 1862, P.R.63.
Emily Carlton, ch. Solymon and w., bp. July 17, 1836, C.R.2.
Harriet G. [———], w. Henry A., Oct. 11, 1834, G.R.1.
Helen Redington, ch. Solymon and w., bp. July 17, 1836, C.R.2.
Henry A., Nov. 17, 1827, G.R.1. [h. Harriet G. (Nickerson), s. Simeon A. and Mary (Hinkley), P.R.63.]
Levi H., s. Simeon A. and Mary (Hinkley), Aug. 30, 1819, P.R.63.
Lydia A., w. Hiram E. Wright, d. Simeon A. and Mary (Hinkley), Mar. 24, 1823, P.R.63.
Mary H., w. Stephen P. Moody, d. Simeon A. and Mary (Hinkley), Mar. 26, 1821, P.R.63.
Samuel C., h. Martha A. (White), s. Simeon A. and Mary (Hinkley), Nov. 14, 1829, P.R.63.
Simeon A., Oct. 26, 1791, in Freetown, Mass., G.R.1. [h. Mary (Hinkley), P.R.63.]
Susan C., w. Spencer W. Mathews, d. Simeon A. and Mary (Hinkley), Mar. 7, 1832, P.R.63. [Susan Church Heath, P.R.64.]
William Solyman, ch. Solymon and w., bp. July 17, 1836, C.R.2.

HENDERSON, James, h. Rosina, ———, 1814, G.R.1.
Mary L., w. ——— Farrow, d. James and Rosina, ———, 1843, G.R.1.
Rosina [———], w. James, ———, 1821, G.R.1.
Sarah R., w. Alexander Crawford, June 16, 1824, G.R.1.

HENRY, Mary Watson, ch. Rufus and Hannah, Dec. 18, 1807.

HERADEN (see Haraden).

HERRICK, Albert L., Aug. —, 1869, G.R.1.
Alfred F., ch. George and Nancy, July 4, 1827.
Amanda M., ch. Joab and Sarah, Feb. 24, 1826.
Barbara A. [———], w. Samuel B., Oct. —, 1830, G.R.1.
Caroline F. (Herick), ch. George and Nancy, Dec. 23, 1830.
Cyntha Abba, ch. Joab and Sarah, Apr. 9, 1829.
David L., Aug. 13, 1832, G.R.13.
Elura Jane, ch. George and Nancy, Nov. 13, 1837.
Frances Hellen, ch. John and Catharine, Oct. 2, 1844.
George, ch. Joab and Sarah, May 24, 1823.
Hannah Augusta, w. James Albert Wilson, Mar. 11, 1836, P.R.95.
Hellen Annette, ch. Joab and Susan (second w.), Aug. 13, 1843.
John Franklin, ch. George and Nancy, Nov. 12, 1835.
Lewis G., ch. George and Nancy, June 13, 1833.
Lucy A. [? m.], Aug. 15, 1835, G.R.13.

HERRICK, Lucy Ann, ch. Joab and Sarah, Aug. —, 1821.
Mary A., Dec. —, 1873, G.R.1.
Melisa A., ch. Joab and Susan (second w.), Dec. 9, 1840. [Melissa A., Dec. 14, G.R.13.]
Oscar F., ch. Joab and Sarah, Feb. 20, 1832.
Pheobe, ch. George and Nancy, Apr. 2, 1825.
Samuel L., May —, 1862, G.R.1.
Sarah E., ch. Joab and Susan (second w.), Nov. 18, 1836.
W[illia]m Harrison, ch. George and Nancy, Feb. 10, 1840.

HERRIMAN (see Harriman), Betsey R. [———], w. Capt. Edwin H., Apr. 11, 1828, G.R.1.
Charles S., Oct. 15, 1856, G.R.1.
Edwin H., Capt., h. Betsey R., July 7, 1827, G.R.1.
Emma F., Mar. 27, 1852, G.R.1.

HERVEY, Ada Elizabeth, w. James C. Swan, d. Calvin and Elizabeth D. (Plummer), Sept. 11, 1849, P.R.25.
Calvin, h. Elizabeth D. (Plummer), Feb. 2, 1818, P.R.25.
Calvina, d. Calvin and Elizabeth D. (Plummer), Dec. 5, 1852, P.R.25.
John Charles, s. Calvin and Elizabeth D. (Plummer), Apr. 19, 1861, P.R.25.
Mary Jeannette, inf. Calvin and Elizabeth D., bp. Feb. 25, 1849, C.R.2. [w. Rufus L. Thatcher, d. Calvin and Elizabeth D. (Plummer), b. Mar. 28, 1848, P.R.25.]
Maurice Campbell, s. Calvin and Elizabeth D. (Plummer), Nov. 10, 1856, P.R.25.

HEWES (see Huse), Ann [———], w. Sylvester C., Sept. 18, 1802, G.R.1.
Henry Pascal, inf. Sylvester and Nancy, bp. Sept. 17, 1837, C.R.2.
Robert Palmer, ch. William and w., Mar. 11, 1826.
Robert Trim, ch. William and w., Nov. 8, 1824.

HEYWOOD, Albert Sibley, ch. Nathan and Lovinia, Aug. 28, 1828.
Almira Louisa, ch. Nathan and Lovinia, July 4, 1830.

HIBBERD, Alfred Ingals (Hibbard), ch. Daniel and Kezia, Oct. 10, 1808.
Charles (Hibbard), ch. Daniel and Kezia, Oct. 10, 1805.
Daniel (Hibbard), ch. Daniel and Kezia, Apr. 11, 1806.
Lydia Ingals, ch. Daniel and Kezia, Feb. 24, 1804.

HICKS, Almira Abigail, ch. Sulivan and Silvia, Sept. 10, 1831. [Sept. 11, G.R.1.]
Rhoda Ann, ch. Sulivan and Silvia, May 15, 1827. [w. Franklin J. Banks, G.R.4.]
Sarah Emeline, ch. Sulivan and Silvia, Oct. 11, 1829.
Silvia Augusta, ch. Sulivan and Silvia, Mar. 7, 1837.
Thomas Franklin, ch. Sulivan and Silvia, Dec. 13, 1833.

HIGGINS, Adeline Dean Prince, inf. Ruth, bp. Mar. 25, 1831, C.R.2.

HILL (see Hills), Bridget [———], w. John, Nov. 15, 1836, G.R.1.
Helen A. [? m.], ———, 1829, G.R.1.
John, h. Bridget, Jan. 17, 1837, G.R.1.
John S., ———, 1825, G.R.1.
Sarah E. [———], Mar. 5, 1828, G.R.1.
William Godfrey, h. Catherine (Power), ———, 1830, in Dublin, Ire., G.R.1.

HILLS (see Hill), Eugene L., May 5, 1886, G.R.1.
Herbert E., Mar. 10, 1869, G.R.1.
Joel Hawes, ch. Joel and Abigail, Nov. 26, 1828.
Joel Hawes, inf. Abigail, bp. Apr. 3, 1831, C.R.2.
Mary [? m.], May 11, 1825, G.R.1.
Mattie Inez, inf. P. R. Jr. and Mattie Ella, bp. Oct. 23, 1881, C.R.3. [b. Aug. 3, G.R.1.]
William Sanford, ch. Joel and Abigail, July 5, 1827.

HILTON, Ann Elisabeth, ch. Ebenezer W. and Permelia, Dec. 28, 1838.
Carrie Isabella, w. William L. Littlefield, d. Enoch Crowell and Caroline Saidie (Haraden), Nov. 7, 1854, P.R.40.
Edward, s. Enoch Crowell and Caroline Saidie (Haraden), Mar. 14, 1849, P.R.40. [s. Enoch W., Mar. 16, P.R.123.]
Emma Jane, w. William P. Thompson Esq., d. Enoch Crowell and Caroline Saidie (Haraden), June 4, 1852, P.R.40.
Enoch Augustus, twin s. Enoch Crowell and Caroline Saidie (Haraden), Feb. 28, 1860, P.R.40.
Enoch G., h. Caroline S., Apr. 1, 1820, G.R.1. [Enoch Crowell Hilton, h. Caroline Saidie (Haraden), h. Sarah A. (Walton), in Hallowell, P.R.40.]
Eugène Crowell, s. Enoch Crowell and Caroline Saidie (Haraden), May 25, 1851, P.R.40.
Helen Maria, d. Enoch Crowell and Caroline Saidie (Haraden), Sept. 22, 1861, P.R.40.

HILTON, Henry Augustus, s. Enoch Crowell and Caroline Saidie (Haraden), Mar. 25, 1847, P.R.40.
Lucy Ann, twin d. Enoch Crowell and Caroline Saidie (Haraden), Feb. 28, 1860, P.R.40.
Mary Hannah, d. Enoch Crowell and Caroline Saidie (Haraden), Apr. 1, 1857, P.R.40.
Wilmot Wood, ch. Ebenezer W. and Permelia, May 13, 1835, in Searsmont.

HINCKLEY (see Hinkley), Emma Frances, ch. Michael S. and Pheobe, Dec. 28, 1845.
Martha Jane, ch. Isaac and Mary, Feb. 28, 1830.
Samuel L., Aug. 21, 1862, G.R.1.

HINDS, Althos, ch. Josiah D. and Hepsebeth, Oct. 6, 1819.
Angela Abba, ch. Daniel G. and Mary, Oct. 29, 1843.
Cornelius, ch. Josiah D. and Hepsebeth, Aug. 14, 1821.
Daniel G., ch. Josiah D. and Hepsebeth, Mar. 22, 1811.
Hannah, ch. Josiah D. and Hepsebeth, Dec. 19, 1823.
Hephzibah G. [———], w. Josiah D., ———, 1780, G.R.1.
Jennet Levinia, ch. Josiah D. and Hepsebeth, May 24, 1807. [Jennette L., w. Capt. Jesse Townsend, G.R.1.]
Joseph D., ch. Josiah D. and Hepsebeth, Mar. 14, 1809. [h. Phebe H., ———, 1810, G.R.1.]
Josiah D., h. Hephzibah G., ———, 1780, G.R.1.
Josiah D., ch. Josiah D. and Hepsebeth, ——— [rec. between ch. b. Feb. 1, 1804 and ch. b. May 24, 1807].
Josiah Daniel, ch. Daniel G. and Mary, Apr. 13, 1846.
Lucelia Anna (see Luselia Anna).
Lucella Jane, ch. Daniel G. and Mary, Oct. 1, 1838.
Lucy, ch. Josiah D. and Hepsebeth, ——— [rec. before ch. b. Feb. 1, 1804].
Luselia Anna, ch. Daniel G. and Mary, Apr. 29, 1840.
Martha, ch. Josiah D. and Hepsebeth, Sept. 19, 1817. [Martha H., G.R.1.]
Phebe H. [———], w. Joseph D., ———, 1816, G.R.1.
Prescott D. (see Josiah D.).
Roxania, ch. Josiah D. and Hepsebeth, Nov. 1, 1815.
Sally, ch. Josiah D. and Hepsebeth, Feb. 1, 1804. [[w. Robert Smart] w. Erastus V. Freeman, G.R.13.]
Watson, ch. Josiah D. and Hepsebeth, Feb. 24, 1813. [Capt., h. Sarah (Farrar), G.R.1.]

HINKLEY (see Hinckley), Mary, w. Simeon A. Heath, Mar. 18, 1793, in Hallowell, G.R.1. [Mar. 18, 1792, P.R.63.]

HINKSON, Hannah, ch. Joseph and Polly, Apr. 7, 1804.
Julian, ch. Joseph and Polly, Aug. 27, 1808.
Loiza, ch. Joseph and Polly, June 1, 1806.
Mary, ch. Joseph and Polly, May 17, 1800.
Millindia, ch. Joseph and Polly, Apr. 23, 1802.

HOBART, Hannah, w. Andrew Leach, Aug. 18, 1758, in Pembroke, Mass., G.R.1.

HODGDON (see Hodsdon), Amelia J., w. George W. Cottrell, Oct. 28, 1831, P.R.99.
David, ch. Robert and Sarah, Feb. 8, 1845.
Deborah Augusta, ch. Rufus (Hodgden) and Deborah, Nov. 24, 1830.
Frank A., June 12, 1849, G.R.1.
Hiram Y. [h. Melissa C.], Oct. 6, 1829, G.R.1.
Leander Normun, ch. Rufus (Hodgden) and Deborah, May 10, 1829.
Mary Elizebeth, ch. Rufus (Hodgden) and Deborah, Aug. 28, 1825.
Melissa C. [———] [w. Hiram Y.], June 13, 1838, G.R.1.
Rufus Augustas, ch. Rufus (Hodgden) and Deborah, Sept. 26, 1827.
Sarah, ch. Robert and Sarah, Aug. 17, 1844.

HODGKINSON, Lillias E. [———], w. Samuel, July 6, 1849, G.R.1.

HODSDON (see Hodgdon), Dorcas, ch. Rev. F. A. and w., May 27, 1845.
Frederick A., "Chaplin 24th Me. Reg.," h. Martha A., Nov. 15, 1804, G.R.1.
Martha A. [———], w. Frederick A., June 24, 1805, G.R.1.

HOIT (see Hoyt), Augusta Ann, ch. Josiah and Mary Ann, Dec. 20, 1811.
Tho[ma]s Pickard, ch. Josiah and Mary Ann, May 29, 1815.
William Chapman, ch. Josiah and Mary Ann, Feb. 22, 1813.

HOLBROOK, Esther, w. Gorham Lancaster, Apr. 30, 1808, P.R.108.
John F., h. Lucy Ann (Lancaster), May 12, 1806, P.R.108.

HOLMES, Alonzo, h. Hannah P., Mar. 10, 1843, G.R.3.
Catherine (see Catherine M. Burgess).
Cyntha, ch. John and Judith, May 18, 1807.
Eleanor [———] [w. Joel], Jan. 13, 1768, P.R.51.

HOLMES, Eliza (see Eliza H. McKeen).
Eliza A., w. Capt. Richard Hopkins, ———, 1822, G.R.1.
George O. [h. Laura I.], Oct. 13, 1841, G.R.3.
Gervenius Henderson, ch. Ezra and Mary, Jan. 28, 1840.
Hannah P. [———], w. Alonzo, Jan. 25, 1845, G.R.3.
Harrit, ch. John and Judith, Oct. 10, 1809.
Joel [h. Eleanor], ———, 1768, P.R.51.
John, ch. John and Judith, Nov. 26, 1811.
Laura, ch. John and Judith, Apr. 14, 1805.
Laura I. [———] [w. George O.], Aug. 7, 1851, G.R.3.
Mary F., w. Charles H. Mitchell, May 7, 1848, G.R.1.
Roxana, ch. John and Judith, May 18, 1814.
Sallie R., w. Henry Whitman Cunningham, Apr. 4, 1807, in Machias, G.R.1.
———, d. George O. and Laura I., Oct. 24, 1887, G.R.3.

HOLT, Albert, s. Richard and Elizabeth, Mar. 5, 1826, P.R.32.
Charles Augustus Crosby, ch. Jonah J. and Elisabeth H., Apr. 25, 1841.
Charles Francis, ch. Elbridge G. and Sarah, Jan. 24, 1846.
Cha[rle]s William, ch. William 2d and Mary [Mary A. (Batson), P.R.31.], Jan. 18, 1840.
Francis D., Oct. 23, 1828, G.R.1. [Francis Davis Holt, h. Mary Hellen Mathews, s. William and Hannah P. (Shute), P.R.29.]
Frederick Augustus, ch. Elbridge G. and Sarah, Jan. 25, 1844.
George, Jan. 8, 1819, G.R.1. [s. Richard and Elizabeth, P.R.32.]
Hannah Jane, w. Josiah D. Freeman, w. Elerson Patterson, d. William and Hannah P. (Shute), Sept. 20, 1830, P.R.29.
Harriet A., ch. William 2d and Mary, Aug. 1, 1842. [w. Charles Bray, d. William and Mary A. (Batson), P.R.31.]
James, s. Richard and Elizabeth, July 17, 1817, P.R.32.
James Edward, grand ch. William and Hannah P. (Shute), Mar. 24, 1860, P.R.29.
James William, ch. William and Hannah, Feb. 23, 1826. [h. Mary Eliza (Wiley), s. William and Hannah P. (Shute), P.R.29.]
Jane R., w. Harvey H. Smalley, June 10, 1833, G.R.1. [d. Richard and Elizabeth, P.R.32.]
Margaret A., Mar. 13, 1835, G.R.1. [Margaret Ann, d. Richard and Elizabeth, P.R.32.]
Mary E., d. Richard and Elizabeth, Feb. 2, 1822, P.R.32.
Mary Eleanor, ch. William and Hannah, Apr. 28, 1824. [w. Allen Orcutt, d. William and Hannah P. (Shute), P.R.29. w. Allen Orcutt, P.R.30. P.R.70.]

HOLT, Melissa Auburn, w. Lewis Ulmer, d. William and Hannah P. (Shute), Sept. 24, 1841, P.R.29.
Nellie Cora, grand ch. William and Hannah P. (Shute), Oct. 4, 1857, P.R.29.
Richard, h. Elizabeth [(Patterson)], Nov. 7, 1793, G.R.1. P.R.32.
Samuel B., h. Annette A. (Patterson), h. Ida M. Robinson, s. William and Mary A. (Batson), Apr. 20, 1847, P.R.31. [s. William Jr., Apr. 22, P.R.123.]
Sarah H., Jan. 11, 1840, G.R.1. [Sarah Hellen, d. Richard and Elizabeth, Jan. 19, P.R.32.]
William, h. Hannah P. (Shute), June 4, 1792, P.R.29.
William, h. Mary A. (Batson), h. Susan C. Wheeler, Dec. 12, 1815, P.R.31. [s. Richard and Elizabeth, P.R.32.]
William P. 2d, h. Margaret E. (Houston), s. Samuel B. and Annette A. (Patterson), Oct. 4, 1869, P.R.31.

HOPKINS, Anna, ch. George and Lydia, Nov. 22, 1799.
Fitz W., ———, 1840, G.R.1.
George Jr., ch. George and Lydia, July 10, 1802.
Harry E., ———, 1879, G.R.1.
Lovinia, ch. George and Lydia, ——— [rec. after ch. b. May 16, 1811].
Ralph Cross Johnson, ch. George and Lydia, May 25, 1808.
Ralph M., ———, 1881, G.R.1.
Richard, Capt., h. Eliza A. (Holmes), ———, 1814, G.R.1.
Rufus Allyn, ch. George and Lydia, May 16, 1811.
Washington, ch. George and Lydia, July 6, 1805.

HOUSTIN (see Houston), Albert Boyce, ch. Benjamin and w., Dec. 20, 1827.

HOUSTON (see Houstin), Albert Boyce, s. Benjamin and Janette, bp. Sept. 1, 1833, C.R.2.
Alexander, ch. Samuel Jr. and Sally, Aug. 22, 1799.
Ann Rebecka, ch. William and Peggy, Mar. 27, 1811.
Benjamin, ch. Robert and Hannah, Sept. 28, 1797.
Caroline, ch. Samuel Jr. and Sally, ——— [rec. after ch. b. Apr. 17, 1801].
David, ch. Robert and Hannah, Aug. 2, 1793.
Eleanor Maria, ch. Robert and Hannah, Dec. 20, 1807.
Elizabeth, ch. Robert and Hannah, May 9, 1791.
Esther, ch. William and Peggy, Mar. 28, 1793.
Esther, ch. Joseph and Hannah, Feb. 25, 1798.
Fanny, ch. Joseph and Hannah, Feb. 1, 1796.
Franklin, ch. Joseph and Hannah, Mar. 12, 1804.

HOUSTON, Hannah, ch. William and Peggy, Mar. 6, 1808.
Hannah Mitchell, ch. Joseph 2d and Susan, Mar. 6, 1831.
Harriot, ch. William and Peggy, Oct. 13, 1805.
Helen Rebecca, ch. Joseph and w., bp. Oct. 13, 1836, C.R.2.
Horace Heath, s. Benjamin and w., bp. May 18, 1836, C.R.2.
  [s. Benj[amin] and Jennette D., b. Nov. 1, 1835, G.R.6.]
James, ch. Robert and Hannah, June 19, 1789.
James, ch. Samuel Jr. and Sally, Dec. 10, 1793.
Jane, ch. Robert and Hannah, June 12, 1800.
Jenney, ch. Samuel Jr. and Sally, Sept. 17, 1798. [Jennette D.,
  w. Benj[amin] Houston, Sept. 17, 1797, G.R.6.]
John, ch. William and Peggy, Mar. 13, 1799.
John Kidder, ch. Robert W. and Mary, May 22, 1831.
John M., ch. Robert and Hannah, July 20, 1795.
Joseph, ch. Samuel and Esther, Apr. 25, 1775.
Joseph, ch. Robert and Hannah, July 10, 1802.
Louisa, ch. Joseph and Hannah, Apr. 8, 1801.
Margaret E., w. William P. Holt 2d, Apr. 3, 1872, P.R.31.
Martha, ch. Samuel Jr. and Sally, June 3, 1788.
Martha N., ch. Joseph and Hannah, Mar. 25, 1809.
Mary, ch. William and Peggy, Apr. 13, 1801.
Mary, ch. Joseph and Hannah, Apr. 20, 1806.
Nathan Foster, ch. Joseph 2d and Susan, Oct. 20, 1829.
Nathan Foster, ch. Joseph and w., bp. Oct. 13, 1836, C.R.2.
Peggy, ch. William and Peggy, July 14, 1803.
Rob[er]t, ch. Samuel Jr. and Sally, Oct. 9, 1789.
Robert Wilson, ch. Robert and Hannah, Jan. 24, 1805.
Sally, ch. Samuel Jr. and Sally, Oct. 23, 1796.
Samuel, ch. Samuel Jr. and Sally, Sept. 21, 1791.
Sarah Jennette, inf. Benjamin and w., bp. Sept. 25, 1839,
  C.R.2.
Thomas, ch. William and Peggy, Mar. 7, 1795.
William, ch. Samuel Jr. and Sally, Aug. 17, 1801.
William Hale, ch. Joseph 2d and Susan, Mar. 2, 1833.
William Hale, ch. Joseph and w., bp. Oct. 13, 1836, C.R.2.

HOWARD, A. J., ———, 1829, G.R.1.
Addie L., d. Sanford and Addie (Clements), Oct. 10, 1879,
  P.R.102.
Caroline W., w. Joseph L. Moody, ———, 1808, G.R.7.
Elijah C., h. Mae E. Clements, s. Sanford and Addie (Clem-
  ents), Feb. 25, 1882, P.R.102.
Elisabeth S. P. [S. P. *in later handwriting*], ch. William and
  Rebecca, Dec. 13 [3 *in later handwriting over* 7], 1827.

HOWARD, Gerald W., h. Mabel G. Ellingwood, s. Sanford and Addie (Clements), Nov. 12, 1875, P.R.102.
Ira L., Oct. 22, 1854, G.R.1.
Julia Ann Amanda, ch. William and Rebecca, Mar. 28, 1824.
Mary Emily, d. Sanford and Addie (Clements), Aug. 11, 1877, P.R.102.
Richard Henry P. [P. *in later handwriting*], ch. William and Rebecca, July 16, 1822.
Sanford, h. Addie (Clements), Feb. 29, 1852, P.R.102.
Sanford Lee, h. Bertha M. Shields, s. Sanford and Addie (Clements), June 23, 1887, P.R.102.
William S. A. [S. A. *in later handwriting*], ch. William and Rebecca, Mar. 31, 1830.

HOWES, Asa A., h. Augusta J. (Moody), h. Hattie E., Sept. 21, 1831, in Augusta, P.R.144.
Frances Augusta, w. Richard P. Whitman, d. James H. and Mary (Hazeltine), Feb. 2, 1890, P.R.86.
Harry E., s. Asa A. and Augusta J. (Moody), Aug. 6, 1873, P.R.144.
James H., h. Mary (Hazeltine), s. Asa Abbott and Augusta (Moody), June 9, 1861, P.R.86. [s. Asa A. and Augusta J. (Moody), P.R.144.]
Ralph H., s. Asa A. and Augusta J. (Moody), Mar. 23, 1864, P.R.144.
Willie M., s. Asa A. and Augusta J. (Moody), Oct. 10, 1868, P.R.144.

HOYT (see Hoit), Upham A., Jan. 6, 1845, G.R.1.

HUBBARD, Charles H., June 4, 1845, G.R.1.
Edward Hawkes, ch. Thaddeus and Emma, July 21, 1807.
Erva Dean [———], w. Leslie L., ———, 1869, G.R.1.
Eunes (Hubberd), ch. Thaddeus and Emma, Nov. 18, 1804.
Leslie L., h. Erva Dean, ———, 1873, G.R.1.
Lucy Ann, ch. Thaddeus and Emma, Jan. 25, 1811.
Margaret E. [———], w. C. H., June 12, 1843, G.R.1.
Thomas Jefferson (Hubberd), ch. Thaddeus and Emma, May 3, 1803.

HUESTIS (see Eustis).

HUNT, Fitzalburn, ch. Nahum and Sally, July 23, 1820.
James Wilder, ch. Nahum and Sally, Apr. 15, 1825.
Margaret H. [———], w. Phineas G., Feb. 26, 1838, G.R.9.
Nahum, ch. Nahum and Sally, Dec. 6, 1821.

HUNT, Phineas G., h. Margaret H., Mar. 30, 1837, G.R.9.
Thomas Ginn, ch. Nahum and Sally, Aug. 14, 1823.
William Parker, ch. Nahum and Sally, Dec. 16, 1826.
———, d. Elijah, Dec. 25, 1847, P.R.123.

HUNTER, Lucretia, w. W[illia]m O. Poor, Sept. 1, 1817, G.R.1.
[Lucretia McClure Hunter, in Bristol, P.R.143.]

HUNTOON, Woodman C., "Co. G. 1st Me. Heavy Art.," June 17, 1827, G.R.1.

HURD, Andrew A., "Co. A. 26 Me. Reg.," Feb. 9, 1844, G.R.1.

HUSE (see Hewes), Emela, ch. John and Mehitable, Mar. 26, 1805.
George, ch. Caleb and Sarah, Aug. 23, 1807.
Harriote, ch. John and Mehitable, Nov. 27, 1808.
John Adams, ch. John and Mehitable, Feb. 28, 1802.
Stephen, ch. John and Mehitable, Jan. 29, 1807.

HUSSEY, Helen M. (see Helen M. Kilgore).

HUTCHINGS (see Hutchins), George Owen, ch. Harrison and Mary, May 23, 1840.
Jos[eph] Franklin, ch. Harrison and Mary, July 13, 1842.

HUTCHINS (see Hutchings), George A., Dec. 8, 1848, G.R.1.
Jeremiah, ———, 1825, G.R.1.

HUTCHINSON, Annie Whittier, w. Samuel Greenleaf Thurlow, July 22, 1816, P.R.159.
Julia M., d. Harvey and Ann, Dec. 24, 1857, G.R.1.
H[illegible], Frank L., ch. Benj[amin] F. and Eliza A., Jan. 1, 1870.
Jennette M., ch. Benj[amin] F. and Eliza A., Feb. 5, 1875.

IDRIS, Levaughn, ———, 1867, G.R.1.

JACKSON, Almira Pander, ch. Samuel Jr. and Lydia, Sept. 25, 1823.
Benjamin Hazeltine, ch. Samuel and Mary, Oct. 10, 1821.
Daniel Henry, ch. Samuel Jr. and Lydia, Aug. 23, 1827.
Elvira F. [———], w. Simon, Sept. 26, 1856, G.R.1.
Henry, ch. Samuel and Mary, Feb. 3, 1812.
Isa E., July 18, 1886, G.R.13.
James I., Jan. 1, 1853, G.R.13.

JACKSON, Jane Cunningham, ch. Samuel and Mary, Jan. 26, 1819.
Mary Eleanor, ch. Samuel and Mary, June 24, 1809.
Mary Elleanor, ch. Samuel Jr. and Lydia, July 20, 1825.
Nettie C., Feb. 17, 1887, G.R.13.
Samuel Haraden, ch. Samuel Jr. and Lydia, Aug. 24, 1830.
Simon, h. Elvira F., Sept. 9, 1852, G.R.1.
Warren C., June 9, 1833, G.R.1.
———, s. Isaac T., Sept. 8, 1849, P.R.123.

JEFFRY, Elizabeth, w. Nathan Read, ———, 1772, G.R.1.

JEWETT, John Parker, ch. Parker and Mary, Nov. 17, 1834.
Judson W., " Co. I. 26 Me. Regt.," Mar. 28, 1840, G.R.1.
Mary Elizabeth, ch. Parker and Mary, Nov. 11, 1832.

JOHNSON, Abigail, ch. Portius and Thais, Nov. 6, 1833.
Alfred, h. Sarah (Cross), July 27, 1766 [in Plainfield, Conn.], P.R.1.
Alfred Jr., h. Nancy (Atkinson), s. Alfred and Sarah (Cross), Aug. 13, 1789 [in Freeport], P.R.1.
Alfred, s. Alfred Jr. and Nancy (Atkinson), Aug. —, 1818, P.R.1.
Alfred, ch. Alfred W. and Annie M., July 29, 1863, G.R.1.
Alfred 2d, ch. Alfred W. and Annie M., Dec. 24, 1864, G.R.1. [s. Alfred W. and Anna Maria (Crosby), P.R.1.]
Alfred, s. Alfred W. and Anna Maria (Crosby), June 11, 1868, in Paris, France, P.R.1.
Alfred Waldo, ch. Alfred Jr. and Nancy, Dec. 20, 1824. [Dec. 24, G.R.1. h. Anna Maria (Crosby), s. Alfred Jr. and Nancy (Atkinson), Dec. 20, P.R.1.]
Ann Sarah, ch. Alfred Jr. and Nancy, Dec. 21, 1821. [w. Nahum Parker Monroe, d. Alfred Jr. and Nancy (Atkinson), P.R.1.]
Arbella, ch. Horatio H. and Ann Frances, Sept. 21, 1842.
Bessie E., ch. Andrew and Lizzie, Feb. 9, 1891.
Carrie A., ch. Andrew and Lizzie, Feb. 27, 1885.
Edward, ch. Alfred Jr. and Nancy, June 30, 1840. [h. Georgiana P. (Miller), s. Alfred Jr. and Nancy (Atkinson), P.R.1.]
Frances Emily, ch. Alfred Jr. and Nancy, Aug. 26, 1828. [w. Charles Allen Lambard, d. Alfred Jr. and Nancy (Atkinson), Aug. 27, P.R.1.]
Fred D., ch. Andrew and Lizzie, Oct. 8, 1880.
George Atkinson, ch. Alfred Jr. and Nancy [(Atkinson) P.R.1.], June 5, 1827.

JOHNSON, Horatio H. Jr., ch. Horatio H. and Ann Frances, Dec. 30, 1844. [Horatio Huntington Johnson, M.D., Jan. 30, 1845, G.R.I.]
Horatio Huntington, Dec. 10, 1808 [in Plainfield, Conn.], G.R.I.
Laura Augusta, ch. Portius and Thais, Feb. 6, 1837.
Lillian E., ch. Andrew and Lizzie, Dec. 10, 1883.
Martha K., ch. Andrew and Lizzie, May 20, 1889.
Mary A., ch. Andrew and Lizzie, Oct. 6, 1887.
Mary Louisa, ch. Alfred Jr. and Nancy, Aug. 9, 1833. [w. Jean Gabriel de Sibourg, d. Alfred Jr. and Nancy (Atkinson), Aug. 9, 1832, P.R.I.]
Nathanial, ch. Daniel and Jane, Mar. 18, 1802.
Ralph, ch. Daniel and Pheobe, June 13, 1835.
Ralph Cross, s. Alfred and Sarah (Cross), Sept. 25, 1790 [in Freeport], P.R.I.
Ralph Cross, ch. Alfred Jr. and Nancy, Dec. 8, 1819. [h. Julia Elizabeth (Lambard), s. Alfred Jr. and Nancy (Atkinson), P.R.I.]
Ralph Cross, ch. Ralph C. and Sarah W., Sept. 1, 1843.
William A., ch. Andrew and Lizzie, Jan. 24, 1878.

JONES, Betsey [———], ———, 1797, G.R.I.
Charlotte B. [———], w. William H., formerly w. Capt. Philip Eastman, Nov. 2, 1807, G.R.I.
Emma, w. Joseph W. Perkins, June 10, 1824, G.R.I.
Frances L., w. Charles B. Hazeltine, Apr. 30, 1832, in Camden, P.R.26.
Francis [sic] Caroline, ch. John and Eliza Ann, Oct. 22, 1841.
Hannah W. [———], w. Verrell S., ———, 1823, G.R.I.
James R., ———, 1827, G.R.I.
John W., Mar. 28, 1853, G.R.I.
Linwood Stewart, s. John W. and Lily Sarah (Stewart), grand ch. John Nelson Stewart and Sarah Ellen (Whitmore), Sept. 16, 1891, P.R.60.
Minnie Evelyn [? m.], ———, 1865, G.R.I.
Pliny M., ———, 1835, G.R.I.
Sophia M., Oct. 26, 1845, in Camden, G.R.I.
Verrell S., h. Hannah W., ———, 1820, G.R.I.
———, d. Solomon V., Jan. 18, 1847, P.R.123.

JORDAN, Lizzie P., w. T. S. Heagan, Sept. 17, 1851, G.R.I.

JOY, Olivia, ch. Benjamin and Fanney, Aug. 20, 1808.

KALER, Annie K., d. Joseph H. and Emily P. (Brooks), Oct. 10, 1864, P.R.128.

KALER, Henry Edward, s. Joseph H. and Emily P. (Brooks), Feb. 12, 1856, P.R.128.
Joseph, h. Mary, Mar. —, 1782 [? in Waldoboro], P.R.127.
Joseph H., s. Joseph and Mary, Oct. 4, 1821 [? in Waldoboro], P.R.127. [h. Emily P. (Brooks), P.R.128.]
Marcella, d. Joseph H. and Emily P. (Brooks), Aug. 5, 1860, P.R.128.
Mary [――――], w. Joseph, Oct. 3, 1782 [? in Waldoboro], P.R.127.
Mary Katherine, d. Joseph and Mary, Mar. 31, 1818 [? in Waldoboro], P.R.127.
Sarah Matilda, d. Joseph and Mary, Jan. 20, 1809 [? in Waldoboro], P.R.127.
Sukey, d. Joseph and Mary, July 25, 1813 [? in Waldoboro], P.R.127.
W[illia]m Ludwig, s. Joseph and Mary, Mar. 20, 1811 [? in Waldoboro], P.R.127.

KEARNEY, John, ch. Patrick and Sarah, Feb. 25, 1833.
William Franklin, ch. Patrick and Sarah, Apr. 30, 1835.

KEEN, Mary E. Ellis [――――], w. W. H., Aug. 9, 1856, G.R.1.

KEITH, Eliza Jane, ch. Samuel S. and Thankful, Dec. 31, 1830.
Rachal Emily, ch. Samuel S. and Thankful, Oct. 18, 1822.
Samuel Stillman, ch. Samuel S. and Thankful, Aug. 20, 1826.
Sarah Ann, ch. Samuel S. and Thankful, Oct. 26, 1828.
Thankful Caroline, ch. Samuel S. and Thankful, Mar. 11, 1824.

KELLAY (see Kelley), Mary E. [? m.], Apr. 19, 1866, G.R.1.

KELLEY (see Kellay), Adelia P. (Kelly), ch. William and Mary, Aug. 13, 1836.
Benjamin, ch. Benjamin and Catharine, Jan. 4, 1834. [[h. Laura A. (Rankin), h. Mary E. (Rankin)] G.R.1.]
Charlotte Eastman, ch. Benjamin and Catharine, Mar. 11, 1838. [Charlotte C., w. Walter B. Rankin, G.R.1.]
Elizabeth Jane, ch. Benjamin and Catharine, Feb. 4, 1836. [Lizzie J., d. Maj. Benj[amin] and Catharine, G.R.1.]
Fannie Banks [? m.], ――――, 1855, G.R.1.
James Edward, ――――, 1858, G.R.1.
James M. W. (Kelly), ch. William and Mary, Aug. 21, 1838.
James Wilmot (Kelly), ch. Benjamin and Catharine, June 13, 1840.
Jane Ann, ch. Benjamin and Catharine, May 1, 1829.
Lizzie J. (see Elizabeth Jane).
Louira H., s. Maj. Benj[amin] and Catharine, Jan. 15, 1844, G.R.1.

KELLEY, Mary Jane (Kelly), ch. William and Mary, Apr. 27, 1842.
Pheobe Jane (Kelly), ch. William and Mary, July 21, 1835.
Philander (Kelly), ch. William and Mary, Oct. 8, 1833.
Thomas Campbell (Kelly), ch. Benjamin and Catharine, Aug. 28, 1831.
Walter Edward, ——, 1888, G.R.1.
Wilmot, ch. Benjamin and Catharine, Mar. 31, 1824.

KELLOCK, Susan L., w. George A. Miller, Jan. 15, 1812, in Thomaston, P.R.21.
——, s. Horrace, Dec. 29, 1848, P.R.123.

KELLY (see Kellay, Kelley).

KELSEY, David Bosworth, ch. Robert and Mary, bp. Sept. 28, 1821, C.R.2.
Earl Sturtevant, ch. Robert and Mary, bp. Sept. 28, 1821, C.R.2.
James Ramsey, ch. Robert and Molly, Oct. 27, 1809.
James Ramsey, ch. Robert and Mary, bp. Sept. 28, 1821, C.R.2.
Mary Moor (Kelsoy), ch. Robert and Molly, Nov. 19, 1804.
Robert, ch. Robert and Molly, Jan. 1, 1807.
William, ch. Robert and Mary, bp. Sept. 28, 1821, C.R.2.

KENDALL, Mary Emeline, ch. John P. and Emeline, Jan. 29, 1842.
Moses Wilson Sampson, ch. Uzziah and Abigail, May 25, 1815.
W[illia]m Henry, ch. John P. and Emeline, July 21, 1839.

KENISTON, Caroline C., w. Charles N. Bean, Nov. 22, 1824, G.R.1.

KILGORE, Helen M. [——], w. Henry H., Mar. 26, 1847, G.R.1. [d. John Hussey, P.R.123.]
Henry H. [h. Helen M.], Aug. 6, 1841, G.R.1.
Mary Francis, d. Henry H. and Helen M., Apr. 29, 1882, G.R.1.

KIMBALL, Abigail Field, ch. John S. and Ann, Oct. 11, 1823.
Ann [——], w. Charles C., May 1, 1811, G.R.1.
Caroline Maria, ch. John S. and Ann, Oct. 7, 1825.
Catharine H., ch. John S. and Ann, Apr. 30, 1827.
Charles C., h. Ann, Apr. 27, 1806, G.R.1.
Charles T., Nov. 12, 1845, G.R.1.
Charles T., Apr. 9, 1847, G.R.1.
Deborah P. [——], w. Edwin C., June 4, 1810, G.R.1.
Edwin C., h. Deborah P., May 5, 1813, G.R.1.

KIMBALL, Edwin S., Sept. 10, 1837, G.R.1.
John Edwin (Kimbal), ch. John S. and Ann, Oct. 17, 1820.
John S., h. Ann D., Dec. 27, 1783, in Plaistow, N. H., G.R.1.
Mary E. [? m.], Feb. 16, 1841, G.R.1.
Susan Sawyer, ch. John S. and Ann, Dec. 5, 1818.
William Crosby (Kimbal), ch. Ruben and Deborah, Mar. 13, 1802.

KING, Cora Amelia, w. William C. Crawford, Apr. 17, 1866, G.R.1.

KINGSBURY, Samuel H., Sept. 10, 1818, G.R.1.

KIRKPATRICK, Anna, ch. Daniel and Mary, Apr. 8, 1805.
Eliza, ch. Daniel and Mary, Mar. 22, 1813.
Hannah, ch. Daniel and Mary, Oct. 8, 1803.
Mary, ch. Daniel and Mary, Aug. 13, 1811.
Mehitable, ch. Daniel and Mary, Feb. 12, 1807.
Samuel, ch. Daniel and Mary, Apr. 13, 1809.

KNIGHT, Adelbert, Jan. 16, 1841, G.R.1.
Bertha M., Dec. 5, 1871, G.R.1.
Orilla C., w. Alonzo Shute, Dec. 24, 1866, P.R.45.
Oscar F., Feb. 3, 1870, G.R.1.
Rebecca, first w. David Lancaster, Apr. 22, 1818, P.R.108.
Sarah A. [? m.], May 12, 1843, G.R.1.
Susan, w. James Lancaster, Jan. 13, 1810, P.R.108.

KNOWLES, Amanda M., ch. Jonathan and Mary, June 29, 1835.
Angela, ch. Jonathan and Mary, Oct. 15, 1839.
Catharine, ch. Simon Jr. and Lydia, Jan. 9, 1818.
Elisha P., ch. Simon Jr. and Lydia, Apr. 1, 1839.
Eliza Jane, ch. Lafayette and Eliza, June 28, 1825.
Emeline, ch. Lafayette and Eliza, Oct. 28, 1834.
Eunice, ch. Simon Jr. and Lydia, Aug. —, 1826.
Frances H., ch. Jonathan and Mary, Sept. 30, 1841.
Frederick, ch. Simon Jr. and Lydia, Apr. 2, 1830.
Fuller, ch. Simon Jr. and Lydia, Dec. 16, 1822.
Harriet, ch. Lafayette and Eliza, Oct. 31, 1835.
Henry W., ch. Jonathan and Mary, July 21, 1827.
James O., ch. Simon Jr. and Lydia, May 21, 1835.
Jasper, ch. Jonathan and Mary, Sept. 1, 1837.
Jeremiah, ch. Lafayette and Eliza, July 6, 1838.
John S., ch. Simon Jr. and Lydia, Mar. 13, 1832.
Jonathan Jr., ch. Jonathan and Mary, Feb. 6, 1833.

KNOWLES, Joseph, ch. Simon Jr. and Lydia, Oct. 5, 1820.
Keziah F., ch. Jonathan and Mary, Mar. 2, 1844.
Lafayette Jr., ch. Lafayette and Eliza, Sept. 6, 1827 [*sic*, see Martha A.].
Laura Ann, ch. Lafayette and Eliza, June 28, 1824.
Lydia Ellen, ch. Lafayette and Eliza, Jan. 24, 1832.
Maria Josiphine (Knowls), ch. Simon Jr. and Lydia, Jan. 10, 1844.
Martha A., ch. Lafayette and Eliza, Mar. 31, 1828 [*sic*, see Lafayette Jr.].
Martha Adaline, ch. Lafayette and Eliza, Nov. 13, 1846.
Mary E., ch. Jonathan and Mary, July 15, 1829.
Mary Olivia, ch. Lafayette and Eliza, Jan. 4, 1843.
Nancy Adaline, ch. Lafayette and Eliza, Mar. 4, 1841.
Orlando S., ch. Jonathan and Mary, Feb. 17, 1846.
Philomon, ch. Simon Jr. and Lydia, Feb. 8, 1837.
Raymond, ch. Jonathan and Mary, Apr. 2, 1831.
Rhoda Ann, ch. Simon Jr. and Lydia, July 4, 1841.
Richmond P., ch. Simon Jr. and Lydia, Feb. 21, 1834.
Robert, ch. Simon Jr. and Lydia, Dec. 5, 1821.
Simon 3d, ch. Simon Jr. and Lydia, Oct. —, 1824.
Tristram, ch. Lafayette and Eliza, May 24, 1830.

KNOWLTON, Alonzo O., ch. W[illia]m H. and Betsey J., Apr. 4, 1851, P.R.101.
Amy E., ch. W[illia]m H. and Betsey J., Aug. 16, 1870, P.R.101.
Anna [w. Amos Atkinson], Nov. 15, 1762 [in Newbury, Mass.], P.R.1.
Aseneth E. [———], w. J. Watson, ———, 1840, G.R.1.
Betsy S. [———], Nov. 21, 1829, G.R.1. [Betsey J., w.W[illia]m H., P.R.101.]
Caroline J., w. Charles P. Hazeltine, d. L. A. and C. E. (Pendleton), Sept. 20, 1849, P.R.66.
Cha[rle]s Edward, s. Lewis A. and Elizabeth Eaton (Pendleton) (second w.), Aug. 31, 1860, P.R.67.
Charlotte, ch. W[illia]m H. and Betsey J., July 27, 1849, P.R.101.
Clarence, ch. W[illia]m H. and Betsey J., June 21, 1863, P.R.101.
Delmont, June 13, 1855, G.R.1. [ch. W[illia]m H. and Betsey J., P.R.101.]
Eddie, ch. W[illia]m H. and Betsey J., Apr. 6, 1867, P.R.101.
Elisha P., Jan. 19, 1837, G.R.13.
Emma F., ch. W[illia]m H. and Betsey J., Aug. 19, 1853, P.R.101.

KNOWLTON, Ernest, ch. Frederick and Elizabeth, May 8, 1864, G.R.1.
Ethel W., w. [Samuel Merrill Ray] Locke, ——, 1872, G.R.1.
Fannie [——], w. B. H., ——, 1847, G.R.13.
Frank B., ——, 1834, G.R.1.
Fred W., ch. Frederick and Elizabeth, Feb. 18, 1856, G.R.1.
Frederick A., Oct. 23, 1826, G.R.1.
G. Merton, ——, 1884, G.R.1.
Henrietta, ch. W[illia]m H. and Betsey J., Dec. 31, 1847, P.R.101.
Herbert Eugene, s. Lewis A. and Elizabeth Eaton (Pendleton) (second w.), Feb. 28, 1866, P.R.67.
J. Watson, h. Aseneth E., ——, 1838, G.R.1.
Lewis A., h. Caroline E. (Pendleton), ——, 1825, G.R.1. [Feb. 21, in Northport, P.R.66.]
Lucinda B., ——, 1836, G.R.1.
Mabell, ch. W[illia]m H. and Betsey J., Apr. 6, 1865, P.R.101.
Marsell, ch. W[illia]m H. and Betsey J., Sept. 21, 1857, P.R.101.
Martha J., ch. W[illia]m H. and Betsey J., Mar. 23, 1845, P.R.101.
Sanford, ch. W[illia]m H. and Betsey J., Feb. 23, 1860, P.R.101.
Sarah E. [? m.], Dec. 28, 1835, G.R.13.
Warren W., Sept. 2, 1871, G.R.1.
William H., Feb. 4, 1818, G.R.1. [h. Betsey J., P.R.101.]
——, s. John W., Jan. 20, 1847, P.R.123.

LADD, Acelia Alice Swazey, ch. Joseph P. and Mehetable C., Oct. 26, 1817.
Almaetia Mary, ch. Joseph P. and Mehetable C., Aug. 28, 1809.
Arnaldo Morearta, ch. Joseph P. and Mehetable C., Mar. 2, 1820.
Attilius Alexis, ch. Joseph P. and Mehetable C., Dec. 7, 1815.
Aurelia Frances, ch. Joseph P. and Mehetable C., Sept. 11, 1811.
Aurelius Towne, ch. Joseph P. and Mehetable C., Nov. 24, 1813.

LAMPHER, Arthur G., h. Lovicy C. [(Stephenson)], ——, 1818, G.R.1.

LANCASTER, Ann Eliza, d. David and Lucy Margaret (Dean) (second w.), Mar. 27, 1858, P.R.108.
Asa Nudd, s. George R. and Sarah (Hasey) (first w.), Nov. 25, 1864, P.R.108.

LANCASTER, Charles W., s. David and Lucy Margaret (Dean) (second w.), June 30, 1851, P.R.108.
David, h. Rebecca (Knight), h. Lucy Margaret (Dean), s. Humphrey and Lucy (Elwell), Nov. 10, 1814, P.R.108.
Eliza Ann, w. Ferdinand Dodge, d. James and Susan (Knight), May 29, 1835, P.R.108.
Ella Angelett, w. Llewellyn Sleeper, d. Francis Marion and Angelett O. (Brown), Mar. 26, 1847, P.R.108.
Francis M., h. Angelett O. (Brown), ———, 1817, G.R.1. [Francis Marion, s. Humphrey and Lucy (Elwell), Nov. 27, P.R.108.]
George Frederick, s. George R. and Sarah (Hasey) (first w.), Jan. 5, 1850, P.R.108.
George R., h. Sarah (Hasey), h. Lucy T. Torrey, s. Humphrey and Lucy (Elwell), June 28 [dup. June 25], 1820, P.R.108.
Gorham, h. Esther (Holbrook), s. Humphrey and Lucy (Elwell), Mar. 12, 1805, P.R.108.
H. N., June 29, 1809, G.R.1. [Humphrey N., h. Mary Amelia (Torrey), s. Humphrey and Lucy (Elwell), P.R.108.]
Humphrey, h. Lucy (Elwell), h. Arena Mansfield, Sept. 25, 1779, P.R.108.
Humphrey N. (see H. N.).
James, h. Susan (Knight), s. Humphrey and Lucy (Elwell), Jan. 31, 1807, P.R.108.
John Albert, h. Mary (Robinson), s. Humphrey and Lucy (Elwell), July 26, 1823, P.R.108.
Lucy Adella, second w. Hartshorn C. Pitcher, d. David and Rebecca (Knight) (first w.), June 9, 1844, P.R.108.
Lucy Ann, w. John F. Holbrook, d. Humphrey and Lucy (Elwell), Mar. 28, 1812, P.R.108.
Lucy T. [———] [w. ———], formerly w. William L. Torrey, June 10, 1832, G.R.1. [second w. George R. Lancaster, P.R.108.]
Lydia Ann, first w. Hartshorn C. Pitcher, d. David and Rebecca (Knight) (first w.), Dec. 4, 1840, P.R.108.
Mary Nickels, w. Edward A. Perry, d. Gorham and Esther (Holbrook), Mar. 13, 1849, P.R.108.
———, twin d. Gorham and Esther (Holbrook), Mar. 18, 1845, P.R.108.
———, twin s. Gorham and Esther (Holbrook), Mar. 18, 1845, P.R.108.

LANE, Caroline August, ch. John H. and Jane, June 25, 1835.
Daniel Haraden, ch. John H. and Jane, June 18, 1837.
Franklin Horatio, ch. Daniel and Julia, Oct. 25, 1819.

LANE, George C., h. Merinda M. (Ellis), Feb. 14, 1858, G.R.1.
John E., ch. John T. and Ellen, July 24, 1866.
John H., h. Sarah J., Sept. 23, 1805, G.R.1.
John Haraden, ch. John H. and Jane, Mar. 31, 1832.
John Kellum, ch. John H. and Jane, Sept. 18, 1842.
Lucy Jane, ch. John H. and Jane, May 10, 1833.
Mary Ann, ch. John H. and Jane, Sept. 2, 1830. [w. ——
  Kaler, Sept. 3, G.R.1.]
Sarah J. [——], w. Jonn H., Aug. 6, 1811, G.R.1.
Willie J., ch. John T. and Ellen, Apr. 26, 1869.
——, s. William D., Aug. 8, 1848, P.R.123.

LANGILL, William F., Oct. 18, 1864, G.R.1.

LARABEE (see Larrabee), ——, d. ——, Apr. 10, 1850, P.R.123.

LARRABEE (see Larabee), Augusta A. [? m.], Mar. 27, 1875, G.R.1.
Lizzie G., inf., bp. June 27, 1877, C.R.3.
Mary J. [? m.], Dec. 1, 1873, G.R.1.

LEACH, Andrew, h. Hannah (Hobart), Feb. 11, 1753, in Glenluce, Scot., G.R.1.
William Henry, ch. W[illia]m B. and Luri Ann, Jan. 11, 1846.

LEIGHTON, Christina C., d. Thomas and Persis T., ——, 1829, G.R.1.
Persis T. [——], w. Thomas, ——, 1807, G.R.1.
Stephen H., ——, 1835, G.R.1.
Thomas, h. Persis T., ——, 1804, G.R.1.

LELAND, Orinda Elizabeth, w. Cornelius Samuel Bullen, ——, P.R.100.

LENNAN, Ansel Jr., ch. Ansel and Mary M., Oct. 18, 1847.
Eva Armanda, ch. Ansel and Mary M., Aug. 3, 1845.

LEONARD, James E., ——, 1875, G.R.1.
Robert C., Mar. 21, 1869, G.R.1.

LEVENSALER, Charles L., ——, 1827, G.R.1.
Llewellyn, ——, 1855, G.R.1.
Marion, ——, 1852, G.R.1.
Wilfred, ——, 1859, G.R.1.

LEWIS, Augustus, ch. Frederic A. and Sally F., May 16, 1827.
Frederic, ch. Frederic A. and Sally F., Sept. 10, 1834.
George W., h. Sarah R. (Black), May 4, 1834, G.R.1.

LEWIS, Helen I., w. Clarence W. Ripley, July 19, 1864, G.R.1.
Henrietta, ch. Frederic A. and Sally F., July 11, 1825.
James, ch. Frederic A. and Sally F., Feb. 24, 1829.
Justus A., bp. June —, 1885, C.R.1.
Kate B., bp. June —, 1885, C.R.1.
Sanford S., ch. James C. and Fannie, Sept. 26, 1865.

LIBBY, Alfred J., ch. Abraham and Betsy, Sept. 28, 1819.
Betsy H., ch. Abraham and Betsy (third w.), Dec. 27, 1830.
Clarisa H., ch. Abraham and Betsy, Sept. 5, 1805.
David, ch. Abraham and Betsy, Sept. 16, 1803.
David H., ch. David and Mary, Aug. 19, 1827.
Elias [dup. adds L.], ch. Abraham and Betsy, Jan. 14 [dup. Jan. 11], 1810.
Helen L., ch. Capt. Elias and Nancy, Oct. 17, 1836.
John A., ch. David and Mary, May 20, 1830.
John Conner, ch. Abraham and Betsy, July 14 [dup. July 12], 1808.
Mary A., ch. Capt. Elias and Nancy, Mar. 30, 1841.
Mary E., ch. David and Mary, Oct. 24, 1832.
Millie T., w. Elijah Souther Shuman, June 22, 1855, P.R.47.
Sally, ch. Abraham and Betsy, Aug. 6, 1801.
Samuel H., ch. Abraham and Betsy, June 12, 1812.
Stephen B., ch. David and Mary, July 7, 1825.
Susan [dup. adds H.], ch. Abraham and Betsy, Apr. 16, 1807.

LIMEBURNER (see Lymburner), Carrie E. [————], w. Oscar L., ——, 1859, G.R.1.
Frank W., Capt., ——, 1852, G.R.1.
Hannah E. [? m.], ——, 1824, G.R.1.
Mary W. [————], w. Capt. Robert, ——, 1825, G.R.1.
Oscar L., h. Carrie E., ——, 1851, G.R.1.
Robert, Capt., h. Mary W., ——, 1822, G.R.1.
Thomas S., ——, 1814, G.R.1.

LISCOMB, Abby Maria, ch. Nath[anie]l and w., July 8, 1833.
John Thomas, ch. Nath[anie]l and w., Aug. 20, 1831.

LITTLEFIELD, Grace E., w. Charles R. Decrow, Feb. 22, 1888, G.R.1.
Jeremiah B., ——, 1833, G.R.1.
Martha Jane, w. Albert Gammans, July 4, 1843, G.R.1.
W. L., Apr. 18, 1853, G.R.1.

LOCKE, Annie Maria, ch. Sam[ue]l Wesley and Frances I., Nov. 22, 1856.

LOCKE, Cha[rle]s Augustine, ch. Samuel and Jenett, Feb. 19, 1834.
Charles Wesley, ch. Sam[ue]l Wesley and Frances I., Dec. 24, 1854.
Horatio Johnson, ch. Samuel and Jenett, Nov. 4, 1837.
John L., ch. Samuel and Jenett, July 6, 1832.
Margaret Jane, ch. Samuel and Jenett, Nov. 4, 1829.
Samuel W., ch. Samuel and Jenett, Oct. 9 [9 *written above* 10 *crossed out*], 1827.

LONG, Almena, ch. William and Mary, Mar. 14, 1846.
William Wallace, ch. William and Mary, Jan. 9, 1843.
———, d. Hezekiah, Aug. 17, 1849, P.R.123.

LONGFELLOW, Amelia, ch. Stephen and Debby, May 31, 1812.
Caroline, ch. Stephen and Debby, Oct. 27, 1805.
Mary Elizabeth, w. Sherburne Sleeper, Apr. 18, 1818, in Hallowell, P.R.146.
Rosilla, ch. Stephen and Debby, Mar. 16, 1804.

LORD, Georgie Geraldine, w. Edgar Fillmore Hanson, d. Henry Lunt and Celeste Ann (Walker), Feb. 22, 1873, P.R.174.
Grace Agnes, d. Henry Lunt and Celeste Ann (Walker), Oct. 12, 1868, P.R.174.
Henry Lunt, h. Celeste Ann (Walker), Sept. 18, 1838, in Portland, P.R.174.
Maurice Walker, s. Henry Lunt and Celeste Ann (Walker), Sept. 3, 1882, P.R.174.
Samuel Henry, h. Myrtle Hayes Forbes, s. Henry Lunt and Celeste Ann (Walker), Dec. 10, 1876, P.R.174.

LOTHROP, Ann Frances, w. Horatio H. Johnson, d. Ansel and Lois (Whittier), Jan. 3, 1819, in Searsmont, P.R.92.
Ann P., ch. Sumner P. and Ann M., Nov. 15, 1861.
Ansel, ———, 1780, G.R.1. [h. Lois (Whittier), Sept. 2, P.R.92.]
Ansel Jr., h. Ann Sarah (Borland), s. Ansel and Lois (Whittier), Jan. 2, 1821, in Searsmont, P.R.92.
Ansel, h. Marcia Wellman, s. Thomas Whittier and Sophia Matilda (Beckett), Feb. 25, 1849, P.R.91.
Ansel Mayo, s. Thomas Whittier Jr. and Helen W. (Herger), May 25, 1890, in Buffalo, N. Y., P.R.91.
Benjamin W., h. Frances (Washburn), s. Ansel and Lois (Whittier), Jan. 10, 1823, in Searsmont, P.R.92.

LOTHROP, David W., ———, 1807, G.R.1. [h. Mary Jane (White), h. Mary Ann (Durham), s. Ansel and Lois (Whittier), Oct. 4, in Nobleboro, P.R.92.]
Elizabeth, w. Gardner Ludwig, d. Ansel and Lois (Whittier), Jan. 5, 1817, in Searsmont, P.R.92.
Julia M., d. Ansel and Lois (Whittier), Sept. 10, 1828, in Searsmont, P.R.92.
Lizzie L., ch. Sumner P. and Ann M., Sept. 22, 1851. [w. Fred W. Pote, G.R.1.]
Lois [————], ———, 1785, G.R.1. [Lois (Whittier), w. Ansel, Dec. 2, P.R.92.]
Lois, w. Robert White, d. Ansel and Lois (Whittier), Mar. 5, 1811, in Searsmont, P.R.92.
Lois Whittier, d. Thomas Whittier and Sophia Matilda (Beckett), Mar. 15, 1847, P.R.91. [Lotrop, P.R.123.]
Mary B., ———, 1853, G.R.1. [Mary Beckett Lothrop, d. Thomas Whittier and Sophia Matilda (Beckett), Mar. 21, P.R.91.]
Pamelia B., w. Eben[eze]r W. Hilton, w. David Putnam, d. Ansel and Lois (Whittier), Apr. 27, 1809, in Nobleboro, P.R.92.
Sumner P., h. Ann M. (Sargent), s. Ansel and Lois (Whittier), May 16, 1826, in Searsmont, P.R.92.
Sumner W., ch. Sumner P. and Ann M., Jan. 6, 1858, in Boston.
Thomas W., ———, 1813, G.R.1. [Thomas Whittier Lothrop, h. Sophia Matilda (Beckett), Oct. 31, in Searsmont, P.R.91.
Thomas W., h. Sophia M. (Becket), s. Ansel and Lois (Whittier), Oct. 31, in Searsmont, P.R.92.]
Thomas Whittier Jr., h. Helen W. (Herger), s. Thomas Whittier and Sophia Matilda (Beckett), July 6, 1860, P.R.91.

LOURAN, Peter, h. Jane, Oct. 25, 1827, G.R.1.

LOW, ———, s. Abraham, Sept. 8, 1848, P.R.123.

LOWNEY, Caroline Frances, ch. Nathaniel M. and Frances, Sept. 1, 1828.
Fanny, ch. Nathaniel M. and Frances, Apr. 18, 1841.
Hannah Rowe (Louney), ch. Nathaniel M. and Frances, May 7, 1833.
Mary Ellen (Louney), ch. Nathaniel M. and Frances, June 27, 1835.
Nath[anie]l Oscar, ch. Nathaniel M. and Frances, Nov. 3, 1831.

LUCAS, Mary A., w. C. Y. Cottrell, Sept. 1, 1822, in Montville, P.R.133. [Mary Ann, w. Christopher Y. Cottrell, P.R.134.]

LUCE, Albert Shaw, h. Henrietta M., Sept. 3, 1842, G.R.I.
Henrietta M. [———], w. Albert Shaw, Oct. 21, 1842, G.R.I.

LUDWIG, Gardiner, M.D., ———, 1813, G.R.I.

LUFKIN, Amanda Mudgett [? m.], Nov. 15, 1850, G.R.I.

LYMBURNER (see Limeburner), Jenney, ch. John and Janney, Mar. 29, 1799.
Peggy, ch. John and Janney, Dec. 27, 1803.
Robert, ch. John and Janney, Mar. 6, 1801.

McAULIFF, Nettie Alta [———], w. John H., Sept. 22, 1891, G.R.I.

McCABE, William A., h. Lizzie (Owen), ———, 1852, G.R.I.

McCARTY, Norman W., Oct. 23, 1870, G.R.I.
Velzora [———], w. W[illia]m H., Feb. 28, 1846, G.R.I.
W[illia]m H., Capt. [h. Velzora], Mar. 11, 1841, G.R.I.

McCASLIN, ———, d. William, Sept. 27, 1848, P.R.123.

McCLINTOCK (see McClyntock), James Y., h. Rachel A., ———, 1802, G.R.I.
Rachel A. [———], w. James Y., ———, 1815, G.R.I.

McCLURE (see McLure).

McCLYNTOCK (see McClintock), Arixene, ch. James Y. and Rachael A., Nov. 10, 1839. [Arixene L. McClintock, G.R.I.]

McCORISON, Henry H., ———, 1877, G.R.4.

McCOY, Horatio Nelson, ch. Gilbert and Huldah, Feb. 9, 1808.
Thomas Jefferson, ch. Gilbert and Huldah, July 1, 1805.

McCRILLIS, Anna J. (see Nancy Ann Judson McCrillis).
Aurinda B. [———], w. Geo[rge] D., ———, 1832, G.R.I.
Charles Henry, ch. James and Jane [(Durham) P.R.138.], Apr. 15, 1827.
Clarissa Bruce, ch. James and Jane [(Durham) P.R.138.], Mar. 20, 1822.
Cora B., w. D. G. Richards, d. Geo[rge] D. and Aurinda B., June 26, 1857, G.R.I.
George D. Boardman, ch. James and Jane, July 16, 1829. [h. Aurinda B., G.R.I. s. James and Jane (Durham), P.R.138.]
James, h. Jane (Durham), Jan. 16, 1780, in Meredith, N. H., P.R.138.

McCRILLIS, James Harvey, ch. James and Jane [(Durham) P.R.138.], Oct. 16, 1812.
John Tolford, ch. James and Jane [(Durham) P.R.138.], July 10, 1817.
Lorinda Eveleth, ch. James and Jane, June 4, 1824. [w. Horatio H. Carter, G.R.1. d. James and Jane (Durham), P.R.138.]
Mary Ann, ch. James and Jane [(Durham) P.R.138.], Dec. 5, 1819.
Nancy Ann Judson, ch. James and Jane, Sept. 10, 1833. [Anna J., w. J. M. Trussell, G.R.1. Anna J., d. James and Jane (Durham), Sept. 16, P.R.138.]
Nancy Durham, ch. James and Jane, Mar. 20, 1815. [d. James and Jane (Durham), in Knox, P.R.138.]
Orinda B. (see Aurinda B.).
Sarah Jane, ch. James and Jane [(Durham) P.R.138.], June 24, 1809.
——, d. Capt. James, May 5, 1848, P.R.123.

McDONAL (see McDonald, McDonel), Alexander, ch. Rodrick and Polly, June 11, 1809.
Mary, ch. Nathan and Clarisa, Nov. 17, 1809.
Rodrick P., ch. Rodrick and Polly, Oct. 28, 1805.

McDONALD (see McDonal, McDonel), A. A., ——, 1848, G.R.1.
Adelle, ch. George and Sarah, Oct. 2, 1847.
Blanch, Oct. 14, 1873, G.R.1. [Blanche, d. E. S. and Jennie N. (Patterson), P.R.23.]
Carle, s. E. S. and Jennie N. (Patterson), Feb. 13, 1882, P.R.23.
Charles Davis, ch. George and Sarah, Oct. 8, 1830.
Edith, Feb. 11, 1891, G.R.1. [d. E. S. and Jennie N. (Patterson), P.R.23.]
Ella Kimball, ch. Benjamin B. and Dolly E., Dec. 4, 1845.
George Augustus, ch. George and Sarah, Jan. 12, 1829.
Harriet Frances, ch. George and Sarah, July 13, 1832.
Helen Augusta, d. Joseph and Lydia, ——, 1844, G.R.1.
Henry Horatio, ch. George and Sarah, May 26, 1835. [Horatio H., G.R.1.]
Horace Eugene, ch. George and Sarah, Oct. 12, 1842.
Horatio H. (see Henry Horatio).
Joseph, Sept. 19, 1801, G.R.1.
Lucius Franklin, ch. George and Sarah, Sept. 14, 1837.
Mellen Drew, Apr. 3, 1875, G.R.1. [s. E. S. and Jennie N. (Patterson), P.R.23.]

McDONALD, Sarah Brown, ch. George and Sarah, May 2, 1827.
Sarah W. [———], w. George, ———, 1806, G.R.1.
Simon Edgar, ch. George and Sarah, Oct. 12, 1844.
Thomas Dawes, ch. Benjamin B. and Dolly E., May 29, 1841.
W[illia]m Oliver Greely, ch. George and Sarah, Dec. 12, 1839.

McDONEL (see McDonal, McDonald), Charles Davis, ch. Simon and Betey, May 24, 1809.
Fanney Baxter, ch. Simon and Betey, Nov. 30, 1803.
George, ch. Simon and Betey, Dec. 29, 1802. [McDonald, h. Sarah W., G.R.1.]

McDOWELL, Clarrie S., w. Sanford H. Mathews, July 28, 1833, P.R.89.

MACE, Ida, inf., bp. Mar. 1, 1874, C.R.3.
John A., h. Nancy B., June 17, 1828, G.R.1.

McFARLAND, Charles, ch. Moses and Rhoda, Mar. 13, 1841.
Eliza, ch. Ephrim and Elizabeth, Aug. 23, 1802.
Elizabeth [———], w. Capt. Ephraim, Oct. 4, 1775, G.R.1.
Ephrim, ch. Ephrim and Elizabeth, Feb. 24, 1800.
Hariet, ch. Moses and Rhoda, May 10, 1843.
John, ch. Ephrim and Elizabeth, Dec. 4, 1797.
Mary Reid, ch. Ephrim and Elizabeth, Nov. 10, 1804.
Sarah Ann, ch. Ephrim and Elizabeth, Sept. 18, 1807.
William Edwin, ch. Moses and Rhoda, Apr. 21, 1839.

McKEEN, Abbie A. [? m.], July 20, 1831, G.R.1.
Abner, ch. Abner and Sally, ———.
Albert J., Feb. 18, 1885, P.R.93.
Alice E., Dec. 13, 1883, P.R.93.
Benjamin Franklin, ch. Ephrim and Lucy, Apr. 18, 1803.
Clarence E., Aug. 27, 1886, P.R.93.
Eliza (see Eliza Gilmore).
Eliza H. [———], w. Joseph A., Dec. 18, 1804, G.R.1. [Eliza (Holmes), Dec. 14, P.R.46.]
Eliza M., d. Joseph and Eliza (Holmes), Dec. 4, 1836, P.R.46.
Emma F., w. Capt. J. H. Perkins, Dec. 17, 1844, G.R.1. [w. James H. Perkins, d. Joseph and Eliza (Holmes), Dec. 7, P.R.46.]
Eph[rai]m, h. Sarah J. (Nickerson), s. Joseph and Eliza (Holmes), Oct. 13, 1826, P.R.46.
Etta E. [———], Dec. 11, 1862, G.R.1.
Freddy A., s. Joseph and Eliza (Holmes), May 21, 1851, P.R.46.

McKEEN, Hazel H., Oct. 27, 1831, G.R.1. [Hazael H., h. Amanda A. (Harris), s. Joseph and Eliza (Holmes), P.R.46.]
Isaac, ch. Ephrim and Lucy, May 8, 1797.
James F., s. Joseph and Eliza (Holmes), Sept. 4, 1829, P.R.46.
James F., " Co. I. 26 Me. Regt.," ———, 1834, G.R.1. [h. Julia G. (Miller), s. Joseph and Eliza (Holmes), July 17, P.R.46.]
Jenney, ch. Abner and Sally, ———.
John, ch. Ephrim and Lucy, Mar. 10, 1793.
Joseph, ch. Ephrim and Lucy, Mar. 4, 1799.
Joseph A., h. Eliza H., July 17, 1805, G.R.1. [h. Eliza (Holmes), P.R.46.]
Joseph A., s. Joseph and Eliza (Holmes), Sept. 29, 1839, P.R.46.
Kezia, w. Joseph Eayrs, Dec. 16, 1769.
Lucy Maria, ch. Ephrim and Lucy, Nov. 5, 1808.
Nancy, ch. Ephrim and Lucy, June 16, 1791.
Nancy, ch. Ephrim and Lucy, Mar. 4, 1801. [w. ——— Ryan, G.R.1.]
Nathaniel, ch. Abner and Sally, ———.
Ralph H., ch. Hazael and Abbie A., May 21, 1868.
Rhoda M., w. Leander J. Staples, w. ——— Dennett, d. Joseph and Eliza (Holmes), Oct. 13, 1841, P.R.46.
Sally, ch. Abner and Sally, Mar. 27, 1804.
Samuel, ch. Ephrim and Lucy, Dec. 29, 1794.
Starret, ch. Abner and Sally, ——— [rec. before ch. b. Mar. 27, 1804].
Susie [———], w. W[illia]m H., ———, 1857, G.R.1.

McKINLEY, Edwin Cole, ch. John and Dolly, May 28, 1824.
Jane Catharine, ch. John and Dolly K., Oct. 19, 1819.
Jane Catharine, ch. John and Dolly, bp. Aug. 26, 1821, C.R.2.
John, ch. John and Dolly K., Feb. 23, 1821.
John, ch. John and Dolly, bp. Aug. 17, 1823, C.R.2.
Martha Ann, ch. John and Dolly K., July 14, 1815.
Martha Ann, ch. John and Dolly, bp. Aug. 26, 1821, C.R.2.
Robert George, ch. John and Dolly K., June 17, 1817.
Thomas, ch. John and Dolly K., Sept. 22, 1813.
———, s. Thomas, July 15, 1849, P.R.123.

McKNIGHT, David, h. Arabelle May (Perkins), Nov. 25, 1858, G.R.1.

McLAUGHLIN (see Malaughlen), Susan Worth, second w. Ebenezer Newell Jr., Aug. 17, 1830, in China, P.R.81.

McLELLAN, Catharine Roxana, ———, 1866, G.R.1.
William Henry, h. Angeline (Nickels), ———, 1832, G.R.1.

McLURE, Martha R. [w. Salathiel Nickerson], Aug. 8, 1780, P.R.14.

McMARTIN, Marjorie [? m.], ———, 1840, in Scotland, G.R.1.

McMILLAN, Archibald, s. Alex[ander] and Susanna, bp. June 3, 1798, C.R.2.
John, s. Alexander and Susanna, bp. Apr. 22, 1802, C.R.2.

MADDOCKS, Alex[ander] H., "vol 26 Me Reg. & 1st Me. Heavy Art.," ———, 1830, G.R.1.
Anna W., w. Horace W. Littlefield, d. Samuel and Eliza (Weed), July 25, 1850, P.R.164.
Daniel R., h. Mary, ———, 1811, G.R.2. [Daniel Rowe Maddocks, s. John and Elizabeth (Kennedy), Dec. 5, 1810, P.R.132.]
Daniel W., h. Charity W. (Thompson), s. Samuel and Eliza (Weed), Feb. 6, 1824, P.R.164.
Elizabeth, w. Benj[amin] W. Philbrook, d. Samuel and Eliza (Weed), Oct. 17, 1829, P.R.164.
Ellen P., w. George F. Ryan, d. Samuel and Eliza (Weed), May 25, 1842, P.R.164.
Emery L., Apr. 25, 1882, G.R.1.
Ephraim, s. John and Elizabeth (Kennedy), July 4, 1797, P.R.132.
Ephriam, h. Sarah A. (Harper), s. Samuel and Eliza (Weed), Aug. 1, 1834, P.R.164.
Henrietta, twin ch. John and Mary, Dec. 5, 1834.
Henry Monroe, twin ch. John and Mary, Dec. 5, 1834.
James Augustus, twin ch. John and Mary, Apr. 17, 1841.
Jane Augusta, twin ch. John and Mary, Apr. 17, 1841.
John, s. John and Elizabeth (Kennedy), Mar. 4, 1800, P.R.132.
John, h. Eliza J. (Keith), s. Samuel and Eliza (Weed), Mar. 19, 1828, P.R.164.
Julia Ann, d. John and Elizabeth (Kennedy), Dec. 31, 1813, P.R.132. [w. Alexander Shibles, P.R.161.]
Maria F., w. Tolford Durham, d. Samuel and Eliza (Weed), Sept. 25, 1846, P.R.164.
Martha, d. Samuel and Eliza (Weed), Jan. 8, 1836, P.R.164.
Mary [———], w. D. R., ———, 1807, G.R.2.
Mary A., w. Salathiel N. Otis, June 23, 1833, G.R.1. [Mary Ann Maddox, P.R.14.]

MADDOCKS, Mary W., w. Paul Hanson Cleary, d. Samuel and Eliza (Weed), Nov. 8, 1825, P.R.164.
Olive R., w. John L. Hunter, d. Samuel and Eliza (Weed), Dec. 2, 1832, P.R.164.
Patty, d. John and Elizabeth (Kennedy), Dec. 4, 1792, P.R.132.
Phebe, d. John and Elizabeth (Kennedy), July 8, 1791, P.R.132.
Sally Kennedy, d. John and Elizabeth (Kennedy), Nov. 22, 1807, P.R.132.
Samuel, h. Harriet Ann Way, s. Samuel and Eliza (Weed), Nov. 28, 1839, P.R.164.
Samuel Lampson, s. John and Elizabeth (Kennedy), May 1, 1805, P.R.132.
Susan G., ch. John and Mary, Apr. 13, 1833.

MAGEE, Susan H., w. Charles R. Stevens, ———, 1846, G.R.1.

MAHONEY, F. E., w. Mark Welch, Oct. 14, 1828, P.R.96.
Genevra Jenkins, w. George Irving Mudgett, Apr. 22, 1860, P.R.109.
George Dickey, h. Ida Albertine (Wilson), Jan. 4, 1849, in Northport, P.R.95.
Georgia E., ———, 1878, G.R.1. [d. George Dickey and Ida Albertine (Wilson), Dec. 3, P.R.95.]

MALAUGHLEN (see McLaughlin), Polly, ch. Daniel and Polly, Mar. 16, 1805.

MANSFIELD, Almeda R., ch. Newhall and Elizabeth [Newell and Elizabeth H., G.R.1.], June 25, 1839.
Augustine P., ch. Newhall and Elizabeth, Jan. 15, 1847. [Augustine Paul, ch. Newell and Elizabeth H., C.R.2. A. P., ch. Newell and Elizabeth H., G.R.1. s. Newell, P.R.123.]
Augustus M., ch. Newhall and Elizabeth [Newell and Elizabeth H., G.R.1.], July 8, 1844.
Effie L., ch. Newhall and Elizabeth, May 19, 1856. [Effie Lizzie, ch. Newell and Elizabeth H., C.R.2. Effie L., ch. Newell and Elizabeth H., G.R.1.]
Eleanor C., ch. Newhall and Elizabeth, Nov. [Nov. *written after* June *crossed out*] 17, 1841.
Elizabeth H. [———], w. Newell, July 24, 1816, G.R.1.
Harriet M. [———], w. Newell, July 3, 1833, G.R.1.
Newell, h. Elizabeth H., h. Harriet M., Nov. 13, 1812, G.R.1.

MARDEN, Emma, w. ——— West, June 29, 1845, G.R.2.

MARRINER, Abbie E., w. Alonzo J. Drinkwater, ——, 1845, G.R.I.
Ada Augusta, w. George Lucas Bowman of Boston (b. Boston), d. Henry Wadsworth and Ann Maria (Donnell), Feb. 13, 1882, P.R.167.
Ann Maria (see Maria A.).
Henry W. [h. Maria A.], May 2, 1841, G.R.I. [Henry Wadsworth Marriner, h. Ann Maria (Donnell), s. Alden and Sybil (Lakin), in Lincolnville, P.R.167.]
Maria A. [———] [w. Henry W.], July 26, 1841. [Ann Maria, d. Samuel Donnell and Eliza (Wyman), in Searsmont, P.R.167.]
———, s. H. W. and M. A., Mar. —, 1872, G.R.I. [s. Henry Wadsworth and Ann Maria (Donnell), Mar. —, 1873, P.R.167.]

MARSH, Alfred Henry, s. Warren E. and Prudence Clara, May 8, 1870, P.R.38.
Charles Warren, s. Warren E. and Prudence Clara, May 14, 1857, in Taunton, Mass., P.R.38.
Everett Abner, s. Warren E. and Prudence Clara, Aug. 6, 1861, in Roxbury, Mass., P.R.38.
George Ernest, s. Warren E. and Prudence Clara, Dec. 18, 1874, P.R.38.
George Thomson, h. Margaret Gibson (Bullen), July 30, 1830, P.R.100.
Lucy Frances, d. George Thomson and Margaret Gibson (Bullen), Sept. 7, 1859, P.R.100.
Prudence Clara [———], w. Warren E., Jan. 25, 1839, in Dartmouth, Mass., P.R.38.
Rufus Harold, s. Warren E. and Prudence Clara, Feb. 4, 1879, P.R.38.
Warren E., h. Prudence Clara, May 6, 1834, in Windsor, P.R.38.

MARSHALL, Anniebell, ch. Thomas H. and Emily S., Sept. 4, 1857. [Annabell, w. ——— Hendershott, G.R.I.]
Frank Elmer, s. Samuel and Climena, Jan. 4, 1863, G.R.I.
James Augustas, ch. Thomas and Susan, Dec. 10, 1831.
Kate Susan, d. W[illia]m C. and Lois, Sept. 30, 1871, G.R.I.
Melville T., ch. Thomas H. and Emily S., Aug. 3, 1855.
Sarah Abigail, ch. Thomas and Susan, Jan. 8, 1824.
Susan Maria, ch. Thomas and Susan, Apr. 13, 1822.
Thomas, h. Susan (Colburn), July 3, 1789, in Tewksbury, Mass., P.R.107.
Thomas Henny, ch. Thomas and Susan, Feb. 10, 1826.

MARSHALL, William Colburn, ch. Thomas and Susan, Aug. 17, 1827. [[h. Lois Rhodes] G.R.1. s. Thomas and Susan (Colburn), P.R.107.]

MASON, Andrew J., ——, 1842, G.R.1.
Blanche E., w. Ralph W. Pattershall, ——, 1877, G.R.1.
Edith L., w. Herman O. Stevens, ——, 1879, G.R.1.
Ernest W., ——, 1870, G.R.1.
Ethel L., ——, 1874, G.R.1.
Howard F., h. Clara F. Moore, ——, 1848, G.R.1.
Isaac F., ch. Isaac and Mary, Feb. 13, 1835.
James C., ch. Isaac and Mary, July 28, 1836.
Martha Ann, ch. Isaac and Mary, Aug. 7, 1829.
Philena C., ch. Isaac and Mary, Sept. 21, 1831.
——, d. Henry, Nov. 10, 1847, P.R.123.

MATHER, Albert Increase, h. Augusta Clara (Cunningham), ——, G.R.1.
Harry A., s. Albert Increase and Augusta Clara (Cunningham), ——, G.R.1.

MATHEWS (see Matthews), Asa, ch. Samuel and Sarah, bp. —— [rec. between Oct. 6, 1805 and June —, 1817], C.R.2.
Clara Avis, w. Edward J. Morison, d. Spencer Walcott and Susan Church (Heath), Jan. 26, 1855, P.R.64.
Cora Susan, d. Spencer Walcott and Susan Church (Heath), June 16, 1861, P.R.64.
Deborah, ch. Samuel and Sarah, bp. —— [rec. between Oct. 6, 1805 and June —, 1817], C.R.2.
Edward, ——, 1854, G.R.1.
Elizabeth, ch. Samuel and Sarah, bp. —— [rec. between Oct. 6, 1805 and June —, 1817], C.R.2.
Frank B., Oct. 8, 1863, G.R.1. [h. Addie L. (Richmond), s. Sanford H. and Clarrie S. (McDowell), P.R.89.]
George, ch. Samuel and Sarah, bp. —— [rec. between Oct. 6, 1805 and June —, 1817], C.R.2.
Hannah, ch. Samuel and Sarah, bp. —— [rec. between Oct. 6, 1805 and June —, 1817], C.R.2.
Joseph, ch. Samuel and Sarah, bp. —— [rec. between Oct. 6, 1805 and June —, 1817], C.R.2.
Lillie Belle, d. Spencer Walcott and Susan Church (Heath), July 9, 1856, P.R.64.
Mabel R., twin ch. Sanford H. and Clarrie S. (McDowell), Apr. 1, 1869, P.R.89.
Maude E., twin ch. Sanford H. and Clarrie S. (McDowell), Apr. 1, 1869, P.R.89.

MATHEWS, Samuel, ch. Samuel and Sarah, bp. ——— [*rec. between* Oct. 6, 1805 *and* June —, 1817], C.R.2.
Sanford H., May 6, 1832, G.R.1. [h. Clarrie S. (McDowell), P.R.89.]
Sarah, ch. Samuel and Sarah, bp. ——— [*rec. between* Oct. 6, 1805 *and* June —, 1817], C.R.2.
Sarah W. [———], w. N., June 19, 1823, G.R.1.
Spencer Hinkley, s. Spencer Walcott and Susan Church (Heath), Nov. 18, 1864, P.R.64.
Spencer Walcott, h. Susan Church (Heath), Feb. 10, 1829, P.R.64.
Stoddard, ch. Samuel and Sarah, bp. ——— [*rec. between* Oct. 6, 1805 *and* June —, 1817], C.R.2.

MATTHEWS (see Mathews), Asa, s. Samuel and Sarah, bp. Apr. 1, 1804, C.R.2.
Carrie A., ———, 1859, G.R.1.
George, ch. Samuel and Sarah, bp. Jan. 5, 1802, C.R.2.
Hannah Parker, ch. Samuel and Sarah, bp. Jan. 5, 1802, C.R.2.
Martha A., ———, 1840, G.R.1.
Priscilla [? m.], ———, 1849, G.R.1.
Stoddard, ch. Samuel and Sarah, bp. Jan. 5, 1802, C.R.2.

MAXFIELD, Huldah (see Huldah M. Gammans).

MAYHEW, Vinal, Capt., h. Martha J., Mar. 11, 1804, G.R.2.

MAYO, Sarah Isabell [———], w. James C., Aug. 2, 1831, G.R.1.

MEEK, Andrew, h. Margaret A., ———, 1810, G.R.1.
Margaret A. [———], w. Andrew, ———, 1809, G.R.1.

MERCHANT, Mary A., w. William C. Coombs, ———, 1834, G.R.1.
Nathaniel, h. Susan, ———, 1801, G.R.1.
Susan [———], w. Nathaniel, ———, 1796, G.R.1.

MERRIAM, Eli C., Capt., "33rd U. S. C. T.," h. Jennie E., Dec. 31, 1839, G.R.2.
George Washington, ch. John and Patience, Dec. 29, 1805.
James Franklin, ch. John and Patience, Feb. 23, 1818.
John Chase, ch. John and Patience, Nov. 23, 1811.
Patience, ch. John and Patience, May 11, 1803.
Persis, ch. John and Patience, May 2, 1801.
W[illia]m Thacher, ch. John and Patience, Feb. 7, 1815.

MERRILL, Adams Huse, ch. Wiggen, Sept. 3, 1806.
Amelia D. G., [? twin] ch. Wiggin and Meria, ——— [? July 16, 1801].
Ammi Cutter, ch. Wiggen, July 6, 1808.
Caroline W. [———], w. Nathaniel, Nov. 20, 1819, G.R.1.
George Eugene, ch. Daniel and Mary G., May 23, 1838.
Helen, ch. Nathaniel and Caroline, Dec. 13, 1841.
Julia, ch. Nathaniel and Caroline, Apr. 11, 1844.
Mary C., ch. Nathaniel and Caroline, Aug. 26, 1839.
Moses Daniel, ch. Daniel and Mary G., Apr. 6, 1829.
Moses Daniel G., ch. Daniel and Mary G., Feb. 26, 1836.
Moses Greeley, ch. Daniel and Mary G., Nov. 19, 1830.
Samuel Cole, ch. Wiggin [dup. Wiggen] and Meria, Oct. 28, 1802.
Susan Mary G., ch. Daniel and Mary G., Mar. 18, 1827.
———, [? twin] s. Wiggin and Meria, July 16, 1801.

MICHAELS, Ada E., ch. Stephen and Sarah E., Dec. 3, 1859.
George E., ch. Samuel and Mary A., Jan. 29, 1859.
Mary E., ch. Samuel and Mary A., Feb. 26, 1853.
Philip, ch. Samuel and Mary A., Feb. 12, 1862.

MILLER, Ada Sophia, [twin] ch. George Anson and Susan, Jan. 21, 1850. [w. Edward H. Colby, [twin] d. George A. and Susan L. (Kellock), P.R.21. [twin] d. George Anson and Susan L. (Kellock), P.R.59.]
Albert Wilson, ch. Leslie P. and Mabel Lennie (Wilson), Oct. 28, 1891, P.R.95.
Alice I., d. Charles Hall and Isabella C. (Kimball), Oct. 5, 1848, P.R.59.
Ann W. [———] [w. Joseph], ———, 1755, G.R.1.
Anna G. [———] [w. Wales L.], ———, 1837, G.R.1.
Annabelle, d. Wales Lewis and Annie G. (Lewis), Mar. 28, 1857, P.R.59.
Benjamin, ch. James and Elizabeth, Apr. 27, 1802.
Benjamin Franklin, ch. Patience, bp. Mar. 1, 1831, a. 5, C.R.2.
Betsy, ch. Joseph and Anne, bp. ——— [*rec. between* Oct. 6, 1805 *and* June —, 1817], C.R.2.
Caro Maria, d. Justus Gorham and O. Maria (Lewis), Nov. 7, 1849, P.R.59.
Charles Hall, ch. Samuel W. and Nancy, Dec. 1, 1819. [s. Samuel W. and Nancy (Brown), P.R.56. h. Isabella C. (Kimball), s. Samuel W. and Nancy (Brown), P.R.59.]
Charlotte E. [———] [w. Samuel F.], ———, 1818, G.R.1.

MILLER, David Houston, ch. James and Elizabeth, Nov. 18, 1807.
Edith H., d. Stephen Wier and Susan B. (Staples), July 6, 1850, P.R.59.
Elizabeth, ch. James and Elizabeth, May 18, 1800.
Ella Sarah, ch. Samuel F. and Charlotte E. [Sam[ue]l Freeman and Charlotte E. (Wording), P.R.59.], Mar. 14, 1844.
Ellen, inf. Joseph and w. of Waldo, bp. Nov. 9, 1841, C.R.2.
Frederick W., s. Stephen Wier and Susan B. (Staples), Jan. 10, 1845, P.R.59.
George Anson, ch. Samuel W. and Nancy, Apr. 9, 1815. [h. Susan L. (Kellock), P.R.21. s. Samuel W. and Nancy (Brown), P.R.56. h. Susan L. (Kellock), s. Samuel W. and Nancy (Brown), P.R.59.]
Georgiana Parker, w. Edward Johnson, d. Dr. Erasmus Darwin and Louisa (Clarke), Dec. 23, 1842, in Franklin, Mass., G.R.1.
Isabella Alice, d. Cha[rle]s H. and Isabella C., bp. Feb. 5, 1849, C.R.2.
James, ch. James and Elizabeth, Jan. 3, 1796.
James, ch. George Anson and Susan, Dec. 13, 1851. [s. George A. and Susan L. (Kellock), P.R.21. s. George Anson and Susan L. (Kellock), Dec. 13, 1852, P.R.59.]
Jane Matilda, d. Sam[ue]l Freeman and Charlotte E. (Wording), Oct. 26, 1848, P.R.59.
John, ch. Joseph and Anne, bp. ——— [*rec. between* Oct. 6, 1805 *and* June —, 1817], C.R.2.
Jonathan N., ch. James and Elizabeth, July 11, 1798.
Joseph [h. Ann W.], ———, 1756, G.R.1.
Joseph, ch. Joseph and Anne, bp. ——— [*rec. between* Oct. 6, 1805 *and* June —, 1817], C.R.2.
Joseph Henry, ch. Patience, bp. Mar. 1, 1831, a. 2, C.R.2.
Julia G., ch. George Anson and Susan, Nov. 21, 1843. [w. James F. McKeen of Swanville, d. George A. and Susan L. (Kellock), P.R.21. d. George Anson and Susan L. (Kellock), P.R.59.]
Justus Gorham, ch. Samuel W. and Nancy, Oct. 17, 1824. [———, 1825, G.R.1. h. O. Maria (Lewis), s. Samuel W. and Nancy (Brown), Oct. 17, 1824, P.R.59.]
Lucinda, ch. Joseph and Anne, bp. ——— [*rec. between* Oct. 6, 1805 *and* June —, 1817], C.R.2. [b. ———, 1790, G.R.1.]
Margaret, ch. Joseph and Anne, bp. ——— [*rec. between* Oct. 6, 1805 *and* June —, 1817], C.R.2. [b. ———, 1782, G.R.1.]
Margaret Sophia, ch. Patience, bp. Mar. 1, 1831, a. 9, C.R.2.

MILLER, Mary, ch. James and Elizabeth, July 11, 1804.
Mary Jane, ch. Samuel W. and Nancy, Oct. 8, 1817. [———,
    1818, G.R.1. d. Samuel W. and Nancy (Brown), Oct. 8,
    1817, P.R.56. P.R.59.]
Matilda H. (see Nancy Matilda).
Maud, w. James Bliss Coombs, Nov. 16, 1866, G.R.1.
Nancy B. [———], w. Samuel W., ———, 1784, G.R.1. [Nancy
    (Brown), Dec. 20, 1783, in Gorham [N. H.], P.R.56.]
Nancy Maria, [twin] ch. George Anson and Susan, Jan. 21,
    1850. [w. Henry C. Marden, [twin] d. George A. and
    Susan L. (Kellock), P.R.21. [twin] d. George Anson and
    Susan L. (Kellock), P.R.59.]
Nancy Matilda, ch. Samuel W. and Nancy, Feb. 15, 1822.
    [Matilda H. [w. ——— Pitcher], G.R.1. Nancy Matilda,
    d. Samuel W. and Nancy (Brown), P.R.56. Nancy Matilda, w. Charles A. Pitcher, d. Samuel W. and Nancy
    (Brown), P.R.59.]
Samuel, ch. Joseph and Anne, bp. ——— [rec. between Oct. 6,
    1805 and June —, 1817], C.R.2.
Samuel Freeman, ch. Samuel W. and Nancy, May 11, 1811.
    [[h. Charlotte E.] G.R.1. s. Samuel W. and Nancy (Brown),
    P.R.56. h. Charlotte E. (Wording), s. Samuel W. and
    Nancy (Brown), P.R.59.]
Samuel W., h. Nancy B.,———, 1785, G.R.1. [h. Nancy (Brown),
    Aug. 2, in Sharon, N. H., P.R.56.]
Samuel W., ch. George Anson and Susan [Susan L. (Kellock),
    P.R.21. P.R.59.], Aug. 22, 1845.
Samuel Wier, inf. Patience, bp. Mar. 1, 1831, C.R.2.
Sarah, w. Josiah Mitchell, Apr. 13, 1821, G.R.1.
Sarah Ann, ch. Patience, bp. Mar. 1, 1831, a. 10, C.R.2.
Sheriden F. B., ch. George Anson and Susan, Nov. 13, 1841.
    [Sheridan F. B., s. George A. and Susan L. (Kellock),
    P.R.21. Sheridan Frances [sic] Bates Miller, s. George
    Anson and Susan L. (Kellock), P.R.59.]
Sherrie Frances, ———, 1861, G.R.1. [Sherrie Francis Bates
    Miller, ch. Wales Lewis and Annie G. (Lewis), July 20,
    1863, P.R.59.]
Sophia, ch. Joseph and Anne, bp. ——— [rec. between Oct. 6,
    1805 and June —, 1817], C.R.2.
Stephen Wier, inf. Joseph and w. of Waldo, bp. May 18, 1836,
    C.R.2.
Stephen Wire, ch. Samuel W. and Nancy, Jan. 13, 1813. [s.
    Samuel W. and Nancy (Brown), P.R.56. Stephen Wier
    Miller, h. Susan B. (Staples), s. Samuel W. and Nancy
    (Brown), P.R.59.]

MILLER, Thomas Nesmith, ch. James and Elizabeth, ———
[*rec. after ch. b.* Nov. 18, 1807].
Wales Lewis, ch. Samuel W. and Nancy, Aug. 29, 1827. [ch. Sam[ue]l W. and Mary [*sic*], C.R.2. [h. Anna G.] G.R.1. h. Annie G. (Lewis), s. Samuel W. and Nancy (Brown), P.R.59.]

MILLIKEN, Lavina [? m.], ———, 1792, G.R.1.
Mary Moody, ch. Heard and Abigail, June 23, 1826.
Seth Llewellyn, Dec. 12, 1831, G.R.1.
Thomas, ———, 1791, G.R.1.

MITCHELL, Allice, ch. Robert and Martha, Apr. 14, 1799.
Betey, ch. Robert and Martha, Aug. 17, 1796.
Edwin, h. Elma A., Sept. 8, 1849, G.R.2.
Elma A. [———], w. Edwin, Nov. 23, 1847, G.R.2.
Florence Louise, d. Charles and Mary, Dec. 14, 1880, G.R.1.
George, ch. Robert and Martha, June 15, 1794.
James, May 24, 1843, G.R.1.
James H., Nov. 1, 1848, G.R.1.
John, ch. Robert and Martha, Sept. 8, 1792.
John Archibald, s. James and Etta (Stewart), June 7, 1876, P.R.60.
Joseph, ch. Robert and Martha, Dec. 23, 1801.
Josiah, Feb. 22, 1816, G.R.1.
Rebecca B., w. Willis S. Hatch, Oct. 24, 1854, G.R.2.
Sarah Margaret, d. James and Etta (Stewart), Jan. 8, 1880, P.R.60.
William Stewart, s. James and Etta (Stewart), May 9, 1873, P.R.60.
William Wyle, ch. Robert and Martha, Oct. 10, 1790.

MIXER, Frances Martha, d. Geo[rge] T. and Sarah C. R., bp. Apr. 3, 1831, C.R.2.
Isaac, Apr. 25, 1847, G.R.2.
Sarah Jane, d. Geo[rge] T. and Sarah C. R., bp. Apr. 3, 1831, C.R.2.

MONROE (see Munro, Munroe), Alfred Johnson, ch. Nahum Parker and Ann Sarah (Johnson), Oct. 2, 1849, P.R.1.
Frances Anna, ch. Nahum Parker and Ann Sarah (Johnson), Sept. 6, 1846, P.R.1.
Frank Philip, ch. Nahum Parker and Ann Sarah (Johnson), Nov. 2, 1852, P.R.1.
Lizzie May, ch. Nahum Parker and Ann Sarah (Johnson), May 15, 1857, P.R.1.

MONROE, Lucelia Avesta, w. John Warren Ferguson, May 7, 1842, G.R.1. [in E. Whately, Mass., P.R.5.]

MOODY, Abigail Soule, w. ——— Coffin, d. Joseph L. and Caroline W. (Howard), ———, G.R.7.
Augusta Jane, ch. Dr. Richard and w., bp. Sept. 17, 1839, C.R.2. [w. Asa A. Howes, d. Richard, M.D., and Eliza Jane (Hall), b. June 4, 1836, P.R.85. first w. Asa A. Howes, b. June 4, 1836, P.R.144.]
Caroline Elizabeth, ch. Joseph L. and Caroline W. (Howard), ———, 1834, G.R.7.
Clara Luella, ch. Joseph L. and Caroline W. (Howard), Sept. 5, 1841, G.R.7.
Fannie Boyd, d. Elbridge G., Nov. 15, 1849, P.R.85.
Frank J., Mar. 15, 1844, G.R.7.
Harlus Wetherell, ch. William P., Mar. —, 1855, P.R.85.
James B., s. Stephen P. and Mary H. (Heath), July 23, 1849, P.R.63.
James L., h. Mary A. Ripley, h. Mary E. Shepard, ———, 1818, G.R.7.
Joseph L., h. Caroline W. (Howard), Nov. 29, 1805, G.R.7.
Josephine (see Mary Josephine).
Mary A. Ripley [———], w. James L., ———, 1815, G.R.7.
Mary E. Shepard [———], w. James L., ———, 1833, G.R.7.
Mary Elizabeth, ch. William and Paulina, Dec. 13, 1806.
Mary Josephine, bp. Feb. —, 1841, C.R.2. [Josephine, d. Richard, M.D., and Eliza Jane (Hall), b. Nov. 10, 1840, P.R.85.]
Mary L., d. Stephen P. and Mary H. (Heath), Oct. 6, 1852, P.R.63.
Ortela Ashley, ch. Stephen P. and Mary H. (Heath), Oct. 17, 1855, P.R.63.
Richard, M.D., h. Eliza Jane (Hall), Mar. 8, 1803, in Saco, P.R.85.
Richard Henry, s. Richard and Eliza J., bp. Oct. 18, 1852, C.R.2. [b. July 8, 1847, G.R.1. s. Richard, M.D., and Eliza Jane (Hall), b. July 8, 1847, P.R.85.]
Sarah Elizabeth, ch. Dr. Richard and w., bp. Sept. 17, 1839, C.R.2. [d. Richard, M.D., and Eliza Jane (Hall), b. Feb. 26, 1839, P.R.85.]
Stephen E. A., s. Stephen P. and Mary H. (Heath), Feb. 24, 1858, P.R.63.
William Hall, s. Richard, M.D., and Eliza Jane (Hall), Dec. 8, 1842, P.R.85.

MOODY, William Lord, s. Elbridge G., Dec. 18, 1845, P.R.85.
William Lowell, s. William P., Oct. 9, 1859, P.R.85.

MOORE, Abbie, w. Sewall A. Black, May 24, 1840, G.R.1.
Albion E., ch. A. K. P. and Mary M., Nov. 19, 1872.
Cha[rle]s Franklin, ch. Charles and Hannah E., Nov. 3, 1832.
Charles Franklin, ch. Charles and w., bp. May 20, 1838, C.R.2.
Charles Henry (Moor), ch. John and Susanna, Dec. 14, 1811.
Elisa (Moor), ch. John and Susanna, July 26, 1804.
Ellen, ch. Cha[rle]s and w., bp. Nov. 9, 1841, C.R.2.
Ellen Maria, ch. Charles and Hannah E., Aug. 14, 1836.
Ellen Mariah, ch. Charles and w., bp. May 20, 1838, C.R.2.
Hannah E., ch. Charles and Hannah E., Aug. 8, 1834.
Hannah Elizabeth, ch. Charles and w., bp. May 20, 1838, C.R.2.
Ja[me]s, ch. Cha[rle]s and w., bp. Nov. 9, 1841, C.R.2.
John Cheverns, ch. Micheal and Martha, June 9, 1832.
John Newton, ch. Charles and Hannah E., Mar. 17, 1843.
Mary Ann (Moor), ch. John and Susanna, Sept. 29, 1807.
Oliver Gordon, ch. Charles and Hannah E., Oct. 2, 1838.
Patience Miller, ch. Cha[rle]s and w., bp. Nov. 9, 1841, C.R.2.
Samuel C., ch. A. K. P. and Mary M., Oct. 15, 1870.
Sarah L. [———], w. Calvin, Apr. 30, 1825, G.R.1.
Sarah Lenora, ch. Charles and Hannah E., Apr. 15, 1841.
 [Sarah Leonora, C.R.2.]
Thomas, ch. Micheal and Martha, July 29, 1833.
———, s. ———, July 1, 1847, P.R.123.

MORANG (see Moranng), Nancy P. (see Nancy P. Burgess).

MORANNG (see Morang), ———, d. John, Apr. 13, 1849, P.R.123.

MORELAND, Emma, w. Cha[rle]s H. Field, Mar. 29, 1858, G.R.1.

MOREY, Albert G., May 15, 1815, G.R.1.
Maria P. [? m.], May 1, 1826, G.R.1.

MORISON, Avis Mathews, d. Edward J. and Clara A. (Mathews), Oct. 6, 1879, P.R.65.
Cora Susan Mathews, d. Edward J. and Clara A. (Mathews), Dec. 22, 1886, P.R.65.
Edward J., h. Clara A. (Mathews), May 9, 1851, P.R.65.
Eloise Mathews, d. Edward J. and Clara A. (Mathews), Mar. 8, 1878, P.R.65.
Evelyn Philbrook, d. Edward J. and Clara A. (Mathews), Jan. 30, 1885, P.R.65.

MORRILL, Caroline Ester, ch. Elijah and Prisilla, Nov. 24, 1808.
Elijah, ch. Elijah and Prisilla, Dec. 11, 1804.
Ellen M., d. Elijah and Lois, June 19, 1846, G.R.1.
George, ch. Elijah and Prisilla, Mar. 27, 1816.
Jennet, ch. William and Susanna, Feb. 2, 1808. [Jennette, w. Capt. Isaac Clark, Feb. 2, 1809, G.R.1.]
Margret Houston, ch. Elijah and Prisilla, Oct. 8, 1806.
Mary, ch. William and Susanna, July 9, 1806.
Mary Elizabeth, ch. Elijah and Prisilla, Oct. 9, 1810.
Naby, ch. Elijah and Prisilla, July 25, 1803.
Priscilla, ch. Elijah and Prisilla, Feb. 7, 1814.
Stephen, ch. William and Susanna, Oct. 26, 1804.
Warren, ch. William and Susanna, Aug. 10, 1802.
William Frothingham, ch. Ephraim T. and Caroline, Dec. 10, 1827.
William P., ch. Elijah and Lois, Oct. 10, 1842.
William Plummer (Morill), ch. William and Susanna, Jan. 22, 1810.

MORRISON (see Morison).

MORSE, Eunice R., w. John Cochran, Dec. 28, 1804, G.R.1.
Leander, Aug. 20, 1826, G.R.1.
———, d. John, Feb. 13, 1850, P.R.123.

MOSSMAN, Allan A., Mar. 10, 1843, P.R.78.

MOULTON, Nancy Maria, Sept. 7, 1863, in York, G.R.1.
Samuel A., Sept. 4, 1800, in York, G.R.1.

MUDGETT, George I., Jan. 18, 1855, G.R.1. [George Irving Mudgett, h. Genevra Jenkins (Mahoney), in Prospect, P.R.109.]
Grace H., Mar. 28, 1888, G.R.1. [Grace Harriman Mudgett, d. George Irving and Genevra Jenkins (Mahoney), P.R.109.]
Henry M., Apr. 18, 1858, G.R.1.
Henry Milton, s. George Irving and Genevra Jenkins (Mahoney), Sept. 5, 1890, P.R.109.
W. L., Aug. 10, 1840, G.R.1.

MUNRO (see Monroe, Munroe), Abria Morrill, ch. Benja[min] and Polly, Jan. 8, 1806.
Benja[min] Gates, ch. Ben[jamin] and Polly, Jan. 18, 1808.
George Hanson, ch. Benja[min] and Polly, Jan. 5, 1822.

BELFAST BIRTHS

MUNRO, Lucretia (Monro), ch. Benja[min] and Polly, Apr. 15, 1820.
Mary Adaline, ch. Benja[min] and Polly, Sept. 4, 1809.
Matilda, ch. Benja[min] and Polly, Nov. 16, 1815.
Polly, ch. Benja[min] and Polly, Jan. 2, 1813.
William Augustus (Monro), ch. Benj[amin] and Polly, May 21, 1818.

MUNROE (see Monroe, Munro), Lovina M. [———], w. E. J., Mar. 8, 1875, G.R.1.

MURCH, Charles Augustus, ch. Lewis C. and Louis, Aug. 24, 1832.
Cha[rle]s Augustus, ch. Lewis C. and Louis, Apr. 7, 1842.
Frances H. [? m.], ———, 1843, G.R.1.
Isaac Allard, ch. Lewis C. and Louis, Sept. 17, 1830.
Mary Elizabeth, ch. Lewis C. and Louis, July 21, 1834.
Susan A., ch. Lewis C. and Louis, Oct. 3, 1836.

MURPHY, E. Bertha [? m.], July 22, 1859, G.R.1.
Theodore H., Rev., Oct. 24, 1857, G.R.1.

MURRY, Emeline Johnson, ch. David and Margret, Oct. 26, 1808.

NASH, Amanda Jane, ch. Francis and Rebecca, Mar. 9, 1831.
Charlotte F., d. J. R. and Alzada B., Dec. 2, 1880, G.R.1.
John W., "Co. I. 26 Me. Vol.," ———, 1840, G.R.1.
Lucinda Brooks, ch. Francis and Rebecca, Apr. 19, 1827.
Mary Lewis, ch. Francis and Rebecca, June 1, 1833.
Samuel Lewis, ch. Francis and Rebecca, May 24, 1829.

NEAL, Benj[amin] F., h. Clara A., Apr. 1, 1841, G.R.1.
Clara A. [———], w. B. F., Aug. 18, 1849, G.R.1.

NESMITH, Benjamin, ch. Benjamin and Martha, July 15, 1802.
Benjamin, ch. James and Nancey, June 1, 1806.
Clarissa, ch. James and Nancey, Dec. 28, 1803.
Esther, ch. Benjamin and Martha, Dec. 5, 1799.
James Esq., May 23, 1764, G.R.1.
Jane Dunlap, ch. James and Nancey, Jan. 31, 1811.
Jonathan, ch. James and Nancey, Jan. 25, 1802.
Maria, ch. James and Nancey, Sept. 19, 1808.
Nancy, ch. Benjamin and Martha, Oct. 23, 1797.

NEWELL, Agnes Imogene, d. Atwood Milton and Marion W. (McLaughlin), Aug. 28, 1873, in Unity, P.R.81.

NEWELL, Atwood Milton, h. Marion W. (McLaughlin), s. Ebenezer Jr. and Olive G. (Record) (first w.), Mar. 14, 1845, in Montville, P.R.81.
Basil Herbert Staples (see Basil Herbert Staples).
Ebenezer Jr., h. Olive G. (Record), h. Susan Worth (McLaughlin), May 1, 1811, in Camden, P.R.81.
George, s. Ebenezer Jr. and Olive G. (Record) (first w.), ——, 1835, in Montville, P.R.81.
Olive Gertrude, d. Atwood Milton and Marion W. (McLaughlin), May 20, 1877, in Unity, P.R.81.
Olivet, w. Josiah E. Staples, ——, 1855, P.R.33. [w. Josiah E. Staples, w. Levi Clay, d. Ebenezer Jr. and Susan Worth (McLaughlin) (second w.), May 13, in Montville, P.R.81.]
Robert Theodore, s. Ebenezer Jr. and Olive G. (Record) (first w.), Feb. 22, 1840, in Montville, P.R.81.
Roberta Theodora, d. Ebenezer Jr. and Susan Worth (McLaughlin) (second w.), July 27, 1865, P.R.81.

NICHOLS (see Nickels), Franklin, h. Isabella Gordon Brown, June 24, 1863, G.R.1.
Nancy Pendleton, ch. Alexander and Prudence, bp. ——— [*rec. between* Oct. 6, 1805 *and* June —, 1817], C.R.2.
Peleg Pendleton, ch. Alexander and Prudence, bp. ——— [*rec. between* Oct. 6, 1805 *and* June —, 1817], C.R.2.

NICKELS (see Nichols), Alexander, s. Alex[ander] and Prudence, bp. May 7, 1803, C.R.2.
Angeline, w. William Henry McLellan, ——, 1840, G.R.1.
David, s. Alex[ander] and Prudence, bp. May 7, 1803, C.R.2.
James, s. Alex[ander] and Prudence, bp. May 7, 1803, C.R.2.
Peleg Pendleton, s. Alexander and Prudence, bp. Apr. 22, 1804, C.R.2.

NICKERSON, Aaron [h. Margaret P.], Apr. 4, 1805, G.R.1.
Albert Telemachus, s. Salathiel and Martha R. (McLure), Oct. 30, 1813, P.R.14. [ch. Salathiel and Martha Rogers, P.R.15.]
Alice F., ch. Sears and Mary A., Sept. 15, 1872.
Celia A., ch. Sears and Mary A., Nov. 28, 1875.
Eliza M., w. Samuel Otis, July 28, 1812, G.R.1. [Eliza Maria, d. Salathiel and Martha R. (McLure), P.R.14. Eliza Maria, ch. Salathiel and Martha Rogers, P.R.15.]
Frances Ellen, Apr. 19, 1840, P.R.15.
Frederick Augustus, Mar. 2, 1848, P.R.15.
Frederick Augustus, June 7, 1849, P.R.15.
Isa M., ch. Sears and Mary A., Apr. 26, 1878.

NICKERSON, James A., ch. Sears and Mary A., June 2, 1869.
Joshua, ch. Joshua (Nickesen) and Tabitha, Sept. 15, 1812.
Margaret McLure, d. Salathiel and Martha R. (McLure), Apr. 8, 1819, P.R.14. [ch. Salathiel and Martha Rogers, P.R.15.]
Martha Ellen, d. Salathiel and Martha R. (McLure), July 17, 1823, P.R.14. [ch. Salathiel and Martha Rogers, P.R.15.]
Salathiel [h. Martha R. (McLure)], Nov. 1, 1789, P.R.14.
Salathiel Clarendon, s. Salathiel and Martha R. (McLure), Oct. 19, 1815, P.R.14. [ch. Salathiel and Martha Rogers, P.R.15.]
Salathiel Clarendon, Nov. 22, 1875, P.R.14. [great grand ch. Salathiel Nickerson and Martha Rogers, P.R.15.]
Thomas, s. Salathiel and Martha R. (McLure), Aug. 31, 1817, P.R.14. [ch. Salathiel and Martha Rogers, P.R.15.]

NORRIS, Herbert R., ——, 1875, G.R.1.

NORTEN (see Norton), ——, s. Moody P., Jan. 27, 1847, P.R.123.

NORTON (see Norten), ——, s. Moody P., Jan. 12, 1848, P.R.123.
——, s. David, Aug. 23, 1848, P.R.123.

NOYES, A. N., Feb. 22, 1812, G.R.1.
Alice, ch. Joseph S. and Jane (Haraden), Oct. 23, 1860, P.R.87.
Ann Maria, ch. Abraham N. and Mary Jane, Apr. 26, 1838.
Arthur Haraden, ch. Joseph S. and Jane [(Haraden) P.R.87.], Mar. 13, 1857.
Elizabeth Sophia, ch. Henry and Rebecca, Oct. 1, 1836.
Henry Erastus, ch. Henry and Rebecca, Aug. 23, 1839.
Horace Colmore, ch. Abraham N. and Mary Jane, Jan. 29, 1837, in Jonesboro.
James F., ——, 1853, in Concord, N. H., G.R.1.
Joseph S., h. Jane (Haraden), Nov. 2, 1824, P.R.87.
Lucy Eleanor, ch. Henry and Rebecca, Sept. 7, 1834, in Boston.
——, ch. Joseph S. and Jane (Haraden), May 5, 1862, P.R.87.

O'CONNELL, Daniel (see Daniel O. Connell).

ORCUTT, Allen, Capt., ——, 1819, G.R.1. [h. Mary E. [(Holt)], Sept. 4, 1818, P.R.30. P.R.70.]
Ann E. [? m.], ——, 1772, G.R.1.
Damaetta Havilla, ch. Allen and Mary Eleanor (Holt), grand ch. William Holt and Hannah P. (Shute), Dec. 22, 1843, P.R.29. [w. Isaac Adelbert Conant, Dec. 22, 1845, P.R.70.]

ORCUTT, Eleanor Jane, ch. Allen and Mary Eleanor (Holt), grand ch. William Holt and Hannah P. (Shute), Apr. 14, 1846, P.R.29. [w. George Dyer, P.R.30.]

OSBORN (see Osborne), Abigail (see Nabby).
Alonzo (Osben), ch. John and Abigail, Oct. 24, 1801. [Osborn, ch. Dr. John S. and Nabby, P.R.8. Osborne, h. Isabella (Tilden), P.R.9.]
Elizabeth Maning (Osben), ch. John and Abigail, Oct. 28, 1806. [Elizabeth Manning Osborn, ch. Dr. John S. and Nabby, Oct. 8, P.R.8.]
Hannah Abigail, ch. John and Lucy C., Aug. 12, 1839.
Harriet S., ch. John and Abigail [Dr. John S. and Nabby, P.R.8.], Nov. 27, 1810.
John (Osben), ch. John and Abigail, Jan. 28, 1799. [Osborn, ch. Dr. John S. and Nabby, P.R.8.]
John (Osben), ch. John and Abigail, Oct. 25, 1803. [Osborn, ch. Dr. John S. and Nabby, Oct. 26, P.R.8.]
John S., Dr., h. Nabby, Sept. 19, 1770 [in Epsom, N. H.], P.R.8.
John Sumner, ch. John and Lucy C., Aug. 16, 1832.
Lucy Amelia, ch. John and Lucy C., Nov. 24, 1833.
Mary Ann (Osben), ch. John and Abigail, —— 21, 1808. [Osborn, ch. Dr. John S. and Nabby, Nov. 22, P.R.8.]
Nabby [———], w. Dr. John S., Apr. 11, 1770 [? in Belfast], P.R.8.
Sukey (Osben), ch. John and Abigail, May 2, 1797. [Nabby Osborn, ch. Dr. John S. and Nabby, Aug. 2, P.R.8.]
Thomas, ch. Dr. John S. and Nabby, Sept. 17, 1792, P.R.8.

OSBORNE (see Osborn), Albert Alonzo, s. Alonzo and Isabella (Tilden), Nov. 18, 1829, P.R.9.
Carrie L. [d. George T. and Helen M. (Pattershall)], Dec. 29, 1860, P.R.9. P.R.12.
Ella N., w. Jos[eph] S. Thombs, [twin] d. Alonzo and Isabella (Tilden), Apr. 17, 1836, P.R.9.
Emma, w. Charles W. Tilden, [twin] d. Alonzo and Isabella (Tilden), Apr. 17, 1836, P.R.9.
George Tobin, h. Helen M. (Pattershall), s. Alonzo and Isabella (Tilden), Jan. 25, 1838, P.R.9.
Harriet L., w. Francis H. Sleeper, d. Alonzo and Isabella (Tilden), July 4, 1827, P.R.9.
Isabella Frances, w. Alfred Frederic Adams, d. Alonzo and Isabella (Tilden), Dec. 19, 1831, P.R.9.
Isaphine Marshall, d. Alonzo and Isabella (Tilden), Sept. 16, 1847, P.R.9.

OSBORNE, John Walker, h. Minnie Bentz, s. Alonzo and Isabella (Tilden), May 19, 1841, P.R.9.
Juliet Maria, w. Charles W. Tilden, d. Alonzo and Isabella (Tilden), May 21, 1834, P.R.9.
Thomas T., s. Alonzo and Isabella (Tilden), Mar. 15, 1826, P.R.9.

OSGOOD, Joseph, h. Frances C. (Hanson), Sept. 6, 1829, G.R.1.

OTIS, Abby Nickerson, July 19, 1857, P.R.14. [great grand ch. Salathiel Nickerson and Martha Rogers, P.R.15.]
Albert Boyd, s. Samuel and Eliza M. (Nickerson), June 24, 1839, P.R.14. [grand ch. Salathiel Nickerson and Martha Rogers, P.R.15.]
David, h. Jean (Boyd), h. Helen Otis, s. Samuel of Bristol, Oct. 22, 1766, P.R.13.
David, s. David and Jean (Boyd), Apr. 15, 1817, in Wiscasset, P.R.13.
Diana, w. Henry Colburn, July 27, 1807, G.R.1. [d. David and Jean (Boyd), in Wiscasset, P.R.13.]
Faney, d. David and Jean (Boyd), Feb. 24, 1814, in Wiscasset, P.R.13.
James, [twin] s. David and Jean (Boyd), Apr. 18, 1812, in Wiscasset, P.R.13.
Margaret, d. David and Jean (Boyd), Jan. 13, 1809, in Wiscasset, P.R.13.
Martha Jane, d. Samuel and Eliza M. (Nickerson), Nov. 5, 1846, P.R.14. [grand ch. Salathiel Nickerson and Martha Rogers, P.R.15.]
Salathiel N., h. Mary A. (Maddocks), Feb. 2, 1834, G.R.1. [h. Mary A. (Maddox), s. Samuel and Eliza M. (Nickerson), P.R.14. Salathiel Nickerson Otis, grand ch. Salathiel Nickerson and Martha Rogers, P.R.15.]
Samuel, h. Eliza M. (Nickerson), May 25, 1805, G.R.1. [s. David and Jean (Boyd), in Wiscasset, P.R.13.]
Samuel Boyd, Sept. 13, 1855, P.R.14. [great grand ch. Salathiel Nickerson and Martha Rogers, P.R.15.]
Thomas, [twin] s. David and Jean (Boyd), Apr. 18, 1812, in Wiscasset, P.R.13.
William B., Apr. 15, 1800, G.R.3. [s. David and Jean (Boyd), in Wiscasset, P.R.13.]

OWEN, Lizzie, w. William A. McCabe, ——, 1866, G.R.1.

PAGE, Frederic Augustus, ch. Oshea and Susan, Mar. 13, 1827.

PAGE, Henry Oshea, ch. Oshea and Susan, July 9, 1823.
John L., May 8, 1843, G.R.I.
Mary E. [————], w. Alva, Dec. 19, 1815, G.R.I. [w. William
  F. Whitten, w. ———— Page, d. Robert Patterson and
  Joanna, P.R.11.]
Mary Helen, ch. Oshea and Susan, Aug. 30, 1825.
Myra E. [————], w. W. E., ————, 1849, G.R.I.
William Lord, ch. Oshea and Susan, Sept. 24, 1821.

PALMER, Catharine, ch. Josiah and Rachel, Oct. 29, 1813.
Charles, Jan. 31, 1800, G.R.I.
Charles Edward, ch. Charles and Zilpha, Oct. 6, 1850.
Dwight P., ch. Lemuel R. and Susannah, Sept. 13, 1839.
  [Dwight Parker Palmer, C.R.2. Dwight Parker Palmer,
  ch. Lemuel R. and Susannah R. (Hanford), P.R.79.]
Dwight P., ch. Lemuel R. and Susannah, Mar. 31, 1843.
  [Dwight Parker Palmer, ch. Lemuel R. and Susannah R.
  (Hanford), P.R.79.]
Edwin Beaman, ch. Lemuel R. and Susannah, Sept. 25, 1833.
  [ch. Lemuel and Susanna, C.R.2. ch. Lemuel R. and Su-
  sannah R. (Hanford), P.R.79.]
Frances A. [————] [w. L. R.], ————, 1820, G.R.I.
George, ch. Benja[min] and Mary, July 7, 1805.
Horatio N., Nov. 28, 1807, in Bristol, G.R.I.
John Alden, ch. John and Susan, Feb. 21, 1824.
Joseph [h. Sarah], ————, 1783, G.R.I.
Joseph Hunt, inf. Lemuel R. and Mary H., bp. Sept. 7, 1851,
  C.R.2. [ch. Lemuel R. and Mary P. D. (Hanford), b.
  Nov. 22, 1850, P.R.79.]
L. R. [h. Susannah R., h. Mary P., h. Frances A.], Feb. 22,
  1809, G.R.I. [Lemuel R., h. Susannah R. (Hanford), h.
  M. D. P. (Hanford), Feb. 22, 1807 [dup. 1809], P.R.79.]
Lucy A. E., ch. Lemuel R. and Susannah, May 19, 1845.
  [Lucy Ann Eaton Palmer, ch. Lemuel R. and Susannah
  R., C.R.2. Lucy Ann Eaton Palmer, ch. Lemuel R. and
  Susannah R. (Hanford), P.R.79.]
Mary E., ch. Lemuel R. and Susannah, Sept. 11, 1837. [Mary
  Eliza, ch. Lemuel and Susanna, C.R.2. Mary Eliza, ch.
  Lemuel R. and Susannah R. (Hanford), P.R.79.]
Mary Eleaner, ch. Charles and Zilpha, Sept. 16, 1848.
Mary Elenor, ch. Benja[min] and Mary, May 18, 1807.
Mary Eliza (see Mary E.).
Mary P. [————] [w. L. R.], Apr. 3, 1810, G.R.I.
Priscilla, w. Thomas Pickard, ————, 1796, G.R.I.
Sarah [————] [w. Joseph], ————, 1781, G.R.I.

PALMER, Susan Elizabeth, ch. John and Susan, Feb. 5, 1820.
Susan M., ch. Lemuel R. and Susannah, Sept. 7, 1835. [Susan Maria, ch. Lemuel and Susanna, C.R.2. Susan Maria, ch. Lemuel R. and Susannah R. (Hanford), P.R.79.]
Susan Whorf, ch. Charles and Zilpha, Mar. 11, 1854.
William, ch. Benja[min] and Mary, Sept. 2, 1809.
Zilpha [? m.], June 22, 1818, G.R.1.

PARKE, Edward Horace, inf. Horace and Lizzie M., bp. Oct. 20, 1878, C.R.2.
Mabel Agnes, inf. Horace and Lizzie M., bp. Oct. 20, 1878, C.R.2.

PARKER, A. V., Feb. 26, 1813, G.R.1.
Delia [w. Horatio Palmer Thompson], Oct. 19, 1839, G.R.1. [Delia Wood Parker, d. Rev. Wooster and Wealthy Ann (Pond), P.R.165.]
Edward E., Feb. —, 1865, G.R.1. [s. Israel W. and Sarah J. (Stephenson), P.R.82.]
Eva A., Nov. 29, 1851, G.R.1.
George F. A., July 8, 1827, in Northport, P.R.78.
Harriet, w. Rufus P. Hassell, July 8, 1823, in Warren, P.R.34.
Harry, Apr. —, 1875, G.R.1. [s. Israel W. and Sarah J. (Stephenson), Apr. 28, P.R.82.]
Henry S., Nov. 28, 1829, G.R.1.
Israel W., h. Sarah J. (Stephenson), Jan. 4, 1832, P.R.82.
Josephine E. [———], ———, 1879, G.R.1.
Julietta S., w. Barker B. Glidden, Dec. 8, 1833, in Camden, P.R.78.
Mary E., w. Horatio P. Thompson, Jan. 21, 1842, G.R.1. [Mary Elizabeth, d. Rev. Wooster and Wealthy Ann (Pond), P.R.165.]
Nellie S., w. Willis B. Fletcher, d. Israel W. and Sarah J. (Stephenson), Mar. 9, 1866, P.R.82.
Ralph L., s. Israel W. and Sarah J. (Stephenson), Dec. 29, 1869, P.R.82.
S. Augustus, Dec. 1, 1861, in Northport, P.R.78.
Samuel S., ———, 1825, G.R.1. [Feb. 8, in Northport, P.R.78.]
Sarah, Oct. —, 1873, G.R.1. [d. Israel W. and Sarah J. (Stephenson), P.R.82.]
Sarah J. [———], w. I. W., Mar. 23, 1842, G.R.1. [Sarah J. (Stephenson), w. Israel W., P.R.82.]
Sarah May, d. Israel W. and Sarah J. (Stephenson), May 2, 1879, P.R.82.

PARKER, Sibyl [——], w. Capt. Silas, Sept. 6, 1800, in Northport, P.R.78.
Silas, Capt., h. Sibyl, May 30, 1799, in Islesborough, P.R.78.
Silas H., Nov. 28, 1829, in Northport, P.R.78.
Sophronia B. [? m.], ——, 1834, G.R.1.
T. Frank, Aug. 27, 1874 [dup. 1873], P.R.78.
Wooster, h. Wealthy Ann (Pond), ——, 1807, G.R.1.

PARTRIDGE, Ella M. (see Ella M. Twombly).
George O., ——, 1858, G.R.1. [s. Joshua Eustis and Mary Abbie (Arnold), Sept. 23, 1859, in Stockton, P.R.129.]
J. A., Capt., Sept. 16, 1832, G.R.1.
James B., ——, 1858, G.R.1. [s. Joshua Eustis and Mary Abbie (Arnold), Mar. 4, in Stockton, P.R.129.]
Joshua E., h. Mary A., ——, 1825, G.R.1. [Joshua Eustis Partridge, h. Mary Abbie (Arnold), May 18, in Stockton, P.R.129.]
Nellie E. [——], w. E. J., ——, 1863, G.R.1.

PATERSHALL (see Pattershall), Blanch E., Sept. 28, 1878, P.R.12.
Evaline R., w. Alexander Graisbury, d. Doane and Lovina (Larabee), Aug. 15, 1854, P.R.12.
George W., h. Effie E. Patterson, s. Doane and Lovina (Larabee), Feb. 11, 1848, P.R.12.
Helen M., w. George T. Osborne, d. Doane and Lovina (Larabee), June 11, 1840, P.R.12.
Martha A., w. Joseph H. Darby, d. Doane and Lovina (Larabee), Nov. 3, 1844, P.R.12.
Mary L., w. James A. Curtis, d. Doane and Lovina (Larabee), Oct. 15, 1837, P.R.12.
Ralph M., Aug. 7, 1875, P.R.12.
Valentine Harrison, h. Grace E. (White), s. Doane and Lovina (Larabee), Feb. 14, 1851, P.R.12.

PATTERSHALL (see Patershall), Arthur, Capt., Nov. 29, 1879, G.R.1. [Arthur M. Patershall, P.R.12.]
Fred D., Capt., h. Laura A., ——, 1843, G.R.1. [Frederick Doane Pattershall, h. Laura A. (Knowlton), s. Doane and Lovina (Larabee), Nov. 27, 1842, P.R.12.]
Laura A. [——], w. Capt. Fred D., ——, 1845, G.R.1.
Melvin A., Mar. 26, 1867, P.R.12.
Ross H., May 4, 1883, P.R.12.
Roxanna H. [? m.], ——, 1785, in Wellfleet, P.R.12.

PATTERSON, A. F., "Co. H. 8th Me. Regt.," ——, 1842, G.R.2.

PATTERSON, Abigail Jane [————], w. Cyrus, ———, 1812, G.R.1.
  [Abigail Jane (Cunningham), Aug. 28, P.R.74.]
Albert, ch. George and Hannah, July 14, 1842.
Albert Clarendon (see Bertie Clarendon Patterson).
Alexis G. [dup. Elexis Volantine], [twin] ch. George and Hannah, Sept. 4, 1834.
Alfred, ch. Robert 2d and Jenney [Jane, C.R.2.], Oct. 5, 1808. [h. Mary, G.R.1.]
Alfred, ch. George and Hannah, Dec. 4, 1823 [dup. 1824].
Alice D., ch. Capt. F. A. and M. D., ———, 1851, G.R.2.
Alonzo H., ———, 1830, G.R.1. [s. David, Aug. 27, P.R.57.]
Amasa F., ch. Robert and Joanna, Aug. 18, 1812, P.R.11.
Andrew, ch. Robert and Elizabeth, July 3, 1780.
Andrew M., h. Rouena M., h. Caroline G. (Patterson), Oct. 29, 1836, G.R.1.
Andrew N., ch. Andrew and Mary, Feb. 25, 1811.
Ann, ch. John M. and Mary, Sept. 15, 1811.
Ann Maria, ch. Robert 4th and Peggy, ——— [*rec. after ch. b.* Oct. 21, 1809]. [w. William G. Crosby, Dec. 31, 1811, G.R.1.]
Ann Maria, ch. John T. and Jane, Feb. 13, 1834. [second w. Harvey Hutchinson, d. John Tufts and Jane (Ferguson), Feb. 1, P.R.119.]
Ann S., ch. George and Hannah, Jan. 7, 1840.
Ann Sarah, ch. Francis A. and Sarah, July 15, 1840.
Anna, ch. William 2d and Polly, Oct. 23, 1788. [Oct. 23, 1785, P.R.57.]
Augusta Ann, ch. Hiram and Betsy, May 23, 1838.
Augusta Jane, ch. Nath[anie]l and Mary E., bp. Dec. 5, 1858, C.R.2.
Augustus, ch. William and Clarisa, Nov. 16, 1840.
Aurelia Whitney, ch. John T. and Jane, Sept. 14, 1839. [w. Philo S. Goud, d. John Tufts and Jane (Ferguson), P.R.119.]
Aurelius, ch. William and Clarisa, July 21, 1842.
Bertie Clarendon, Sept. 15, 1862, P.R.14. [Albert Clarendon Patterson, great grand ch. Salathiel Nickerson and Martha Rogers, P.R.15.]
Betsy, ch. William 4th and Jane, Dec. 18, 1797. [Elizabeth, w. Richard Holt, G.R.1. P.R.32.]
Caroline A., ch. John M. and Mary, Aug. 3, 1826.
Caroline G., w. Andrew M. Patterson, July 28, 1860, G.R.1.
Charles A., ch. John M. and Mary, June 2, 1825.
Charles Barton, ch. James Jr. and Nancy, Feb. 17, 1810.

PATTERSON, Charles Barton, ch. Robert 5th and Sally, Dec. 6, 1833.
Charles Milton, ch. John T. and Jane, Dec. 3, 1828. [h. Helen (McLellan), s. John Tufts and Jane (Ferguson), P.R.119.]
Crosby, ch. George and Hannah, Oct. 4, 1820.
Cyrus, ch. Nathaniel Jr. and Sally, Nov. 4, 1812. [h. Abigail Jane, G.R.1. h. Abigail Jane (Cunningham), P.R.74.]
David, ch. William 2d and Polly, Sept. 5, 1794. [———, 1791, G.R.1. h. Rhoda N., Sept. 5, 1791, P.R.57.]
David Floyed, ch. Robert 5th and Sally, Aug. 7, 1829.
David M., s. Robert and Joanna, Oct. 30, 1821, P.R.11.
Diana, ch. Robert 3d and Joanna, Feb. 13, 1806. [Dianna, Feb. 13, 1805, P.R.11.]
Edward, ch. Robert 4th and Peggy, July 10, 1805.
Edwin M., ch. Andrew and Mary, June 3, 1805.
Elexis Volantine (see Alexis G.).
Elisha, ch. Robert and Elizabeth, Aug. 17, 1789.
Elison L., ch. John and Hannah, ——— [rec. after ch. b. Apr. 3, 1820].
Eliza, ch. Robert 4th and Peggy, Aug. 9, 1802.
Elizabeth, ch. Robert and Elizabeth, Feb. 18, 1778.
Elizabeth, ch. William 2d and Polly, Oct. 18, 1782. [Oct. 18, 1780, P.R.57.]
Elizabeth (see Betsy).
Elizabeth Ann, ch. Robert and Joanna, May 23, 1829, P.R.11.
Emma J., ch. Francis A. and Sarah, May 25, 1845.
F. A., Capt., h. Mary D., ———, 1800, G.R.2.
F. A. Jr., "Co. K. 4th Me. Regt.," ———, 1844, G.R.2.
Ferris Fitch, ch. Alfred, bp. Nov. 15, 1835, C.R.2. [b. ———, 1830, G.R.1.]
Fitzwilliam, s. Nathaniel and Sally, Sept. 20, 1823, P.R.74.
Fitzwilliam, s. Nathaniel and Sally, Nov. 22, 1825, P.R.74.
Francis A., h. Sarah A. (Patterson), s. Robert and Joanna, Mar. 15, 1819, P.R.11.
Francis Volantine, [twin] ch. George and Hannah, Sept. 4, 1834.
Francis W., s. Nathaniel and Sally, Mar. 24, 1816, P.R.74.
Frank M., ———, 1837, G.R.1. [M. Franklin Patterson, s. David, Sept. 3, P.R.57.]
Frank W., ———, 1839, G.R.1. [s. Cyrus and A. J. (Cunningham), Nov. 10, P.R.74.]
Franklin A., ch. Sulivan and Elmira, Jan. 4, 1841.
Franklin Martin, ch. James Jr. and Nancy, Nov. 19, 1811.
Fredrick, ch. Martin and Allice, Oct. 27, 1801.
Freeman C., ch. Andrew and Mary, Nov. 19, 1820.

PATTERSON, George, ch. Robert and Elizabeth, Apr. 24, 1796.
George A., ——, 1839, G.R.1. [George Albert, s. David, Feb. 18, 1838, P.R.57.]
George Ferguson, s. John Tufts and Jane (Ferguson), Oct. 16, 1844, P.R.119.
George Jackson [dup. *omits* George], ch. George and Hannah, June 20, 1828.
George L., ch. George and Hannah, Apr. 22, 1846.
George William, ch. Robert 5th and Sally, Sept. 28, 1817.
Georgianna, ch. William and Clarisa, June 16, 1844.
Grace, inf. Nath[anie]l and Mary E., bp. Dec. 1, 1861, C.R.2.
Granville A., ch. Sulivan and Elmira, Feb. 17, 1845.
Hannah, ch. Nathaniel and Hannah, Apr. 18, 1782.
Hannah, ch. William 2d and Polly, July 24, 1791. [July 24, 1788, P.R.57.]
Hannah E. (see Hannah E. Beckwith).
Hannah Floyed, ch. Robert 5th and Sally, Apr. 12, 1827.
Hannah J., ch. George and Hannah, June 27, 1838.
Harriet Amanda, d. David, Sept. 4, 1828, P.R.57.
Harriet E. [dup. Harriot Eliza], ch. George and Hannah, May 31 [dup. May 30], 1830.
Harriot, ch. Robert 3d and Joanna, Oct. 20, 1803. [Harriet, P.R.11.]
Henry D., ——, 1852, G.R.1.
Henry Eells, ch. Robert 4th and Peggy, Aug. 12, 1807.
Henry O., ——, 1835, G.R.1. [Henry Otis Patterson, s. David, Feb. 14, P.R.57.]
Hiram, ch. John M. and Mary, Aug. 3, 1808.
Horatio Nelson, ch. Martin and Allice, Aug. 4, 1807.
Ida May, d. R. O. and M. F., Aug. 29, 1856, G.R.1.
Isabel F., ch. Capt. F. A. and M. D., ——, 1854, G.R.2.
Jackson (see George Jackson Patterson).
James, [twin] ch. James and Jenney, Aug. 6, 1786.
James George, ch. James Jr. and Nancy, Dec. 23, 1815.
James William, ch. George and Hannah, June 24 [dup. June 23], 1832.
Jane [———], w. Robert, ——, 1770, G.R.1.
Jane (see Jenney).
Jane, ch. Robert 4th and Peggy, Oct. 21, 1809.
Jane, ch. Robert 2d and Jenney, Oct. 22, 1810.
Jane Frances, [twin] ch. John T. and Jane, Mar. 9, 1831. [Jane Francis, twin d. John Tufts and Jane (Ferguson), P.R.119.]
Jenney, ch. James and Jenney, Aug. 25, 1774.
Jenney, ch. William 2d and Polly, Apr. 5, 1775. [Jane, P.R.57.]
Jenney, ch. Robert and Elizabeth, June 9, 1798.

PATTERSON, Jenney, ch. William 4th and Jane, Feb. 12, 1802.
Jenney, ch. Robert and Elizabeth, Apr. 11, 1804.
Joanna [———], w. Robert, Aug. 20, 1782, P.R.11.
John, ch. Robert and Elizabeth, Nov. 15, 1784.
John, ch. Robert 2d and Jenney, Dec. 8, 1801. [John Tufts Patterson, s. Robert and Jane, C.R.2. John Tufts Patterson, h. Jane (Ferguson), P.R.119.]
John, ch. John M. and Mary, July 14, 1819.
John A., Feb. 4, 1848, G.R.13.
John Calvin, ch. Hiram and Betsy, Feb. 26, 1840.
John F., ch. John and Hannah, Apr. 3, 1820.
John Lewis, ch. John T. and Jane [John Tufts and Jane (Ferguson), P.R.119.], Nov. 24, 1836.
John M., ch. William 2d and Polly, May 26, 1779. [John Mitchel Patterson, May 26, 1778, P.R.57.]
John Sebra, ch. Robert 5th and Sally, Nov. 10, 1819.
Kate Louise, d. Cyrus W., bp. July 4, 1875, C.R.1.
Lewis A., ch. John and Hannah, ———.
Louisa Jane, ch. Martin and Allice, Jan. 21, 1812.
Lydia Emeline, ch. George and Hannah, Feb. 4, 1826 [dup. Feb. 23, 1825].
Lydia S., ch. John and Hannah, ———.
M. Franklin (see Frank M.).
Margaret Augusta, ch. John T. and Jane, Apr. 7, 1827. [first w. Harvey Hutchinson, d. John Tufts and Jane (Ferguson), P.R.119.]
Margret, [twin] ch. James and Jenney, Aug. 6, 1786.
Margret, ch. Robert 2d and Jenney, June 12, 1795. [Margaret, ch. Robert and Jane, G.R.1.]
Martha, ch. Robert and Elizabeth, Nov. 23, 1782.
Martha, ch. Robert and Elizabeth, Feb. 7, 1794.
Martin, ch. Nathaniel and Hannah, Apr. 17, 1777.
Martin, ch. Robert 4th and Peggy, Oct. 11, 1803.
Martin Jamison, ch. Martin and Allice, Jan. 25, 1810.
Martine J., ch. James and Jenney, Jan. 30, 1779.
Mary (see Polly).
Mary, ch. James and Jenney, Mar. 31, 1784.
Mary [———], w. Alfred, ———, 1804, G.R.1.
Mary, ch. John M. and Mary, Apr. 21, 1806.
Mary E., ch. Andrew and Mary, Mar. 5, 1813.
Mary E. [———], w. Nathaniel, ———, 1813, G.R.1.
Mary E. (see Mary E. Page).
Mary E., ———, 1832, G.R.1. [Mary Elizabeth, d. David, Dec. 27, P.R.57.]

PATTERSON, Mary Eleanor, inf. Alfred and w., bp. Nov. 17, 1839, C.R.2. [b. ——, 1839, G.R.1.]
Mary Ellen, ch. Nath[anie]l and Mary E., bp. Dec. 5, 1858, C.R.2.
Mary Frances [————], w. Capt. R. O., Oct. 6, 1835, G.R.1.
Mary J. [? m.], ——, 1842, G.R.1.
Mary L., June 19, 1866, G.R.1.
Mary P., ch. John and Hannah, ———.
Mary S. [? m.], Apr. 2, 1856, G.R.13.
Melvina A., ch. Sulivan and Elmira, Jan. 27, 1843.
Milton, ch. Robert 2d and Jenney [Jane, C.R.2. G.R.1.], Apr. 20, 1805.
Milton, ch. Robert 3d and Joanna, Mar. 20, 1810. [h. Eunice Kinsman Hatch, P.R.11.]
Nancy, ch. John M. and Mary, Dec. 27, 1809.
Nancy A., ch. Andrew and Mary, Aug. 6, 1817.
Nancy Jane, ch. Robert 5th and Sally, Mar. 6, 1822. [w. A. D. Chase, G.R.1. w. Alden Darwin Chase, P.R.75.]
Nathan, ch. Hiram and Betsy, June 5, 1844.
Nathaniel, ch. Nathaniel and Hannah, Oct. 30, 1785. [h. Sally, P.R.74.]
Nathaniel, ch. Robert 2d and Jenney [Jane, G.R.1.], May 10, 1793.
Nathaniel, ch. Robert 2d and Jenney, Jan. 26, 1798. [ch. Rob[er]t 3d and Jane, C.R.2. h. Mary E., G.R.1.]
Orsamus R., ch. Robert and Joanna, Apr. 5, 1817, P.R.11.
Otis, ch. Robert 3d and Joanna, Feb. 5, 1808. [h. Elisa Galvin of Westbrook, P.R.11.]
Paulina, ch. John M. and Mary, Jan. 21, 1809.
Peggy, ch. William 4th and Jane, Feb. 14, 1799.
Peggy, ch. Robert 4th and Peggy, Sept. 24, 1799.
Polly, ch. William 2d and Polly, Nov. 25, 1786. [Mary, Nov. 25, 1782, P.R.57.]
R. O., Capt., h. Mary Frances, Sept. 21, 1824, G.R.1.
Rachael, ch. John M. and Mary, June 21, 1813.
Rachael, ch. Hiram and Betsy, Apr. 2, 1842.
Rebecca N., w. Benjamin P. Ryder, Oct. 5, 1818, in Chatham, P.R.49.
Rhoda N. [————], w. David, July 31, 1796, P.R.57.
Richard E., ch. John and Hannah, ——— [rec. before ch. b. Apr. 3, 1820].
Richard F., h. Salenda, Nov. 29, 1824, G.R.1. [s. Robert and Joanna, P.R.11.]
Robert, ch. Nathaniel and Hannah, June 9, 1771. [h. Jane, G.R.1.]

PATTERSON, Robert, ch. William 2d and Polly, June 14, 1776.
[h. Joanna, June 14, 1775, P.R.11. June 14, 1776, P.R.57.]
Robert, ch. James and Jenney, July 20, 1776.
Robert, ch. Robert and Elizabeth, Feb. 21, 1792. [Robert 5th [h. Polly], G.R.1.]
Rob[er]t, ch. Francis A. and Sarah, Sept. 16, 1843. [Capt. Robert F., h. Viola J., G.R.1.]
Robert Franklin, [twin] ch. John T. and Jane, Mar. 9, 1831. [h. Julia Bradbury, twin s. John Tufts and Jane (Ferguson), P.R.119.]
Robert Otis, ch. Robert 5th and Sally, Aug. 21, 1825.
Roscoe Adelbert, s. John Tufts and Jane (Ferguson), June 1, 1847, in Salem, P.R.119.
Rowena M. [———], w. Andrew M., Apr. 22, 1853, G.R.1.
Rufus King, ch. Martin and Allice, Apr. 28, 1805.
Ruth Ellen, ch. Hiram and Betsy, May 12, 1846.
Sally, ch. Nathaniel and Hannah, Aug. 30, 1779.
Sally, ch. Robert and Elizabeth, Jan. 26, 1786.
Sally [———], w. Nathaniel, Sept. 13, 1786, in Edgecomb, P.R.74.
Sarah Ann, d. Nathaniel and Sally, May 2, 1819, P.R.74.
Sewall (see Suel).
Starrat, ch. Martin and Allice, Sept. 20, 1803.
Starret, ch. Nathaniel and Hannah, Apr. 4, 1774.
Suel, ch. George and Hannah, Jan. 19, 1822 [dup. 1821].
Sullivan, ch. Andrew and Mary, Mar. 2, 1807.
Susan Jane, ch. Alfred, bp. Nov. 15, 1835, C.R.2. [b. ———, 1834, G.R.1.]
Susanna, ch. James and Jenney, July 23, 1781. [Susannah, w. Robert White, P.R.148.]
Susannah M., ch. Andrew and Mary, Aug. 8, 1815.
Thomas Furber, ch. James Jr. and Nancy, Nov. 8, 1813.
Thomas Shute, ch. Robert 5th and Sally, Aug. 28, 1815.
Viola J. [———], w. Capt. Robert F., ———, 1853, G.R.1.
Washington, ch. Andrew and Mary, Feb. 17, 1809.
William, ch. William 2d and Polly, Apr. 1, 1773.
William, ch. Robert and Elizabeth, Nov. 16, 1775.
William, ch. William 4th and Jane, Oct. 5, 1800.
W[illia]m, ch. John M. and Mary, Feb. 15, 1822.
William Elerson, ch. Elerson and Hannah Jane (Holt) (Freeman), grand ch. William Holt and Hannah P. (Shute), Dec. 12, 1858, P.R.29.
———, d. Isaac S., Jan. 15, 1847, P.R.123.
———, d. Henry, Aug. 24, 1847, P.R.123.
———, d. Capt. Robert O., May 11, 1849, P.R.123.

PAUL, Abbie [———] [w. James], ———, 1821, G.R.13.
Caroline, w. John Wight, Oct. 24, 1813.
Edgar, Sept. 20, 1840, G.R.1.
Ella A., d. James and Abbie, ———, 1857, G.R.13.
Flavilla, w. —— Duffie, Aug. 18, 1838, G.R.1.
James [h. Abbie], ———, 1804, G.R.13.
James Nelson, ch. James Jr. and Sabra, Feb. 25, 1834.
Jesse Granville, ———, 1851, G.R.1.
Joel H. [h. Lucinda], ———, 1812, G.R.1.
John S., ch. James Jr. and Sabra, Oct. 1, 1828.
Lucinda [———], [w. Joel H.], ———, 1818, G.R.1.
Mary A., ch. James Jr. and Sabra, Mar. 18, 1832.
Walter, ———, 1860, G.R.13.
Warren H., ch. James Jr. and Sabra, Jan. 13, 1830.
Wilbur, ———, 1859, G.R.13.

PAYSON, Caroline R., ch. Samuel and Rebecca, Nov. 6, 1828.
Eliza, ch. Samuel and Rebecca, May 3, 1840.
Hollis M., ch. Samuel and Rebecca, Feb. 7, 1846.
John, ch. Samuel and Rebecca, Oct. 10, 1830 [*sic*, see Simon A.].
John F., ch. Samuel and Rebecca, Feb. 26, 1833.
Samuel A., ch. Samuel and Rebecca, May 31, 1838.
Simon A., ch. Samuel and Rebecca, Jan. 17, 1831 [*sic*, see John].
Susan, ch. Samuel and Rebecca, Mar. 21, 1836.

PEASE, Sarah, w. Nathaniel Barker, Oct. 3, 1789, in Parsonfield, P.R.76.

PEAVEY, ———, d. Darius, Nov. 30, 1848, P.R.123.

PECK, Elizabeth [———], w. Samuel, ———, 1774, G.R.1.
James Sullivan, ch. Samuel and Elizabeth, Mar. 25, 1808.
Samuel, h. Elizabeth, ———, 1780, G.R.1.
Samuel Soper, ch. Samuel and Elizabeth, Sept. 1, 1804.
William Moody, ch. Samuel and Elizabeth, Mar. 7, 1806.

PEIRCE (see Pierce), Abby C., d. Bailey and Eliza T., Sept. 11, 1824, G.R.1.
Bohan F., ch. Samuel and Rebeckah, Feb. 5, 1803.
David, ch. David and Hannah, Sept. 8, 1813.
Emma Lena (see Lena P.).
Franklin, ch. David and Hannah, Sept. 4, 1815.
Hiram, ch. David and Hannah, Jan. 25, 1819.
John, ch. David and Hannah, Nov. 11, 1811. [h. Sarah Frances (Thorndike), P.R.112.]

PEIRCE, John Frederic, s. John and Sarah Frances (Thorndike), Jan. 21, 1857, P.R.112.
Lena P., w. Charles Woodbury Frederick, July 27, 1863, P.R.120.
Percy C., Mar. 10, 1866, G.R.1.
Robert, ch. David and Hannah, June 1, 1817.
Robert Franklin, h. Carrie Etta (Sylvester), s. John and Sarah Frances (Thorndike), Apr. 17, 1843, P.R.112.
Sarah Elizabeth, w. David Augustus Elwel, d. John and Sarah Frances (Thorndike), Mar. 19, 1840, P.R.112.
Thomas, ch. Thomas and Oliva, Nov. 28, 1801.
Trestum Gilman, ch. Samuel and Rebeckah, Jan. 10, 1804.
William, ch. David and Hannah, Aug. 16, 1810.

PENDLETON, Aurelia [———], w. Henderson, June 30, 1833, G.R.1.
Caroline E., w. L. A. Knowlton, ———, 1826, G.R.1. [July 13, in Islesboro, P.R.66.]
Charles, h. Louisa W. (Eaton), Aug. 5, 1802, P.R.67.
Edith M., Sept. 7, 1870, G.R.1.
Edwin Grey, s. Charles and Louisa W. (Eaton), Feb. 14, 1843, P.R.67.
Elizabeth Eaton, second w. Lewis A. Knowlton, d. Charles and Louisa W. (Eaton), July 20, 1834, P.R.67.
Frederic Clifford, h. Georgia S. Alden, s. Charles and Louisa W. (Eaton), Sept. 21, 1835, P.R.67.
Harriet E., w. Robert H. Coombs, Apr. 13, 1831, P.R.97.
Henderson, h. Aurelia, Oct. 10, 1828, G.R.1.
Herbert A., h. Eva, Apr. 27, 1849, G.R.1.
Joseph T., Dec. 12, 1824, G.R.13.
Leonard R., July 10, 1872, G.R.1.
Mary R., Dec. 10, 1851, G.R.13.
Nathaniel Eaton, s. Charles and Louisa W. (Eaton), June 12, 1841, P.R.67.
Sarah F. [? m.], Nov. 18, 1829, G.R.13.
William Charles, s. Charles and Louisa W. (Eaton), Oct. 22, 1837, P.R.67.
William Lewis, inf. Lewis, M.D., bp. July 4, 1875, C.R.1.

PERKINS, Abbie E. [———], w. Cha[rle]s M., Dec. 7, 1867, G.R.1.
Abbie S. [———], w. B. F., Nov. 25, 1850, G.R.1.
Abigail Mead, w. James B. Patterson of Waldo, d. Joseph and Cyrena (French), Feb. 19, 1823, in Freedom, P.R.158.
Albert, [twin] ch. Edward and Joanna, May 26, 1836.

PERKINS, Arabelle May, w. David McKnight, May 6, 1848, G.R.1.
Augustus, [twin] ch. Edward and Joanna, May 26, 1836.
Bertha M. [―――], w. Edwin S., Sept. 26, 1881, G.R.1.
Bethia, w. Geo[rge] Anderson of Freeport, d. Joseph and Cyrena (French), May 31, 1827, in Freedom, P.R.158.
Cha[rle]s M., h. Abbie E., May 13, 1862, G.R.1. [s. Horace S. and Lucy E. (Burgess), P.R.52.]
Daniel M. True, inf., bp. Aug. 17, 1882, in Northport, C.R.3.
Daniel P., ch. Edward and Joanna, Nov. 25, 1831.
Edward, h. Joanna, Feb. 20, 1804, G.R.13.
Edward Wight, ch. Edward and Joanna, Jan. 26, 1829. [Jan. 26, 1830, G.R.13.]
Edwin S., s. Horace S. and Lucy E. (Burgess), Dec. 1, 1877, P.R.52.
Eliza A. [? m.], Nov. 21, 1845, G.R.13.
Ella G., ―――, 1873, G.R.1. [Ella Catherine, twin d. Horace S. and Lucy E. (Burgess), Dec. 18, P.R.52.]
Emma S., ―――, 1873, G.R.1. [Emma Serena, twin d. Horace S. and Lucy E. (Burgess), Dec. 18, P.R.52.]
Fred W., s. Horace S. and Lucy E. (Burgess), June 10, 1864, P.R.52.
George R., ―――, 1857, G.R.1. [George Robert, s. Horace S. and Lucy E. (Burgess), May 1, P.R.52.]
Gertrude, ―――, 1874, G.R.1.
Hannah Abagail, ch. Edward and Joanna, Oct. 7, 1833. [w. ――― Condon, G.R.13.]
Harriett N., w. Capt. George R. Carter, May 12, 1831, G.R.1. [Harriet Newell Perkins, d. Joseph and Cyrena (French), P.R.158.]
Hiram, ch. Edward and Joanna, Aug. 7, 1840.
Horace Albert, s. Capt. James and Emma F., Feb. 25, 1870, G.R.1.
Horace S., ch. Joseph and Serena, Oct. 8, 1833. [h. Lucy E. (Burgess), P.R.52. Horace Seaver Perkins, s. Joseph and Cyrena (French), Oct. 8, 1832, P.R.158.]
James H., ch. Joseph and Serena, Jan. 3, 1841.
James H., ch. Joseph and Serena, July 13, 1843. [James Henry Perkins, h. Emma F. (McKeen), h. Hattie C. Bradstreet, s. Joseph and Cyrena (French), P.R.158.]
Joanna [―――], w. Edward, Mar. 20, 1803, G.R.13. [Johanna (Wight), d. Edward, P.R.2.]
Joseph, Apr. 23, 1797, G.R.1.
Joseph, s. Edward and Joanna, Apr. 12, 1828, G.R.13.

PERKINS, Joseph, ch. Edward and Joanna, Oct. 7, 1838.
Lizzie M., d. Horace S. and Lucy E. (Burgess), Nov. 12, 1871, P.R.52.
Nellie E., ———, 1867, G.R.1.
Silas M., ch. Joseph and Serena, Mar. 19, 1835. [Silas McKeen Perkins, h. Annie Clark, s. Joseph and Cyrena (French), Mar. 18, P.R.158.]

PERRY, Augustus [h. Jane C.], Apr. 30, 1815, G.R.1. [h. Jane C. (Porter), in Camden, P.R.160.]
Edward A., h. Mary Nickels (Lancaster), Nov. 10, 1844, P.R.108. [Edward Augustus, s. Augustus and Jane C. (Porter), P.R.160.]
Eliza Melissa, ch. John and Eliza, Oct. 25, 1836.
Emily Fowler, d. Augustus and Jane C., bp. Sept. 3, 1847, C.R.2. [w. Phineas Pendleton, b. Feb. 16, G.R.1. w. Capt. Phineas Pendleton, d. Augustus and Jane C. (Porter), b. Feb. 16, P.R.160.]
Hiram H., ch. John and Eliza, Sept. 22, 1840.
Isabella Jane, inf. Augustus and Jane C., bp. Nov. 28, 1852, C.R.2. [w. Clarence O. Poor, d. Augustus and Jane C. (Porter), b. Jan. 14, P.R.160.]
Jane C. [————], w. Augustus, Jan. 13, 1820, G.R.1.
Joseph Franklin, ch. John and Eliza, Oct. 8, 1837.
Julia Margaret, inf. Augustus and Jane C., bp. Aug. 11, 1850, C.R.2. [d. Augustus and Jane C. (Porter), b. June 10, P.R.160.]
Lena Lancaster, d. Edward A. and Mary Nickels (Lancaster), Sept. 20, 1871, P.R.108.
Ralph M., ———, 1865, G.R.1.
Robert Edward, s. Edward A. and Mary Nickels (Lancaster), Sept. 6, 1875, P.R.108.
Sarah C., ch. John and Eliza, Sept. 30, 1844.
Walter Frank, inf. Augustus and Jane C., bp. Sept. 9, 1855, C.R.2. [s. Augustus and Jane C. (Porter), b. Oct. 11, 1854, P.R.160.]

PETTEE, Climenta T. Hanna [————], w. Nathan W., Jan. 4, 1846, G.R.1.
Nathan W., h. Climenta T. Hanna, Oct. 12, 1838, G.R.1.

PHILBRICK (see Philbrook), Charles, Aug. 3, 1815, G.R.1.
Diantha [————], w. Charles, Feb. 20, 1812, G.R.1.
Edmund M., Mar. 2, 1838, G.R.3.

PHILBRICK, Eph[rai]m, h. Hannah, ———, 1803, G.R.2.
Hannah [———], w. Eph[rai]m, ———, 1810, G.R.2.
Melinda M. [———], w. Walter A., Mar. 20, 1833, G.R.2.
Walter A., Aug. 19, 1829, G.R.2.

PHILBROOK (see Philbrick), Hannah T. [———], w. S. V., June 3, 1836, G.R.4.

PHILLIPS, Charlotte Eleanor, ch. Nicholas and Betsy, ——— [*rec. after ch. b.* Apr. 23, 1830].
Eleanor, ch. Nicholas and Betsy, Nov. 12, 1816.
Elijah, h. Elizabeth, June 19, 1854, G.R.13.
Elizabeth [———], w. Elijah, Aug. 6, 1848, G.R.13.
Franklin Tinkham, ch. Nicholas and Betsy, June 26, 1819.
George Greenleaf (Phillip), ch. Nicholas and Betsy, ——— [*rec. after ch. b.* June 26, 1819].
Levinia Ann (Phillip), ch. Nicholas and Betsy, ——— [*rec. before ch. b.* Apr. 23, 1830].
Mary, ch. Nicholas and Betsy, Oct. 14, 1814.
Nicholas Theodore, ch. Nicholas and Betsy, Apr. 23, 1830.
Phebe, ch. Nicholas and Betsy, Dec. 16, 1812.
Susan [———], w. ———, Nov. 21, 1832, G.R.13.

PHINNEY, Albert Alen (Phiney), ch. Timothy and Adaline, June 11, 1831.
Edwin Williams, ch. Timothy and Adaline, Sept. 11, 1829.

PHIPPS, David W., h. Viola J. Varney, h. Annie L. (Davidson), s. Stephen E. and Phebe P. (Warren), Aug. 29, 1837, in Plymouth, P.R.39.
Stephen E., h. Phebe P. (Warren), ———, 1810, P.R.39.

PICKARD, Henry W., "Co. A. 20th Me. Regt.," ———, 1841, G.R.1.
Thomas A., s. Thomas and Priscilla (Palmer), ———, 1821, G.R.1.

PIERCE (see Peirce), Hannah, Apr. 7, 1860, P.R.97.
Joanna, w. Edmund P. Brown, Jan. 18, 1818, G.R.4.
Kingsbury S., Jan. 23, 1890, G.R.1.
Maud G. [? m.], Nov. 17, 1885, G.R.1.

PILLSBURY, Ansel M., h. Catherine C., ———, 1818, G.R.1.
Daniel E., ch. Daniel and w., Apr. 19, 1842.
John Calvin, ———, 1865, G.R.1.
John M., ch. Daniel and w., June 9, 1838.
Margaret R., ch. Daniel and w., May 25, 1840.

PILLSBURY, Richard R., ch. Daniel and w., Aug. 18, 1834.
William M., ch. Daniel and w., June 9, 1836.
PIPER, Charles B., h. Nancy, ———, 1812, G.R.I.
Charles P. Jr., Jan. 6, 1842, G.R.I.
Clarkson R., Mar. 10, 1845, G.R.I.
Nancy [———], w. Charles B., ———, 1814, G.R.I.
PITCHER, Albert A., July 8, 1839, P.R.162.
Ann Cornelia, ch. Jonathan and Elizabeth, June 26, 1819.
Annie M., d. Cha[rle]s A. and Nancy Matilda (Miller), June 24, 1849, P.R.59.
Anson, ch. Calvin 2d and Lydia, Jan. 3, 1844.
Augusta A., ch. William and Sarah, Aug. 12, 1833.
Aura A., ch. William and Sarah, Aug. 30, 1835. [w. E. C. Fletcher, G.R.I.],
Byron L., Feb. 9, 1850, G.R.I. P.R.162.
Calvin, h. Lydia, May 5, 1812, G.R.12.
Calvin Hartshorn, ch. Calvin and Joanna, Dec. 11, 1835. [Hartshorn C., h. Lydia Ann (Lancaster), h. Lucy Adella (Lancaster), P.R.108. Calvin Hartson Pitcher, h. Lydia A. (Lancaster), h. Lucy A. (Lancaster), s. Calvin and Joanna (Prescott), P.R.172.]
Caroline, ch. Calvin and Joanna, Oct. 24, 1829. [Caroline A., w. William C. Frederick, d. Calvin and Joanna (Prescott), P.R.172.]
Cha[rle]s A., ch. Fisher A. and Eliza [(Whittier) P.R.162.], Apr. 14, 1822.
Charles S., ch. Jonathan and Elizabeth, Mar. 29, 1823.
Daniel, ch. Calvin and Joanna [(Prescott) P.R.172], Mar. 15, 1825.
Daniel L., ch. Fisher A. and Eliza [(Whittier) P.R.162.], Dec. 16, 1825.
Edith, d. Hartshorn C. and Lydia Ann (Lancaster) (first w.), Aug. 3, 1866, P.R.108.
Electa, ch. Calvin and Joanna, Nov. 3, 1831. [Electa B., w. Martin Stone, d. Calvin and Joanna (Prescott), P.R.172.]
Eliza [———], w. Fisher A., ———, 1798, G.R.I. [Eliza (Whittier), Sept. 9, in Vienna, P.R.162.]
Eliza, ch. Jonathan and Elizabeth, Sept. 7, 1810.
Eliza A., ch. Fisher A. and Eliza, Mar. 8, 1818. [Eliza Ann, ch. Fisher A. and Eliza (Whittier), P.R.162.]
Elizabeth [———], w. Jonathan, Oct. 4, 1782, in Cohasset, Mass.
Ephraim Adams, ch. William and Betsey, bp. ——— [*rec. between* Oct. 6, 1805 *and* June —, 1817], C.R.2.

PITCHER, Fisher A., h. Eliza, ——, 1784, G.R.1. [h. Eliza (Whittier), Oct. 4, 1786, in Stodard, N. H., P.R.162.]
Freddie, s. Hartshorn C. and Lydia Ann (Lancaster) (first w.), Sept. 28, 1864, P.R.108.
George, ch. Calvin and Joanna [(Prescott) P.R.172.], May 4, 1821.
George S., h. Sarah (Elms), July 19, 1808, G.R.1.
Georgia S., w. James H. Clark, Apr. 6, 1845, G.R.1.
Hartshorn C. (see Calvin Hartshorn Pitcher).
Helen Jane, ch. Calvin 2d and Lydia, Jan. 22, 1841.
Hellen Annette, ch. Calvin 2d and Lydia, Nov. 1, 1846.
Herbert, ch. William and Sarah, Jan. 18, 1840. [Herbert W., ch. William and Sarah W., G.R.1.]
Horatio Gates [dup. *omits* Gates], ch. Jonathan and Eliza [dup. Elizabeth], Apr. 23, 1807.
Isabella T., ch. Fisher A. and Eliza, Feb. 22, 1824. [Isabell T., w. T. D. Manning, d. Fisher A. and Eliza (Whittier), P.R.162.]
Joana, ch. Calvin and Joanna, Dec. 25, 1818. [Joanna, w. Jonathan Pitcher, d. Calvin and Joanna (Prescott), P.R.172.]
John W., Aug. 10, 1842, P.R.162.
Jonathan, h. Elizabeth, June 20, 1777, in Warwick.
Jonathan, ch. Jonathan and Elizabeth, Aug. 31, 1812.
Jonathan, ch. Jonathan and Elizabeth, Nov. 16, 1815.
Josiah Ellis, ch. Calvin and Joanna [(Prescott) P.R.172.], Apr. 30, 1840.
Louise [————], w. O. W., Jan. 6, 1844, G.R.1.
Luther A., ch. Fisher A. and Eliza [(Whittier) P.R.162.], Feb. 15, 1816.
Lydia [————], w. Calvin, Mar. 12, 1819, G.R.12.
Lydia Edith (see Edith).
Marie Louise, ch. William and Sarah, Aug. 14, 1837. [Maria Louise, ch. William and Sarah W., G.R.1.]
Marietta, ch. William and Sarah [Sarah W., G.R.1.], Jan. 31, 1845.
Mary E., ch. Jonathan and Elizabeth, June 29, 1817.
Mary Elizabeth, ch. Jonathan and Eliza [dup. Elizabeth], Oct. 27, 1808.
Mary Elizabeth, ch. Calvin and Joanna, Feb. 13, 1817. [w. Robert Pote, d. Calvin and Joanna (Prescott), P.R.172.]
Nancy, ch. Calvin and Joanna, Apr. 3, 1827. [Nancy M., w. William A. White, d. Calvin and Joanna (Prescott), P.R.172.]

PITCHER, Olivia Maria [———], w. T. W., ———, 1825, G.R.1.
Oscar, ch. William and Sarah, June 19, 1843. [Oscar W., h. Louise, G.R.1.]
Ralph, s. Hartshorn C. and Lucy Adella (Lancaster) (second w.), Apr. 22, 1878, P.R.108.
Sally, ch. Calvin and Joanna, June 19, 1823. [Sally W., w. Noah M. Mathews, d. Calvin and Joanna (Prescott), P.R.172.]
Susan Jane, ch. Jonathan and Elizabeth, ——— [*rec. after ch. b.* Mar. 29, 1823].
Tamesin F., ch. Fisher A. and Eliza, Dec. 4, 1827. [Tamzen W., w. Albert D. Mathews, d. Fisher A. and Eliza (Whittier), P.R.162.]
Thomas W., ch. Fisher A. and Eliza [(Whittier) P.R.162.], Nov. 15, 1830.
William, h. Sarah (Winslow), Dec. 11, 1807, G.R.1.
William H. H., ch. Jonathan and Elizabeth, Oct. 10, 1813.
Wilmot, ch. Calvin 2d and Lydia, Nov. 22, 1842.

PLUMMER, Elizabeth D., w. Calvin S. Hervey, Jan. 16, 1826, P.R.25.

POND, Wealthy Ann, w. Wooster Parker, ———, 1815, G.R.1.

POOR, Andrew P., ———, 1841, G.R.1.
Annabellah Sarah (see Annabellah Sarah Swan).
Benjamin Jr. (see Benj[amin] Poor Swan).
Benjamin (see Benj[amin] Poor Swan).
Benjamin Varnum, ch. James and Ann, June 19, 1818.
Benjamin Varnum, ch. James and Ann, bp. Aug. 26, 1821, C.R.2.
Carrie E., w. [Percy A.] Sanborn, ———, 1845, G.R.1.
Charles Varnum, ch. William, Nov. 1, 1817. [s. William and Sally (Farington), Nov. 2, P.R.142.]
Clarance Osgood, ch. William O. and w., Apr. 28, 1844. [Clarence Osgood Poor, s. William Osgood and L. H., P.R.142. Clarence Osgood Poor, h. Isabella (Perry), s. William Osgood and Lucretia McClure (Hunter), P.R.143.]
Clarissa Prescott, d. William and Sally (Farington), July 10, 1812, in E. Andover, P.R.142.
Clementine N. [———], w. Hollis M. A., July 22, 1836, G.R.1.
Cora V., w. M. A. Stephenson, d. Levi M. and Abbie G., Aug. 31, 1868, G.R.1.
Dolly Joanna (see Dolly Joanna Swan).
Eliza M. [———] [w. John], ———, 1812, G.R.1.

POOR, Francis Farrington, ch. William, Aug. 26, 1821. [Francis Farington Poor, s. William and Sally (Farington), P.R.142.]
Isabella Gordon, ch. William O. and w., June 3, 1859. [ch. William O. and Lucretia H., June 3, 1858, G.R.I. d. William Osgood and Lucretia McClure (Hunter), June 3, 1858, P.R.143.]
James Johnson, ch. James and Ann, bp. Aug. 26, 1821, C.R.2.
John [h. Maria G., h. Eliza M.], ——, 1804, G.R.I.
John, ——, 1871, G.R.I.
John H., ——, 1846, G.R.I.
Lovina Walton [? m.], ——, 1845, G.R.I.
Lydia Tyler (see Lydia Tyler Poor Swan).
Maria G. [————] [w. John], ——, 1806, G.R.I.
Nancy Parker, d. William and Sally (Farington), May 18, 1815, in E. Andover, P.R.142.
Nina Foster, ch. Clarence O. and Isabella J., bp. May 6, 1877, C.R.2.
Sally Kimball, d. William and Sally (Farington), Feb. 12, 1811, in E. Andover, P.R.142.
Sarah, d. William and Sally (Farington), Mar. 26, 1808, in E. Andover, P.R.142.
Walter Osgood, ch. Clarence O. and Isabella J., bp. May 6, 1877, C.R.2.
William, h. Sally (Farington), Sept. 5, 1776, in Andover, Mass., P.R.142.
William O., Sept. 1, 1809, G.R.I. [William Osgood Poor, h. L. H., s. William and Sally (Farington), in E. Andover, P.R.142. William Osgood Poor, h. Lucretia McClure (Hunter), s. William and Sally (Farrington), in E. Andover, P.R.143.]
——, s. B. N., Sept. 18, 1848, P.R.123.
——, d. James, Sept. 20, 1849, P.R.123.

PORTER, Abby C., w. Hon. Albert Pilsbury, Mar. 15, 1817, G.R.I.
Catharine, ch. Robert P. and Roxanna, bp. June 27, 1802, in Mt. Ephraim, C.R.2.
Elizabeth, ch. Robert P. and Roxanna, bp. June 27, 1802, in Mt. Ephraim, C.R.2.
Greenleaf, ch. John and Almira, Jan. 21, 1838.
Hellen, ch. John and Almira, Oct. 21, 1835.
Josiah, ch. Robert P. and Roxanna, bp. June 27, 1802, in Mt. Ephraim, C.R.2.

POTE, A. E., Nov. 12, 1834, G.R.I.
Caroline Augusta, ch. Robert P. and w., June 11, 1826.

POTE, Charles, ch. Robert P. and w., Oct. 25, 1819.
Charles B., ch. Robert and Mary Elizabeth, June 12, 1844.
Edward Augustus, ch. Robert and Mary Elizabeth, Nov. 12, 1834.
Elizabeth Ann, ch. Robert and Mary Elizabeth, Mar. 3, 1836.
Fanny, ch. Robert P. and w., Mar. 19, 1817.
George Pitcher, ch. Robert and Mary Elizabeth, June 4, 1842.
Harriet Jane, ch. Henry and Racheal, June 4, 1831.
Henry Gamaliel, ch. Henry and Racheal, Mar. 23, 1826.
Jane, ch. Robert P. and w., Jan. 17, 1822.
Joseph William, ch. Henry and Racheal, Feb. 23, 1833.
Julia Elizabeth, ch. Robert P. and w., July 30, 1829.
Mary Abigal, ch. Henry and Racheal, Sept. 28, 1828.
Mary Ann, ch. Robert P. and w., Mar. 30, 1809.
Robert, ch. Robert P. and w., Apr. 12, 1814.
Sarah Jane, ch. Robert and Mary Elizabeth, Mar. 15, 1840.
William, ch. Robert P. and w., May 27, 1811.

POTTLE, Alice E. [———], w. Nathaniel J., ———, 1869, G.R.1.
Arbella, ch. William and Elisabeth, July 24, 1858.
Ellen, ch. William and Elisabeth, Oct. 2, 1850.
Emerline, ch. William and Elisabeth, Sept. 25, 1839, in Perry.
George A., ch. William and Elisabeth, Jan. 13, 1845.
Lizzie F., ch. William and Elisabeth, June 8, 1848. [June 8, 1847, P.R.123.]
Nathaniel J., h. Alice E., ———, 1867, G.R.1.
William F., ch. William and Elisabeth, Sept. 28, 1842.

POWER, Catherine, w. William Godfrey Hill, ———, 1828, in Lismore, Ire., G.R.1.

PRATT, Ida Hayford, Oct. 4, 1875, G.R.1.

PRENTISS, Lydia, w. Rev. W[illia]m Frothingham, Apr. 11, 1790, G.R.1. [second w. Rev. William Frothingham, in Reading, P.R.90.]
Rebecca, Aug. 25, 1794, G.R.1.

PRESCOTT, Georgia [———], w. Samuel N., ———, 1844, G.R.1.

PRICE, Henry Naaman, ch. Naaman and Eliza, Feb. 4, 1832.

PRINCE, Emma Albertern Augusta, ch. Isaac and Martha, bp. May 5, 1861, C.R.2.
Mary Elizabeth, d. Joseph, bp. Mar. 2, 1834, C.R.2.
William Joseph, inf. Isaac and Martha, bp. June 4, 1854, C.R.2.

QUIMBY, Ann Elizabeth, ch. Robert W. and Hannah, ———
  [*rec. between ch. b.* Oct. —, 1836 *and ch. b.* Oct. 24, 1845].
Arelia Ann, ch. William and Apha, Nov. 11, 1819.
Augusta S. (see Susan Augusta).
Aurelia Ann (see Arelia Ann).
Charles Giles, ch. Robert W. and Hannah, Oct. —, 1836.
Dan[ie]l [Dan¹ *written in pencil*], ch. Jonathan and Susanna, ———.
Elizabeth Augusta (see Lizzie Augusta).
Ellen Adelaide, ch. William and Apha, Sept. 24, 1832.
Frances Augusta, ch. William and Apha, Aug. 19, 1830.
George A., ch. Phineas P. and Susanah, June 8, 1841. [George Albert, h. Rose A. (———) Quimby, h. Adelaide E. (Chase), s. Phineas P. and Susanna Burnham (Haraden), P.R.118.]
Herbert Converse, ch. William and Apha, Nov. 26, 1840.
John Haraden, ch. Phineas P. and Susanah, Feb. 14, 1829. [h. Annie M. (Noyes), s. Phineas P. and Susanna Burnham (Haraden), P.R.118.]
Julia Maria, ch. William and Apha, Aug. 22, 1821.
Kate Chase, ch. George A. and Adelaide E., Mar. 22, 1887. [Katharine Chase Quimby, d. George Albert and Adelaide E. (Chase), P.R.118.]
Lizzie Augusta, ch. George A. and Adelaide E., Apr. 21, 1888. [Elizabeth Augusta, w. Charles Chipman Pineo, d. George Albert and Adelaide E. (Chase), P.R.118.]
Mary Elisabeth, ch. William and Apha, Sept. 25, 1824.
Olive Francis, ch. Robert W. and Hannah, July 19, 1834.
Pheneas P. [Pheneas P. *written in pencil*], ch. Jonathan and Susanna, ———. [Phineas P., h. Susanna B. [(Haraden)], Feb. 16, 1802, G.R.1. Phineas P., h. Susanna Burnham (Haraden), Feb. 16, 1802, P.R.118.]
Robert White, ch. Jonathan and Susanna, Dec. 11, 1804.
Rose A. [———], w. Geo[rge] A., June 3, 1842, G.R.1.
Sally [Sally *written in pencil*], ch. Jonathan and Susanna, ———.
Sarah Elisabeth, ch. William and Apha, Oct. 8, 1827.
Susan Augusta, ch. Phineas P. and Susanah, Mar. 26, 1833. [w. James W. Frederick, d. Phineas P. and Susanna Burnham (Haraden), P.R.118. Augusta S., second w. James Woodbury Frederick, P.R.120.]
Susan Elizabeth, ch. Robert W. and Hannah, Aug. 26, 1832.
Towle [Towle *written in pencil*], ch. Jonathan and Susanna, ———.

QUIMBY, W[illia]m [W^m *written in pencil*], ch. Jonathan and Susanna, ———. [William, Apr. 30, 1792, G.R.I.]
William Edward, ch. William and Apha, Jan. 16, 1837.
William Henry, ch. Phineas P. and Susanah [S. B., G.R.I.
Susanna Burnham (Haraden), P.R.118.], Apr. 19, 1831.
W[illia]m Henry, ch. Robert W. and Hannah, Oct. 24, 1845.
William Henry, ch. John H. and Annie (Noyes), Oct. 12, 1863. [h. Annie D. (Blodgett), s. John Haraden and Annie M. (Noyes), P.R.118.]

QUINLAN, Elizabeth [? m.], Jan. 10, 1810, G.R.I.

RACKLIFF, Martha A. [———], w. Samuel N., June 11, 1846, G.R.I.
Samuel N., h. Martha A., July 29, 1849, G.R.I.

RANDALL, John M., h. Lena May, May 5, 1870, G.R.I.
Lena May [———], w. John M., June 8, 1864, G.R.I.

RANKIN, Desire E., w. Capt. William Crockett, Apr. 16, 1834, G.R.I.
Elmer Irving, s. Walter B. and Charlotte C. (Kelly), May 24, 1866, P.R.145.
Kate Laura, w. Elmer Alfred Sherman, d. Walter B. and Charlotte C. (Kelly), Mar. 7, 1864, P.R.145.
Laura A. [w. Benjamin Kelley], May 16, 1840, G.R.I.
Mary E. [w. Benjamin Kelley], Sept. 6, 1842, G.R.I.
Walter B., h. Charlotte C. [(Kelley)], Feb. 7, 1836, G.R.I.

RARIDEN, John, ch. Michael and Ellen, June 4, 1851.
Mary E., ch. Michael and Ellen, Apr. 12, 1855.
Michael Jr., ch. Michael and Ellen, Apr. 12, 1849. [Rairaden, Apr. 8, P.R.123.]
Tho[ma]s J., ch. Michael and Ellen, Aug. 18, 1858.
William M., ch. Michael and Ellen, June 30, 1853.

RAYMOND, Eliza Jane, ch. Freeman C. and Mary Jane, Oct. 12, 1827.
Freeman Stewart, ch. Freeman C. and Mary Jane, July 8, 1830.
Louisa Ann, ch. Freeman C. and Mary Jane, Sept. 20, 1828.
———, s. W[illia]m H., Oct. 24, 1847, P.R.123.

READ (see Reed), Arthur Warren, [twin] s. George and Helen (Stanwood), Feb. 3, 1873, P.R.166.
Charles, h. Rosina (Blanchard), s. Nathan and Elizabeth J., ———, 1809, G.R.I.
Charles Julius, ch. Charles and Rosina [(Blanchard) P.R.166.], Apr. 2, 1841.

READ, Charlotte V., ch. Nathan and Elizabeth J., ——, 1811, G.R.1.
Clarence Eugene, s. George and Helen (Stanwood), Dec. 6, 1880, P.R.166.
Edward V., ch. Nathan and Elizabeth J., ——, 1806, G.R.1.
Elizabeth H. [*sic*, ? W.], ch. Nathan and Elizabeth J., ——, 1793, G.R.1.
Elizabeth J., ch. Cha[rle]s and Rosina, ——, 1858, G.R.1. [Elizabeth Jeffry Read, d. Charles and Rosina (Blanchard), Aug. 9, P.R.166.]
Elizabeth W. (see Elizabeth H.).
George, ch. Nathan and Elizabeth J., ——, 1803, G.R.1.
George Tilden, s. Charles and Rosina (Blanchard), Oct. 19, 1846, P.R.166.
Grace S., Feb. 3, 1873, G.R.1. [Grace Stanwood Read, [twin] d. George and Helen (Stanwood), P.R.166.]
Hannah E., ch. Cha[rle]s and Rosina, ——, 1851, G.R.1. [Hannah Elizabeth, d. Charles and Rosina (Blanchard), May 25, P.R.166.]
Helen L., ch. Cha[rle]s and Rosina, ——, 1849, G.R.1. [Helen Latitia, d. Charles and Rosina (Blanchard), Jan. 25, P.R.166.]
Joseph Bowditch, ch. Charles and Rosina [(Blanchard) P.R.166.], July 10, 1839.
Louise Johnson, d. George and Helen (Stanwood), Feb. 9, 1891, P.R.166.
Mary Jane, ch. Charles and Rosina [(Blanchard) P.R.166.], Nov. 6, 1842.
Narcissa Willmaetta, d. Charles and Rosina (Blanchard), Dec. 28, 1855, P.R.166.
Nathan, h. Elizabeth (Jeffry), July 2, 1759, in Warren, Mass., G.R.1.
Norman Allen, s. George and Helen (Stanwood), Jan. 4, 1886, P.R.166.
Rosetta Ellen, d. Charles and Rosina (Blanchard), June 11, 1853, P.R.166.
William J., ch. Nathan and Elizabeth J., ——, 1800, G.R.1.
W[illia]m Jeffrey, ch. Charles and Rosina, Apr. 30, 1838. [William Jeffry Read, s. Charles and Rosina (Blanchard), Aug. 30, P.R.166.]
William Jeffrey, ch. Charles and Rosina [(Blanchard) P.R.166.], Mar. 21, 1845.
Willis Haward, s. Charles and Rosina (Blanchard), Sept. 7, 1865, P.R.166.

RECORD, Olive G., first w. Ebenezer Newell Jr., ——, 1810, in Hebron, P.R.81.

REDMAN, Abba B., ch. John B. and Jane, July 20, 1845.
Alvah S., h. Eliza J., h. Alvira N., Oct. 6, 1828, G.R.1.
Alvira N. [——], w. Alvah S., Nov. 5, 1840, G.R.1.
Eliza J. [——], w. Alvah S., Dec. 8, 1835, G.R.1.
Elvira N. (see Alvira N.).
Mary Etta, May 16, 1868, G.R.1.
Willie S., Oct. 4, 1861, G.R.1.

REED (see Read), Adaline, ch. George W. and Sally, Jan. 17, 1832.
Albert D., ch. George W. and Sally, Oct. 21, 1844.
Ann M., ch. George W. and Sally, Sept. 20, 1842.
Charles, ch. George W. and Sally, Dec. 3, 1827.
Charles H., May 18, 1849, in Industry, G.R.1.
David, ch. Thomas and Sally, Feb. 1, 1796.
Eliza Ann, ch. George W. and Sally, Feb. 9, 1835.
Franklin Patterson (Read), ch. George W. and Sally, Sept. 8, 1830.
George Henry, ch. George W. and Sally, Sept. 19, 1833.
George Washington, ch. Thomas and Sally, Apr. 13, 1803.
James, ch. Thomas and Sally, Dec. 31, 1805.
Jane S., ch. George W. and Sally, Feb. 15, 1837.
Louise (see Louise Riggs).
Lucy Ann, ch. George W. and Sally, Mar. 12, 1839. [w. Otis B. Woods, Mar. 12, 1840, G.R.1.]
Polly, ch. Thomas and Sally, Mar. 9, 1801.
Sally, ch. Thomas and Sally, July 2, 1798.
Thomas, ch. Thomas and Sally, Aug. 20, 1793.
Thomas, ch. George W. and Sally, Apr. 28, 1828.

RHOADES (see Rhodes), Catherine (see Catherine Calderwood).

RHODES (see Rhoades), Lois, w. William Colburn Marshall, Oct. 10, 1837 [dup. 1838], G.R.1.

RICE, Sophia (see Sophia R. Caldwell).

RICH, Mercy [——], w. Nelson, Aug. 13, 1820, G.R.1.
Nelson, h. Mercy, Mar. 26, 1812, G.R.1.
Perry Frank, ch. John Frank and Mary Perry, Feb. 19, 1887.

RICHARDS, Charles T., ch. Samuel and Nancy, Apr. 19, 1838.
Geo[rge] F., Jan. 14, 1873, G.R.1.

RICHARDS, John H. B., ch. Samuel and Nancy, Oct. 1, 1835.
Mary Jane, ch. Samuel and Nancy, Oct. 28, 1833. [w. Luther
   A. Pitcher, G.R.I.]
Sylvanus G., ch. Samuel and Nancy, Mar. 3, 1841.
———, s. James, Nov. 22, 1849, P.R.123.

RICHARDSON, Cha[rle]s Oscar, ch. William B. and Lydia,
   Sept. 26, 1841.
Edwin R., ch. William B. and Lydia, Feb. 3, 1836.
James W[illia]m, ch. William B. and Lydia, May 12, 1838.
Joseph M., ch. William B. and Lydia, Aug. 26, 1843.
Rosina, ch. William B. and Lydia, Nov. 23, 1839.
Zelia, ch. William B. and Lydia, May 19, 1846.
———, d. W[illia]m, July 20, 1847, P.R.123.

RIGGS, Annie T., w. Jacob K. Dennett, d. Asa Franklin and
   Louise (Reed), Dec. 23, 1865, P.R.103.
Asa, h. Louise, Jan. 5, 1827, G.R.I. [Asa Franklin Riggs, h.
   Louise (Reed), P.R.103.]
Frank Andrews, h. Harriet Chapin, s. Asa Franklin and Louise
   (Reed), Aug. 11, 1862, P.R.103.
Jennie E., w. Fred G. Carter, d. Asa Franklin and Louise
   (Reed), Jan. 29, 1855, P.R.103.
Julia C., w. Jordan W. Coombs, d. Asa Franklin and Louise
   (Reed), Apr. 29, 1854, P.R.103.
Louise [———], w. Asa, Apr. 13, 1828, G.R.I. [Louise (Reed),
   w. Asa Franklin Riggs, P.R.103.]
Mary B., w. Roscoe W. Cottrell, d. Asa Franklin and Louise
   (Reed), Feb. 14, 1860, P.R.103.

RINK, Charles Frederick, ch. Charles and Nannette, Sept. 16,
   1857.
Emile Otto, ch. Charles and Nannette, May 16, 1859.

RITCHIE, Margaret, w. Ammi Cutter Sibley, June 14, 1847,
   G.R.I.

ROBBINS, Augustus M., h. Susie J., Sept. 1, 1852, G.R.I.
Elizabeth K., w. Paul De Laney of Cameron, Mo., d. Levi
   Lindley and Matilda Miller (Wight), June 1, 1879,
   P.R.124.
Emerson, July 11, 1838, G.R.I.
Harriet E., w. Rev. A. T. Ringold, d. Levi Lindley and Matilda
   Miller (Wight), Nov. 22, 1871, P.R.124.
Ida, ch. ——— (w. Lewis), June 2, 1885, in Poor House.
Laforest L., h. Bertha Knowlton, s. Levi Lindley and Matilda
   Miller (Wight), Aug. 1, 1874, P.R.124.

ROBBINS, Levi L., h. Matilda M., Oct. 5, 1840, G.R.13. [Levi Lindley Robbins, h. Matilda Miller (Wight), in Union, P.R.124.]
Lilian P., w. F. Wallace Chase of Unity, d. Levi Lindley and Matilda Miller (Wight), Dec. 9, 1867, P.R.124.
Marianna, d. Levi Lindley and Matilda Miller (Wight), Sept. 29, 1869, P.R.124.
Matilda M. [―――], w. Levi L., May 1, 1845, G.R.13. [Matilda Miller (Wight), w. Levi Lindley Robbins, May 5, P.R.124.]
Nathan, ch. ――― (w. Lewis), Nov. 10, 1887, in Poor House.
Sarah L., d. Levi Lindley and Matilda Miller (Wight), Nov. 29, 1881, P.R.124.

ROBERTS, Daniel J., "Co. I. 26th Regt. Me. Vol.," h. Drusilla, h. Laura J., Apr. 2, 1826, G.R.1.
John M., Jan. 11, 1870, G.R.1.
Laura J. [―――], w. Daniel J., Jan. 8, 1827, G.R.1.
Nettie M. [―――], w. W. J., June 5, 1872, G.R.13.

ROBERTSON, Mary L. [? m.], June 2, 1878, G.R.1.

ROBINSON, Annie M., w. William F. Patterson, d. Benjamin and Ellen (Crowell), Aug. 30, 1874, P.R.37.
Arthur, ch. John and Lucy, Mar. 2, 1846.
Augustus H., s. David and Ann (Sconse), Mar. 9, 1854, P.R.36.
Benjamin, ch. David and Ann [(Sconse) P.R.36.], Sept. 3, 1841.
Bennie, s. Benjamin and Ellen (Crowell), Nov. 14, 1878, P.R.37.
David G., ch. David and Ann [(Sconse) P.R.36.], May 6, 1837.
Elsy J., w. Elijah M. Shuman, May 16, 1828, P.R.48.
Geo[rge] Ross, ch. David and Ann [(Sconse) P.R.36.], Aug. 7, 1839.
James Henry, ch. David and Ann [(Sconse) P.R.36.], Oct. 2, 1843.
Jane, d. David and Ann (Sconse), Dec. 15, 1833, P.R.36.
John, ch. John and Lucy, Sept. 17, 1839.
Katie E., w. Roy F. Copeland, d. Benjamin and Ellen (Crowell), Dec. 11, 1879, P.R.37.
Lorana, ch. John and Lucy, Oct. 21, 1824 [? 3 *over* 2].
Mary, w. John Albert Lancaster, Jan. 15, 1826, P.R.108.
Mary E., d. Benjamin and Ellen (Crowell), July 14, 1868, P.R.37.
Mary Elizabeth, ch. David and Ann [(Sconse) P.R.36.], Nov. 28, 1845.
Mary Jane, ch. John and Lucy, Jan. 5, 1842.

ROBINSON, Pliny, ch. John and Lucy, Feb. 5, 1844.
Thomas, h. Fannie A. (Michales), s. Benjamin and Ellen (Crowell), Jan. 31, 1871, P.R.37.
William A., s. Benjamin and Ellen (Crowell), June 24, 1881, P.R.37.
W[illia]m Augustus, ch. David and Ann [(Sconse) P.R.36.], Apr. 2, 1835.

RODERICK, Irvin Levi, Nov. 12, 1887, G.R.1.

ROGERS, Almira E., second w. John P. Bagley, d. Martin and Sarah M. (Grinnell), Mar. 12, 1824, P.R.136.
Byron Martin, h. Annie Adelia Brier, s. William Thomas and Frances Augusta (West), Dec. 28, 1858, P.R.135.
Caroline J. F. [F. *crossed out*], ch. Martin and Sally, Dec. 17, 1826. [Caroline J., w. ——— Howard, Dec. 15, 1827, G.R.1. Caroline J., w. ——— Sargent, w. ——— Howard, d. Martin and Sarah M. (Grinnell), Dec. 17, 1826, P.R.136.]
Catharine, ch. Robert and Mary, Aug. 2, 1812.
Charles Augustus, s. William Thomas and Frances Augusta (West), Jan. 19, 1850, P.R.135.
Charles William, s. William Thomas and Frances Augusta (West), Dec. 3, 1853, P.R.135.
Maria E., ch. Martin and Sally, Feb. 18, 1828. [w. Capt. Pettingill, d. Martin and Sarah M. (Grinnell), Feb. 18, 1829, P.R.136.]
Martin, h. Sarah M. (Grinnell), Apr. 13, 1784, P.R.136.
Martin C., s. Martin and Sarah M. (Grinnell), Aug. 28, 1819, P.R.136.
Mary A., w. Joshua Cottrell (brother of Simon), w. Axel Hayford, d. Martin and Sarah M. (Grinnell), Mar. 24, 1818, P.R.136.
Phebe G., w. Ja[me]s McCrillis, d. Martin and Sarah M. (Grinnell), July 22, 1813, P.R.136.
Sarah P., w. Simon Cottrell, w. John P. Bagley, d. Martin and Sarah M. (Grinnell), May 29, 1815, P.R.136.
William Thomas, h. Frances Augusta (West), Oct. 26, 1821, in Marshfield, Mass., P.R.135. [s. Martin and Sarah M. (Grinnell), P.R.136.]
———, s. Capt. Martin Jr., Nov. 23, 1847, P.R.123.

ROIX, Abbie [———], w. David, Mar. 24, 1835, G.R.1.
Albert A., ———, 1839, G.R.1.
Alfred M., Sept. 21, 1828, G.R.1.
Cora B. [? m.], ———, 1855, G.R.1.

ROIX, David, Capt., h. Abbie, July 10, 1826, G.R.1.
Luella J. [———, ———], w. William A., ———, 1852, G.R.1.
Mary L. [? m.], Jan. 26, 1855, G.R.1.
William A., ———, 1851, G.R.1.
William R., Apr. 7, 1820, G.R.1.
———, d. Eligah, Jan. 26, 1848, P.R.123.

ROLERSON (see Rollerson), Caroline [———], w. Thomas P., Feb. 11, 1828, G.R.1.
Charles A., ch. Joseph and Clara, Dec. 27, 1832.
Clara Frances, ch. Joseph and Clara, Feb. 13, 1839.
Lizzie, d. Thomas P. and Caroline, Sept. 16, 1863, G.R.1.
Mary Francis, ch. Joseph and Clara, Apr. 27, 1836.
Sarah Theodosa, ch. Joseph and Clara, July 13, 1841.
Sarah Theodosa, ch. Joseph and Clara, Oct. 10, 1844.
Susan M., ch. Joseph and Clara, Feb. 13, 1835.

ROLLERSON (see Rolerson), ———, s. Thomas (Irishman), Feb. 8, 1848, P.R.123.

ROSS, Andrew Jackson, ch. Hugh and Eliza, Mar. 15, 1815.
Elizabeth S., ch. Hugh and Eliza, Sept. 28, 1829.
Evelina, ch. Hugh and Eliza, Sept. 13, 1827.
Hannah, ch. Hugh and Eliza, ——— [rec. after ch. b. Oct. 27, 1832].
Hugh Jr., ch. Hugh and Eliza, Oct. 29, 1821.
James, ch. Hugh and Eliza, ——— [rec. between ch. b. Mar. 15, 1815 and ch. b. Oct. 29, 1821].
John Clifford, ch. Hugh and Eliza, Feb. 3, 1809, in Prospect.
Richard S., ch. Hugh and Eliza, Oct. 27, 1832.
Simon, ch. Hugh and Eliza, Aug. 17, 1824.
Susan, ch. Hugh and Eliza, Apr. 12, 1812, in Prospect.

ROUCKS, Alfred, ch. William and w., Sept. 21, 1828.
Charles, ch. William and w., Jan. 8, 1817.
David, ch. William and w., July 10, 1826.
John, ch. William and w., Aug. 15, 1821.
William, ch. William and w., Apr. 7, 1819.

ROWE, Alfred, ch. Robert and Susan, July 15, 1834.
Almira, ch. Peter 2d and Esther, Mar. 28, 1838.
Christopher C., Jan. 26, 1835, G.R.1.
Cyrus, ch. Peter and Joanna H., Nov. 14, 1808, in Standish.
Fanny, ch. Peter and Joanna H., ——— [rec. before ch. b. Nov. 14, 1808], in Standish.
Fanny, ch. Robert and Susan, Oct. 29, 1845. [Fanny L., G.R.4.]
Harrison, ch. Robert and Susan, Jan. 6, 1839.
James L., ch. Peter 2d and Esther, Oct. 31, 1840, in Monroe.

BELFAST BIRTHS

ROWE, Jefferson, ch. Robert and Susan, Sept. 3, 1841.
Joanna, ch. Robert and Susan, Aug. 23, 1835. [w. ——— Brewster, G.R.4.]
Julia A., w. ——— McLean, ———, 1850, G.R.4.
Mary, w. Robert R. Swett, June 30, 1806, in Gorham, P.R.130.
Robert, ———, 1804, G.R.4.
Susan [? m.], ———, 1807, G.R.4.
William, ch. Robert and Susan, May 11, 1843.

RUSS (see Rust), Charles Austin, ch. John and Sally, May 2, 1808.
George Ulmer, ch. John and Sally, Dec. 1, 1800.
John Augustus, ch. John and Sally, Nov. 3, 1804.
John D., s. William and Nancy, Mar. 10, 1825, P.R.44.
Joseph Reed, ch. John and Sally, Sept. 25, 1802.
Martha R., d. William and Nancy, Mar. 10, 1821, P.R.44.
Mary E., d. William and Nancy, Sept. 11, 1827, P.R.44.
Mary Elizabeth, ch. John and Sally, Nov. 3, 1809.
Nancy [———], w. William, May 15, 1801, P.R.44.
Theodore, ch. John and Sally, Aug. 11, 1806.
William, h. Nancy, h. Mary W. (Farrar), June 16, 1796, P.R.44.
———, s. George U., July 1, 1847, P.R.123.

RUSSELL, Frederick, h. Susan F., Nov. 1, 1821, G.R.1.
Ralph D., s. Geo[rge] A. and Angelia E., Dec. 22, 1873.
Susan F. [———], w. Frederick, Feb. 27, 1820, G.R.1.

RUST (see Russ), Albert Smith, s. William (Russ) and Nancy, Mar. 6, 1830, P.R.44.
Alonzo, s. William (Russ) and Mary W. (Farrar), Apr. 28, 1833, P.R.44.
Augusta, d. William (Russ) and Mary W. (Farrar), May 8, 1839, P.R.44.
Emma, w. Silas Brown, d. William (Russ) and Mary W. (Farrar), Mar. 26, 1850, P.R.44.
Eugene, ———, 1851, G.R.1.
Frederick W., ———, 1848, G.R.1.
Jane (see Margaret J. Shute).
Joseph, s. William (Russ) and Nancy, Dec. 19, 1822, P.R.44.
Margaret J. (see Margaret J. Shute).
Maria A., w. ——— Pierce, ———, 1844, G.R.1.
Martha J. [? m.], ———, 1820, G.R.1.
Nancy, d. William (Russ) and Nancy, Apr. 20, 1832, P.R.44.
Oscar, s. William (Russ) and Mary W. (Farrar), Oct. 9, 1837, P.R.44.
William M., ———, 1818, G.R.1. [Russ, s. William and Nancy, Dec. 14, P.R.44.]

RYAN (see Ryon), Adelaide, d. Lewis H. and Martha (Hopkins), ——, 1857, P.R.163.
Alice, d. Lewis H. and Martha (Hopkins), ——, 1862, P.R.163.
Ann Maria, d. William and Nancy (McKeen), July 25, 1820, P.R.163.
Benjaman Franklin, h. Sylvia Ames, s. William and Nancy (McKeen), Jan. 5, 1828, P.R.163.
Catherine, ch. John, Oct. 2, 1778, P.R.10.
Charles, ch. John, July 17, 1783, P.R.10.
Charles F., s. William and Nancy (McKeen), Nov. 13, 1822, P.R.163.
Edwin, s. Lewis H. and Martha (Hopkins), July —, 1855, P.R.163.
Ezra, ch. John, Jan. 18, 1781, P.R.10.
Franklin G., Aug. 6, 1866, G.R.1. [s. George Flowers and Ellen P. (Maddocks), P.R.163.]
George F., Feb. 11, 1832, G.R.1. [George Flowers Ryan, h. Ellen P. (Maddocks), s. William and Nancy (McKeen), P.R.163.]
Irvin D., s. Edward S. and Abbie, Nov. 13, 1879, G.R.1.
James, ch. John, Mar. 21, 1773 [in Edgecomb], P.R.10.
John, ch. John, Feb. 10, 1776, P.R.10.
Lewis H., h. Martha (Hopkins), s. William and Nancy (McKeen), Nov. 26, 1829, P.R.163.
Lillian V., d. George Flowers and Ellen P. (Maddocks), Dec. 12, 1862, P.R.163.
Lucie E., d. George Flowers and Ellen P. (Maddocks), Oct. 15, 1864, P.R.163.
Lucy E., d. William and Nancy (McKeen), Dec. 24, 1825, P.R.163.
Luis, ch. John, Nov. 1, 1785, P.R.10.
Maria M., d. Lewis H. and Martha (Hopkins), ——, 1860, P.R.163.
Mary Edna, d. Lewis H. and Martha (Hopkins), Sept. 21, 1873, P.R.163.
Thomas E., h. Lydia Wyman, s. William and Nancy (McKeen), Jan. 13, 1833, P.R.163.
Thomas E., s. Thomas E. dec'd and Lydia Wyman, Mar. 9, 1863, P.R.163.
William, ch. John, June 7, 1788, P.R.10.
W[illia]m H., ——, 1781, G.R.1.
William Henry, h. Sarah (Cunningham), s. William and Nancy (McKeen), June 21, 1824, P.R.163.

RYDER, Alice C., d. Benjamin P. and Rebecca N. (Patterson), Aug. 10, 1850, P.R.49.
Alice C., d. Benjamin P. dec'd and Lucy W. Temple, Aug. 16, 1860, in Brewer, P.R.49.
Benj[amin] F., s. Benjamin P. and Rebecca N. (Patterson), Dec. 8, 1845, P.R.49.
Benj[ami]n P., ch. David and Hannah, Nov. 15, 1814. [h. Rebecca N. (Patterson), h. Lucy W. Temple, Nov. 15, 1813, in Chatham, P.R.49.]
David Jr., ch. David and Hannah, Oct. 12, 1816.
David, ——, 1817, G.R.1.
David D., s. Benjamin P. and Lucy W. Temple, Feb. 8, 1855, in Rockland, P.R.49.
Elijah Guy, s. Otis K. and Alma J. (Shuman), Dec. 29, 1885, P.R.35. [Guy Elijah, s. Otis K. and Alma Jane (Shuman), P.R.48.]
Ephriam D., ch. David and Hannah, Oct. 17, 1827 [*sic*, see Hannah J.]. [Capt., h. Eunice A. (Ames), Oct. 17, 1827, G.R.1.]
Frederick A., s. Benjamin P. and Rebecca N. (Patterson), Aug. 23, 1847, P.R.49.
Georgianna, ch. David Jr. and Sophrona, May 15, 1845.
Guy Elijah (see Elijah Guy).
Hannah J., ch. David and Hannah, May 17, 1828 [*sic*, see Ephriam D.].
Herbert R., h. Annie (Patterson), s. Otis K. and Alma J. (Shuman), Nov. 25, 1869, P.R.35. [Herbert Ramond Ryder, s. Otis K. and Alma Jane (Shuman), P.R.48.]
Jos[eph] H., ch. David and Hannah, Sept. 21, 1825.
Lena O., d. Otis K. and Alma J. (Shuman), Mar. 23, 1871, P.R.35. [Lena Orrie, d. Otis K. and Alma Jane (Shuman), P.R.48.]
Margarett Frances, w. Henry Cushman Gray, Dec. 2, 1838, in Vinal Haven, P.R.104.
Maria S., ch. David and Hannah, Aug. 27, 1818.
Mary Augusta, ch. David Jr. and Sophrona, Feb. 28, 1842.
Otis K., h. Alma J. (Shuman), Jan. 18, 1840, P.R.35. [s. Benjamin P. and Rebecca N. (Patterson), P.R.49.]
Rebecca T., d. Benjamin P. and Rebecca N. (Patterson), Nov. 10, 1852, P.R.49.
Sarah F., d. Benjamin P. and Lucy W. Temple, Oct. 24, 1856, P.R.49.
Sarah Mariah, d. Benjamin P. and Rebecca N. (Patterson), Oct. 2, 1842, P.R.49.
Simonne, ch. David and Hannah, Sept. 3, 1821.

RYDER, Thomas C., ch. David and Hannah, Aug. 23, 1823.
Viola E., w. Ross L. Stevens, d. Otis K. and Alma J. (Shuman), July 8, 1877, P.R.35. [Viola Elsie, d. Otis K. and Alma Jane (Shuman), P.R.48.]

RYON (see Ryan), Bridget, ch. John Jr. and Rachel, Jan. 22, 1811.
Catherine, ch. John Jr. and Rachel, Jan. 24, 1809.
Lucy, ch. John Jr. and Rachel, May 27, 1813.
Sally, ch. John Jr. and Rachel, June 27, 1804.

SALMOND, Agnes Calista, ch. William and Mary Jane, Dec. 31, 1817.
Edwin, ch. William and Mary Jane, May 6, 1829.
Eunice Bass, ch. William and Mary Jane, Dec. 9, 1819.
Josephine, ch. William and Mary Jane, Sept. 26, 1826.
Julia Antoinette, ch. William and Mary Jane, July 9, 1815.
Lavinia, ch. William and Mary Jane, Apr. 10, 1825.
Lucia [*sic*] Eugene, ch. William and Mary Jane, Dec. 27, 1832.
Mary Park, ch. William and Mary Jane, Oct. 10, 1813.
Urania Jane, ch. William and [dup. *adds* Mary] Jane, Dec. 9, 1812 [dup. 1811].
William Whitman, ch. William and Mary Jane, Feb. 18, 1822.

SANBORN, Eben M., h. Harriet A. (Johnson), s. Josiah and Zibiah P. (Fales), Apr. 25, 1843, P.R.83.
Essie May, d. Eben M. and Harriet A. (Johnson), Nov. 10, 1878, P.R.84.
Fred S., ———, 1874, G.R.1.
Josiah, h. Zibiah P. (Fales), Aug. 24, 1808, P.R.83.
Lena Ada, d. Eben M. and Harriet A. (Johnson), Oct. 29, 1872, P.R.84.
Madge Louise, twin d. Eben M. and Harriet A. (Johnson), Sept. 18, 1884, P.R.84.
Mildred L. [———], w. L. J., Feb. 10, 1885, G.R.1.
Milly Irma, d. Eben M. and Harriet A. (Johnson), Apr. 21, 1874, P.R.84.
Moses K., h. A. M. Phipps, s. Josiah and Zibiah P. (Fales), May 3, 1833, P.R.83.
Olive Anna, w. J. B. Payson, d. Josiah and Zibiah P. (Fales), Oct. 17, 1836, P.R.83.
Percy A., h. Carrie E. (Poor), s. Josiah and Zibiah P. (Fales), Feb. 10, 1849, P.R.83.
Ralph, twin s. Eben M. and Harriet A. (Johnson), Sept. 18, 1884, P.R.84.

SANBORN, Winnifred Johnson, d. Eben M. and Harriet A. (Johnson), July 29, 1888, P.R.84.

SARGEANT (see Sargent, Sergent), Sarah M., ch. Ignatius and Sarah F., Nov. 14, 1844.

SARGENT (see Sargeant, Sergent), Ann Morrill, ch. Herbert R. and Mary Elizabeth, Jan. 21, 1828. [w. ―――― Lothrop, Jan. 21, 1829, G.R.1.]
Benj[amin], Aug. 14, 1816, G.R.1.
Benjamin Butman, ch. John and Joanna, Apr. 28, 1813.
Charles Chapin (Sargeant), ch. Herbert R. and Mary Elizabeth, Feb. 7, 1843.
David, ch. John, Nov. 27, 1821.
Francs [sic] R. (Sargeant), ch. Herbert R. and Mary Elizabeth, Sept. 23, 1845.
George Herbert (Sargeant), ch. Herbert R. and Mary Elizabeth, Oct. 31, 1830.
Helen A. [――――], w. Samuel D., Sept. 11, 1857, G.R.1.
Joanna Butman, ch. John, Mar. 3, 1826.
Lucy F. (Sargeant), ch. Herbert R. and Mary Elizabeth, Oct. 30, 1832.
Margaret Shirley, ch. John, Nov. 2, 1827.
Mary, ch. John and Joanna, Mar. 30, 1817.
Mary E. (Sargeant), ch. Herbert R. and Mary Elizabeth, Sept. 8, 1836.
Mial Butman, ch. John and Joanna, Apr. 13, 1805.
Richard Butman, ch. John and Joanna, Sept. 19, 1809.
Samuel D., h. Helen A., Nov. 30, 1854, G.R.1.
Samuel Winthrop, ch. John and Joanna, Apr. 14, 1815.
Sarah Elizabeth, ch. John, May 26, 1823.
Thomas Woodbury, ch. John and Joanna, Mar. 3, 1807.
William, ch. John and Joanna, Dec. 19, 1810.
――――, s. Benjamin, Sept. 28, 1849, P.R.123.

SAUNDERS, Edward Washington, ch. Edward and Betsey, Mar. 4, 1833.
Mary Elizabeth, ch. Edward and Betsey, Nov. 28, 1834.
Susan Jane, ch. Edward and Betsey, Oct. 24, 1836.

SAVAGE, ――――, ch. Hiram and Lucy (d. John B. Redman), Apr. 20, 1847, P.R.123.

SAWYER, Benjamin, ch. Aaron and Rosanna, July 6, 1811.

SCENDLING, ――――, s. James and w., Mar. 22, 1848, P.R.123.

SENTER, Addiline, ch. Allenson and Sally, May 1, 1807.
Almira, ch. Isaac and Hannah, May 14, 1808.
German, ch. Isaac and Hannah, Oct. 19, 1810.
Hannah, ch. Isaac and Hannah, Aug. 26, 1802.
Isaac Newton, ch. Isaac and Hannah, July 28, 1806.
James M., ch. Isaac and Hannah, July 4, 1812.
Margret, ch. Isaac and Hannah, Dec. 8, 1804.
Sophia, ch. Isaac and Hannah, Oct. 23, 1799.

SERGENT (see Sargeant, Sargent), Polly, ch. Robert L. and Polly, Nov. 24, 1804.
Robert, ch. Robert L. and Polly, Mar. 6, 1803.

SEVENO, Francis Alexei, ch. Frances [sic] A. and Louisa (second w.), Apr. 19, 1846.
Mary E., ch. Frances [sic] A. and Louisa (second w.), Nov. 11, 1844.

SHALES, Alice G., d. Lendal T. and Emily P. (Woods), Sept. 27, 1877, P.R.152.
Emily [———], w. John, Aug. 27, 1818, G.R.2.
Lendall T., h. Emily P. (Woods), May 27, 1847, G.R.1. [Lendal T., P.R.152.]
William A., s. Lendal T. and Emily P. (Woods), Oct. 23, 1889, P.R.152.

SHAW, Ella Frances, ch. Maria A., bp. Dec. 3, 1858, C.R.2.
Francis A., "Co. F. 17 Rigt. Mass. Inft.," Dec. 17, 1831, G.R.13.
Hanson D., Apr. 20, 1827, G.R.1.
Mary [? m.], Feb. 21, 1826, G.R.1.
Mary A. [———], w. Thomas H., ———, 1823, G.R.5.
Mary Mariah, ch. James and Mary, bp. June 18, 1826, C.R.2.
Samuel F., ch. Job and Dorothy, Jan. 14, 1832.
Samuel Scammon Howard, ch. James and Mary, bp. June 18, 1826, C.R.2.
———, twin d. Joseph, Mar. 30, 1849, P.R.123.
———, twin s. Joseph, Mar. 30, 1849, P.R.123.
———, s. Dean, June 8, 1849, P.R.123.

SHEPARD (see Shepherd), Ann B. Hahn [———], w. John, Sept. 11, 1773, G.R.1.
John, Mar. 11, 1771, G.R.1.
John Frederick, s. Lewis F. and Sarah (Dow), Feb. 27, 1832, Exeter, N. H.
Lewis F., h. Sarah (Dow), ———, 1805, in Waldoborough. [Sept. 30, G.R.1.]

SHEPHERD (see Shepard), John Frederick, s. L. Frederick and w., bp. Oct. 7, 1838, C.R.2.

SHERMAN, Abigail Marion, ch. Nathan and Hannah, bp. Nov. 22, ―― [? 1835], C.R.2.
Elizabeth Augusta, ch. Nathan and Hannah, bp. Nov. 22, ―― [? 1835], C.R.2.
Henry, Capt., h. Temperance, ――, 1768, G.R.1.
Isaac H., h. Sarah G. Clark, Sept. 22, 1829, G.R.1.
Lucy Connor, ch. Nathan and Hannah, bp. Nov. 22, ―― [? 1835], C.R.2.
Raymond Richard, s. Elmer Alfred and Kate Laura (Rankin), Nov. 23, 1887, P.R.145.
Sarah G. Clark [――――], w. Isaac H., Nov. 12, 1833, G.R.1.
Temperance [――――], w. Capt. Henry, ――, 1752, G.R.1.
Thomas Franklin, ch. Nathan and Hannah, bp. Nov. 22, ―― [? 1835], C.R.2.
Walter Malcolm, s. Elmer Alfred and Kate Laura (Rankin), Feb. 15, 1891, P.R.145.
William Connor, ch. Nathan and Hannah, bp. Apr. 1, 1840, C.R.2.

SHIBLES, Albert H., h. Augusta F. (Gilman), s. Alexander and Julia A. (Maddocks), Dec. 29, 1834, P.R.161.
Alexander, h. Julia A. (Maddocks), Apr. 1, 1804, P.R.161.
Augusta A., w. William Gardner, d. Alexander and Julia A. (Maddocks), Mar. 18, 1832, P.R.161.
Cha[rle]s N., s. Alexander and Julia A. (Maddocks), Nov. 10, 1847, P.R.161.
Clara A., w. Cha[rle]s A. Merrill, d. Alexander and Julia A. (Maddocks), Nov. 1, 1843, P.R.161.
Florence M., w. Llewellyn Mahar, d. Alexander and Julia A. (Maddocks), May 14, 1855, P.R.161.
Julietta, w. James E. Mosher, d. Alexander and Julia A. (Maddocks), Aug. 6, 1840, P.R.161.
Laura E., d. Alexander and Julia A. (Maddocks), Nov. 2, 1848, P.R.161.
Leonora, d. Alexander and Julia A. (Maddocks), June 15, 1845, P.R.161.
Relief, d. Alexander and Julia A. (Maddocks), Feb. 22, 1837, P.R.161.

SHIRLEY, Betsey, ch. James and Mary, Feb. 1, 1809.
Hugh, ch. James and Mary, Nov. 12, 1796.
James, [twin] ch. James and Mary, May 9, 1804.
Jane, ch. James and Mary, Oct. 22, 1800.

SHIRLEY, John, ch. James and Mary, Oct. 30, 1801.
Margaret H., ch. James and Mary, Aug. 8, 1806.
Mary (see Polly).
Nancy, [twin] ch. James and Mary, May 9, 1804.
Polly [Polly *written above* Mary *crossed out*], ch. James and Mary, Oct. 7, 1798. [Polly, C.R.2.]
SHUMAN, Alma J., w. Otis K. Ryder, June 22, 1849, in Waldoboro, P.R.35. [Alma Jane, d. Elijah M. and Elsy J. (Robinson), P.R.48.]
Anna A., w. Roscoe T. Cross, d. Elijah M. and Elsy J. (Robinson), Dec. 21, 1858, P.R.48.
Caro Florence, d. John Marten and Sarah Mariah, Apr. 23, 1852, P.R.47.
Carrie A., w. Harvey S. Cunningham, Feb. 3, 1855, in Waldoboro, P.R.42. [d. Elijah M. and Elsy J. (Robinson), P.R.48.]
Clarence H. [s. Elijah Souther and Millie T. (Libby) (second w.)], Oct. 5, 1883, P.R.47.
Clarisa Ann, d. John Marten and Sarah Mariah, Oct. 27, 1840, P.R.47.
Elijah M., h. Elsy J. (Robinson), June 22, 1820, P.R.48.
Elijah Souther, h. Arabella R. (Cunningham), h. Millie T. (Libby), h. Ada H. (———) Kimball, s. John Marten and Sarah Mariah, Apr. 5, 1848, P.R.47.
Elsy Ada, d. Elijah M. and Elsy J. (Robinson), Feb. 8, 1853, P.R.48.
Gertrude, d. Elijah M. and Elsy J. (Robinson), Apr. 19, 1865, P.R.48.
Grace, d. Elijah Souther and Arabella R. (Cunningham), Dec. 14, 1874, P.R.47.
James C., s. Elijah M. and Elsy J. (Robinson), Sept. 15, 1850, P.R.48.
James Madison, h. Orinda B. (Savage), s. John Marten and Sarah Mariah, June 10, 1846, P.R.47.
Jennie May, twin d. Elijah Souther and Arabella R. (Cunningham), Feb. 17, 1869, P.R.47.
John Franklin, s. John Marten and Sarah Mariah, Aug. 11, 1843, P.R.47.
John M., twin s. Elijah Souther and Arabella R. (Cunningham), Feb. 17, 1869, P.R.47.
John Marten, h. Sarah Mariah, May 22, 1812, P.R.47.
Mary Emma, d. John Marten and Sarah Mariah, Aug. 8, 1856, P.R.47.
Nancy Ad, d. Elijah M. and Elsy J. (Robinson), Feb. 26, 1852, P.R.48.

SHUMAN, Nettie A. [d. Elijah Souther and Millie T. (Libby) (second w.)], Jan. 14, 1888, P.R.47.
Sarah Catherine, d. John Marten and Sarah Mariah, Aug. 11, 1838, P.R.47.
Sarah Francis, d. John Marten and Sarah Mariah, Nov. 12, 1850, P.R.47.
Sarah Mariah [———], w. John Marten, June 11, 1820, P.R.47.

SHUTE, Alonzo, ch. William and Malinda, May 13, 1832. [Capt. Alonzo L., h. Margaret J., May 13, 1833, G.R.1. Alonzo, h. Margaret J. (Russ), May 13, 1833, P.R.45.]
Azubah A. [———], w. Capt. Thomas R., Mar. 14, 1823, G.R.1.
Clyde R., s. Ralph D. and Orilla C. (Knight), Sept. 10, 1890, P.R.45.
Darius, ch. William and Malinda, May 31, 1834. [Darius F., ———, 1835, G.R.1.]
Flora E., ch. Capt. Alonzo and M. J., Feb. 16, 1856, G.R.1. [Flora Ella, d. Alonzo and Margaret J. (Russ), P.R.45.]
Franklin, ch. William and Malinda, Jan. 15, 1829. [———, 1830, G.R.1.]
Fred A., Jan. 4, 1861, G.R.1. [s. Alonzo and Margaret J. (Russ), P.R.45.]
Hannah P., w. William Holt, Apr. 17, 1806, P.R.29.
Leander P., ———, 1840, G.R.1.
Lucy A. [? m.], ———, 1842, G.R.1.
Lucy A., ———, 1861, G.R.1.
Margaret J. [———], w. Capt. Alonzo L., Dec. 25, 1835, G.R.1. [Jane (Rust), d. William (Russ) and Mary W. (Farrar), Dec. 24, P.R.44. Margaret J. (Russ), Dec. 25, P.R.45.]
Mary Elizabeth, ch. William and Malinda, Sept. 22, 1827.
Melinda [———], w. Capt. William, ———, 1805, G.R.1.
Melinda E., w. ——— Willis, ———, 1870, G.R.1.
Ralph D., h. Orilla C. (Knight), s. Alonzo and Margaret J. (Russ), Sept. 4, 1866, P.R.45.
Sarah A., w. David W. Dyer, ———, 1820, G.R.1.
Thomas R., Capt., h. Azubah A., Jan. 20, 1822, G.R.1.
Vesta J., ch. Capt. Alonzo and M. J., Aug. 7, 1872, G.R.1. [d. Alonzo and Margaret J. (Russ), P.R.45.]
Vesta J., d. Ralph D. and Orilla C. (Knight), Jan. 13, 1889, P.R.45.
William, Capt., h. Melinda, ———, 1800, G.R.1.
William Lewis, ch. William and Malinda, Jan. 27, 1826. [Capt., G.R.1.]
———, s. Capt. Thomas, June 25, 1848, P.R.123.
———, d. Capt. Thomas, Sept. 14, 1849, P.R.123.

SIBLEY, Ammi Cutter, ch. Reuben and Hannah C., bp. July 9, 1848, C.R.2. [[h. Margaret (Ritchie)] b. Sept. 16, 1847, G.R.1.]
Charles Andrews, inf. Reuben and Hannah C., bp. Oct. 16, 1853, C.R.2.
Charlotte, ch. Reuben and Hannah C., bp. July 9, 1848, C.R.2.
Edward, ch. Reuben and Hannah C., bp. July 9, 1848, C.R.2.
Eliphalet Greely, inf. Reuben and Hannah C., bp. Aug. 11, 1850, C.R.2.
Hannah C. [———], w. Reuben, Nov. 2, 1808, G.R.1.
John Read, ch. Reubin and Margaret S., Aug. 21, 1837.
Margaret Cutter, ch. Reubin and Hannah Cushing, June 8, 1840.
Margaret S. [———], w. Reuben, Oct. 12, 1812, G.R.1.
Reuben, Sept. 15, 1807, G.R.1.
William, ch. Reubin and Margaret S., Aug. 24, 1835.

SIDES, George A., h. Mary J., ———, 1830, G.R.3.
George W., s. G. A. and M. J., Sept. 2, 1857, G.R.3.
Mary J. [———], w. George A., ———, 1836, G.R.3.

SIMMONS, Ellen, ch. John Randall and Mary, ———, 1872, G.R.1.
John Randall, h. Mary, ———, 1831, G.R.1.
John Randall, ch. John Randall and Mary, ———, 1860, G.R.1.
Josiah, ch. John Randall and Mary, ———, 1862, G.R.1.
Mary [———], w. John, ———, 1838, G.R.1.
Mary, ch. John Randall and Mary, ———, 1857, G.R.1.
Rachel, ch. John Randall and Mary, ———, 1867, G.R.1.
———, s. Nathaniel and ——— (Moody), Jan. 2, 1848, P.R.123.

SIMPSON, Mary E., first w. John S. Caldwell, Nov. 17, 1818, in York, P.R.156.
William Henry, ch. Josiah Jr. and Susan, Sept. 24, 1825.

SLEEPER, Annie C. [———], Jan. 15, 1839, G.R.1.
Francis Hathaway, s. Sherburne and Mary Elizabeth (Longfellow), Oct. 26, 1843, P.R.146.
Grenville Gleason, s. Sherburne and Mary Elizabeth (Longfellow), Aug. 29, 1847, P.R.146.
Jane Elizabeth (see ——— Sleeper).
Llewellyn, h. Ella Angelett (Lancaster), Apr. 27, ———, P.R.108.
[John Llewellyn Sleeper, s. Sherburne and Mary Elizabeth (Longfellow), Apr. 27, 1845, P.R.146.]

SLEEPER, Mary Elizabeth, d. Sherburne and Mary Elizabeth (Longfellow), July 2, 1853, P.R.146.
Percy Manasseh, s. Sherburne and Mary Elizabeth (Longfellow), Apr. 6, 1859, P.R.146.
Samuel Longfellow, ch. Sherburne and Mary E. [Mary Elizabeth (Longfellow), P.R.146.], Aug. 10, 1838.
Sarah B. [? m.], ———, 1827, G.R.1.
Sherburne, h. Mary Elizabeth (Longfellow), July 4, 1811 [? in Searsmont], P.R.146.
Sherburne A. [h. Laura (Gammans)], July 25, 1841, G.R.1. [Sherburne Augustus, s. Sherburne and Mary Elizabeth (Longfellow), P.R.146.]
Sherburne H., ch. Sherburne A. and Laura J., June 29, 1869.
Waity Ann, ch. Manasseh and Hannah, May 26, 1816.
———, d. Sherburne, June 1, 1849, P.R.123. [Jane Elizabeth, d. Sherburne and Mary Elizabeth (Longfellow), May 31, P.R.146.]

SMALL, Albert, h. Laura A., Feb. 14, 1812, G.R.1.
Alfred A., Jan. 5, 1849, G.R.1.
Caroline F. [———], w. Elmer, M.D., ———, 1843, G.R.1.
Laura A. [———], w. Albert, June 10, 1814, G.R.1.
Ruth W. [———], w. Asa S., Oct. 16, 1818, G.R.1.
Sarah H. [———], w. Joel, June 12, 1820, G.R.1.
———, d. Asa, Jan. 21, 1850, P.R.123.

SMALLEY, A. B., ch. Alex[ander] D. and Eliza W. (Stearns), Aug. 2, 1876, in Jackson, P.R.28.
Alexander D., h. Lida (Stearns), s. Isaac W. and Mary (Farnham), Dec. 2, 1847, P.R.27. [h. Eliza W. (Stearns), P.R.28.]
Annette, ch. Castanus M. and Mary S., July 11, 1881.
Asenath F. [? m.], ———, 1831, G.R.1.
B. B., ch. Alex[ander] D. and Eliza W. (Stearns), Mar. 8, 1887, P.R.28.
Benjamin L., Capt., July 1, 1827, G.R.1.
Castaneous, Jan. 22, 1846, G.R.1. [Castanus, h. Mary S. (Redman), s. Isaac W. and Mary (Farnham), Jan. 22, 1845, P.R.27.]
Castanus M., ch. Castanus M. and Mary S., Aug. 17, 1878.
E. A., ch. Alex[ander] D. and Eliza W. (Stearns), July 14, 1880, in Jackson, P.R.28.
E. L., ch. Alex[ander] D. and Eliza W. (Stearns), Mar. 3, 1884, P.R.28.
Eliza W., Sept, 11, 1853, G.R.1. [Eliza W. (Stearns), w. Alex[ander] D. Smalley, Sept. 11, 1854, in Jackson, P.R.28.]

SMALLEY, Ella Isabel, ch. Castanus M. and Mary S., Mar. 25, 1888.
Frank H., ch. Castanus M. and Mary S., May 22, 1875.
George A., June 14, 1878, G.R.I.
Harvey H. Jr., Aug. 31, 1866, G.R.I.
Isaac W., h. Mary (Farnham), Sept. 30, 1823, in St. George, P.R.27.
Isaac W., s. Isaac W. and Mary (Farnham), May 25, 1859, P.R.27.
John F., h. Nettie G. (Stevens), s. Isaac W. and Mary (Farnham), Dec. 25, 1853, P.R.27.
Lilla V. P., d. Isaac W. and Mary (Farnham), Aug. 23, 1856, P.R.27.
Lulu L., ch. Castanus M. and Mary S., Jan. 9, 1884.
Lycurgus V. Payne, s. Isaac W. and Mary (Farnham), Oct. 12, 1851, P.R.27.
M. E., ch. Alex[ander] D. and Eliza W. (Stearns), Jan. 15, 1878, in Jackson; P.R.28.
Martha J., w. W[illia]m A. Carter, d. Isaac W. and Mary (Farnham), Aug. 14, 1849, P.R.27.
Mary E. [? m.], Oct. 15, 1875, G.R.I.
Mary Etta, d. Isaac W. and Mary (Farnham), Nov. 9, 1860, P.R.27.
Rachel F., w. William O. Cunningham, July 2, 1828, P.R.41.
Sheridan P., twin s. Isaac W. and Mary (Farnham), July 8, 1864, P.R.27.
Sherman T., h. Hattie A. Tenny, twin s. Isaac W. and Mary (Farnham) July 8, 1864, P.R.27.

SMART, Ann Rebeckah, ch. Nehemiah and Sarah, Oct. 28, 1833.
Edward, ch. Nehemiah and Sarah, June 4, 1832.
Hannah, ch. Nehemiah and Sarah, Mar. 12, 1818.
James Covill, ch. Nehemiah and Sarah, Jan. 30, 1826.
Martha Esther, w. Augustine Oliver Stoddard, Dec. 8, 1844, in Swanville, P.R.55.
Martin Lewis, ch. Nehemiah and Sarah, Feb. 28, 1830.
Thomas Crowell, ch. Nehemiah and Sarah, Feb. 8, 1828.

SMITH, Ada Frances [———], w. Francis O., Apr. 22, 1857, G.R.I.
Adeline, w. Horatio N. Palmer, Nov. 20, 1819, G.R.I.
Almira, ch. Caleb and Lydia, bp. ——— [rec. between Oct. 6, 1805 and June —, 1817], C.R.2.
Almyra, ch. Caleb and Lydia, June 13, 1802.

SMITH, Anna Cornelia, ch. Peter H. and Lydia H., Feb. 6, 1817, in New Bedford. [w. William Winslow, Feb. 6, 1816, G.R.1.]
Chadborn, ch. Caleb and Lydia, Sept. 14, 1805.
Charles E., Oct. 11, 1874, G.R.2.
Clara A., Sept. 1, 1860, G.R.1.
Clarance Hurd, ch. Luther M. and Sarah N., bp. June 12, 1856, C.R.2.
Elmer O., Oct. 14, 1862, G.R.1.
Francis O., Sept. 6, 1854, G.R.1.
George F., ch. Peter H. and Lydia S., Jan. 29, 1832, G.R.1.
Gershom Cox, ch. Peter H. and Lydia H., Oct. 7, 1824.
Helen Maria, ch. Peter H. and Lydia H., Aug. 11, 1820.
Henry Shearman, ch. Peter H. and Lydia H., Aug. 29, 1818.
Isaac Tilton, ch. Isaac and Thankful, Feb. 18, 1813.
James, ch. Caleb and Lydia, bp. ——— [rec. between Oct. 6, 1805 and June —, 1817], C.R.2.
John Mariam, ch. Abiatha and Mary, July 24, 1822.
Joseph F., Sept. 22, 1840, G.R.2.
Luther Edgar, ch. Luther M. and Sarah N., bp. June 12, 1856, C.R.2.
Luther M., h. Sarah N., Apr. 5, 1820, G.R.1.
Lydia, ch. Caleb and Lydia, Apr. 16, 1795.
Lydia, ch. Caleb and Lydia, bp. ——— [rec. between Oct. 6, 1805 and June —, 1817], C.R.2.
Lydia Sherman [———], w. Peter H., Sept. 3, 1806, G.R.1.
Mary Ann, ch. Abiatha and Mary, Jan. 19, 1817.
Mary E. [? m.], Apr. 20, 1822, G.R.1.
Mary Frances, ch. Luther M. and Sarah N., bp. June 12, 1856, C.R.2.
Melinda B. [? m.], Mar. 18, 1843, G.R.2.
Nathen, ch. Nathen and Betsy, July 4, 1802.
Nicholas V. D. T., Jan. 6, 1806, G.R.1.
Peter H., h. Lydia Sherman, Aug. 6, 1787, G.R.1.
Sally, ch. Nathen and Betsy, Sept. 12, 1804.
Saphronia Pike, ch. Abiatha and Mary, Nov. 14, 1820.
Sarah Jones, ch. Peter H. and Lydia, Oct. 11, 1826.
Sarah N. [———], w. Luther M., May 23, 1820, G.R.1.
Sophia, ch. Caleb and Lydia, Jan. 10, 1799.
Sophia, ch. Caleb and Lydia, bp. ——— [rec. between Oct. 6, 1805 and June —, 1817], C.R.2.
Sophronia Pike (see Saphronia Pike Smith).
Sylvester, ch. Nathen and Betsy, Feb. 18, 1807.
Viola Elizabeth, ch. Luther M. and Sarah N., bp. June 12, 1856, C.R.2.

SMITH, William Frederick, ch. Peter H. and Lydia H., Apr. 26, 1822.
William Frederick, ch. Peter H. and Lydia H., Aug. 25, 1828.
William Warner, ch. Caleb and Lydia, bp. ———— [rec. between Oct. 6, 1805 and June —, 1817], C.R.2.
————, s. Harvey, Feb. 8, 1848, P.R.123.

SNOW, Edward H., ch. Isreal T. and Susan, Jan. 20, 1858.
Sophronia B., Aug. 26, 1834, in Jackson, P.R.78.

SOULE, Martha Jane Babson, ch. Charles and Phebe, bp. May 28, 1826, C.R.2.

SOUTHER, ————, d. Sam[ue]l, Apr. 9, 1848, P.R.123.
————, s. Rev. Sam[ue]l, Mar. 7, 1850, P.R.123.

SOUTHWORTH, Augusta A., d. D. B. and M. J., Apr. 11, 1877, G.R.1.
Augusta F., Feb. 20, 1846, G.R.1.
Dana B., h. Martha J., May 20, 1836, G.R.1.
Fred M., ————, 1865, G.R.1.
Martha J. [————], w. Dana B., Sept. 10, 1842, G.R.1.

SPEED, Adison, ch. George and Susan, Dec. 3, 1833.
Elizabeth S., d. George W. and Margaret (Batchelder), Jan. 3, 1842, P.R.62.
Fidelia Ann, ch. George and Susan, Aug. 20, 1829.
George H., s. George W. and Margaret (Batchelder), Feb. 24, 1840, P.R.62.
George W., ————, 1804, G.R.1. [h. Margaret (Batchelder), Jan. 27, P.R.62.]
Horace O., s. George W. and Margaret (Batchelder), Jan. 24, 1848, P.R.62.
Leonora, w. David P. Flanders, Feb. 23, 1847, G.R.1. [Leonora S., w. Dr. David P. Flanders, d. George W. and Margaret (Batchelder), P.R.62.]
Mary R., w. Tho[ma]s D. Barr, d. George W. and Margaret (Batchelder), Oct. 10, 1850, P.R.62.
Thomas, ch. George and Susan, Aug. 4, 1827.
William E., s. George W. and Margaret (Batchelder), Nov. 2, 1843, P.R.62.
————, s. George, Jan. 4, 1849, P.R.123.

SPENCER, Aubrey G., h. Sarah A., Sept. 10, 1845, G.R.1.
Sarah A. [————], w. Aubrey G., Aug. 20, 1845, G.R.1.

SPRATT, Sarah W., w. Stephen G. Bicknell, Sept. 5, 1833, G.R.1. [Sept. 4, P.R.114.]

SPRING, Anna Estelle, ch. James H. and Julia A. A., Nov. 28, 1851.

Bitsey Thaxter [Thaxter *in later handwriting*], ch. Samuel and Bitsey, Dec. 3, 1823 [*date in later handwriting*]. [Betsey T., d. Samuel and Betsey (Thaxter) (Colburn), Dec. 3, 1823, P.R.19. Betsy T., d. Samuel and Betsy Colburn, Dec. 3, 1823, P.R.20.]

Charlotte Woodbury, ch. Samuel and Bitsey, Jan. 30, 1819. [d. Samuel and Betsey (Thaxter) (Colburn), P.R.19. w. John W. White, d. Samuel and Betsy Colburn, P.R.20.]

Frederick Hodsdon, ch. James H. and Julia A. A., Sept. 14, 1848.

James Henry, ch. Samuel and Bitsey, Dec. 30, 1820. [s. Samuel and Betsey (Thaxter) (Colburn), P.R.19. h. Julia A. A. (Howard), s. Samuel and Betsy Colburn, P.R.20.]

Lydia Ann, ch. Samuel and Bitsey, Apr. 6, 1826. [d. Samuel and Betsey (Thaxter) (Colburn), P.R.19. d. Samuel and Betsy Colburn, P.R.20.]

Martha Maria, ch. Nahum and Sally, Feb. 10, 1802.

Martha Maria, ch. Samuel and Bitsey, Feb. 20, 1829 [*date in later handwriting*]. [d. Samuel and Betsey (Thaxter) (Colburn), Feb. 20, 1829, P.R.19. d. Samuel and Betsy Colburn, Nov. 20, 1829, P.R.20.]

Samuel, h. Betsey (Thaxter) Colburn, Mar. 12, 1788, P.R.19.

Samuel Jr., ch. Samuel and Bitsey, Aug. 5, 1816. [s. Samuel and Betsey (Thaxter) (Colburn), Aug. 11, P.R.19. s. Samuel and Betsy Colburn, Aug. 11, P.R.20.]

Samuel, ch. James H. and Julia A. A., Oct. 29, 1845.

Samuel Munroe, ch. Samuel and Bitsey, ——— [*rec. after ch. b.* Feb. 20, 1829]. [s. Samuel and Betsey (Thaxter) (Colburn), P.R.19. s. Samuel and Betsy Colburn, Oct. 20, 1831, P.R.20.]

William Henry, ch. James H. and Julia A. A., Mar. 20, 1843.

STANLEY (see Stanly), Clarrisy, ch. Nathaniel and Lucy, Sept. 5, 1802.

Joseph, ch. Nathaniel and Lucy, June 18, 1809.

Ruel, ch. Nathaniel and Lucy, Aug. 26, 1807.

Sophronia, ch. Nathaniel and Lucy, Oct. 22, 1804.

STANLY (see Stanley), ———, d. Capt. Ruel, Dec. 3, 1849, P.R.123.

STANWOOD, Helen, w. Geo[rge] T. Read, Nov. 7, 1853, G.R.I.

STAPLES, Alred, ch. Alfred and Abagail, Sept. 30, 1852.
Andrew W., "Co. E. 19th Me. Regt.," h. Mabel, ———, 1836, G.R.I.
Annie E., d. Miles S. and Sarah (Ellingwood), Aug. 19, 1855 [? in Swanville], P.R.33.
Basil Herbert, s. Josiah E. and Olivet (Newell), June 13, 1878, P.R.33. [Basil Herbert (Staples) Newell, P.R.81.]
Belzora, ch. David and Martha, Feb. 28, 1846.
Carrie A., d. Miles S. and Sarah (Ellingwood), May 13, 1862 [? in Swanville], P.R.33.
Carrie E., d. Miles S. and Sarah (Ellingwood), Oct. 28, 1853 [? in Swanville], P.R.33.
Edwin A., "Co. I. 26th Me. Regt.," July 23, 1842, G.R.I.
Fletcher O., s. Miles S. and Sarah (Ellingwood), Apr. 21, 1867, P.R.33.
Fred F., s. L. and R. M., Oct. 29, 1862, G.R.I.
Fred Miles, h. Fannie E. (Sinnott), s. Miles S. and Sarah (Ellingwood), Nov. 7, 1870, P.R.33.
Freeman Hartwell, ch. Alfred and Abagail, Mar. 23, 1839.
George Wellington, ch. David and Martha, Jan. 30, 1843.
Henry, ch. Alfred and Abagail, June 9, 1847.
Herbert, s. Miles S. and Sarah (Ellingwood), Mar. 21, 1859 [? in Swanville], P.R.33.
Josiah E., h. Olivet (Newell), s. Miles S. and Sarah (Ellingwood), June 23, 1850 [? in Swanville], P.R.33.
Laroy T., ch. Alfred and Abagail, June 26, 1851.
Leander C., ch. Alfred and Abagail, May 1, 1837.
Leroy T. (see Laroy T.).
Mabel [———], w. Andrew W., ———, 1860, G.R.I.
Marion, ch. Alfred and Abagail, Sept. 22, 1843.
Melvin J., h. Lida M. (Crawford), s. Miles S. and Sarah (Ellingwood), Oct. 12, 1851, P.R.33.
Miles S., h. Sarah (Ellingwood), Sept. 18, 1820, in Swanville, P.R.33.
Roscoe, ch. Alfred and Abagail, Nov. 1, 1856.
Simeon, h. Eliza A. (Dyer), June 18, 1815, G.R.I.
William H. Jr., Feb. 17, 1885, G.R.I.
———, d. Hezekiah, Dec. 28, 1847, P.R.123.

STARRETT, Francis James, ch. Henry Atherton and Ellen Mary (Cutter), May 7, 1872, P.R.116.
Henry Atherton [h. Ellen M. (Cutter)], ———, 1833, G.R.I.

BELFAST BIRTHS

STEARNS, Eliza W. (see Eliza W. Smalley).
Vesta A., ch. John Y. and Lois E., Aug. 11, 1877.
William P., ——, 1819, G.R.1.

STEELE, Elizabeth, ch. Robert and Margret, Oct. 25, 1793.
James R., ch. Robert and Margret, July 16, 1800.
John, ch. Robert and Margret, Feb. 9, 1797.
Margret, ch. Robert and Margret, Aug. 11, 1795.
Martha, ch. Robert and Margret, Oct. 5, 1791.
Robert, ch. Robert and Margret, Sept. 7, 1798.

STEPHENSON (see Stevenson), Albion Parris Kent, ch. Francis and Hannah, July 14, 1826.
Alfred J., ch. Caleb and Jenney, May 29, 1810.
Ambrose, ch. Zenes and w., Nov. 18, 1811.
Ann, ch. Thomas and Ann, Apr. 21, 1810.
Benjamin Franklin, ch. Francis and Hannah, Dec. 13, 1816.
Betsy, ch. Caleb and Jenney, Dec. 30, 1793. [Betsey, w. Benjamin Cunningham, Dec. 30, 1792, P.R.110.]
Caleb, ch. Caleb and Jenney, Oct. 22, 1804.
Charles Austin, ch. Jerom Jr. and Polly, Dec. 5, 1815.
Charles C., h. Mary E. (Bean), Oct. 5, 1842, G.R.1.
Charles Edward, Apr. 14, 1847, G.R.1. [s. Charles and Jane (Durham), P.R.123.]
Chester B., ——, 1836, G.R.1.
Chester Barter, ch. Jerom Jr. and Polly, Dec. 22, 1834.
Erastus Bartlett (Stevenson), ch. Jerom Jr. and Polly, Oct. 31, 1812.
Eunice, ch. Zenes and Louis, June 11, 1809.
Fanny, ch. Caleb and Jenney, Apr. 6, 1797.
Fred J., ——, 1861, G.R.1.
Harriet Elisabeth, ch. Francis and Hannah, Dec. 7, 1814.
Harriet L. [? m.], ——, 1858, in Waldo, G.R.1.
Jane M. [————], w. Charles A., ——, 1817, G.R.1.
Jenney, ch. Caleb and Jenney, Sept. 21, 1792.
Jerom 3d, ch. Jerom Jr. and Polly, Apr. 12, 1827.
Joanna, ch. Zenes and w., Dec. 29, 1817.
John, ch. Caleb and Jenney, Aug. 27, 1802.
John Houston, ch. Thomas and Ann, May 19, 1814.
John Loomis, ch. Francis and Hannah, Sept. 26, 1821.
Joshua, ch. Caleb and Jenney, Feb. 28, 1807.
Judith, ch. Zenes and w., Oct. 19, 1815.
Louis, ch. Zenes and Louis, July 10, 1805.
Lovisa Chandler, ch. Jerom Jr. and Polly, June 13, 1824. [Lovicy C., w. Arthur G. Lampher, G.R.1.]

STEPHENSON, Lucius Chandler, ch. Jerom Jr. and Polly, Nov. 28, 1817.
Margaret, twin ch. Francis and Hannah, Apr. 17, 1819.
Martha, ch. Jerom Jr. and Polly, Aug. 5, 1821.
Mary, ch. Thomas and Ann, Dec. 4, 1811. [sister of Jane Brown, G.R.1.]
Ruth, ch. Caleb and Jenney, May 27, 1800.
Sally Crosby, twin ch. Francis and Hannah, Apr. 17, 1819.
Samuel Gilmore, ch. Francis and Hannah, May 17, 1824.
Sarah J. (see Sarah J. Parker).
Sibbil, ch. Jerom Jr. and Polly, Apr. 12, 1820.
Susanna, ch. Caleb and Jenney, Mar. 9, 1795.
Susanna Hallet, ch. Jerom Jr. and Polly, Sept. 4, 1814. [Susannah H., w. ——— Sweetser, G.R.1. Susannah H., w. Samuel L. Sweetser, P.R.124.]
Thomas Lincoln, ch. Francis and Hannah, Apr. 28, 1829.
Warren, ch. Caleb and Jenney, May 17, 1799.
Warren, ch. Zenes and Louis, Mar. 1, 1807.
William H., ch. Caleb and Jenney, July 16, 1812.

STEVENS, Albert T., Jan. 10, 1822, G.R.1.
Albert Varnum, ch. Jonathan and Debbe, bp. ——— [*rec. between* Oct. 6, 1805 *and* June —, 1817], C.R.2.
Annie M. [? m.], Feb. 11, 1833, G.R.1.
Arletta M. [? m.], ———, 1843, G.R.1.
Charles R., h. Susan H. (Magee), ———, 1848, G.R.1.
Debbe Poor, ch. Jonathan and Debbe, bp. ——— [*rec. between* Oct. 6, 1805 *and* June —, 1817], C.R.2.
Dolly Julian, ch. Jonathan and Debbe, bp. ——— [*rec. between* Oct. 6, 1805 *and* June —, 1817], C.R.2.
Eliza Watson, ch. William Esq. and Eliza L. W., Dec. 22, 1826.
Fred A., Feb. 19, 1871, G.R.1.
George Watson, ch. William Esq. and Eliza L. W., Nov. 24, 1832.
John, Dr., June 24, 1840, G.R.1.
Jonathan Peabody, ch. Jonathan and Debbe, bp. ——— [*rec. between* Oct. 6, 1805 *and* June —, 1817], C.R.2.
Lydia [———] [w. ———], Apr. 5, 1795, in N. H., G.R.1.
Nettie G., w. [John F.] Smalley, May 15, 1862, G.R.1.
Samuel F., Oct. 10, 1836, G.R.1.
Susan Louisa, ch. William Esq. and Eliza L. W., Feb. 6, 1830.
Susanna Emely, ch. Jonathan and Debbe, bp. ——— [*rec. between* Oct. 6, 1805 *and* June —, 1817], C.R.2.
William Oliver, ch. William Esq. and Eliza L. W., Feb. 3, 1828.

STEVENSON (see Stephenson), ———, d. Franklin, Apr. 26, 1848, P.R.123.

STEWART (see Stuart), Elizabeth [———], w. Thomas, Nov. 10, 1775.
Emma Isadora, d. John Nelson and Sarah Ellen (Whitmore), Sept. 18, 1849, P.R.60.
Etta, w. James Mitchell, d. John Nelson and Sarah Ellen (Whitmore), Mar. 16, 1853, P.R.60.
John N., ———, 1822, G.R.1. [John Nelson, h. Sarah Ellen (Whitmore), May 3, P.R.60.]
Lily Sarah, w. John W. Jones, d. John Nelson and Sarah Ellen (Whitmore), Oct. 22, 1859, P.R.60.
Mary Hannah, w. Francis W. Whitmore, d. John Nelson and Sarah Ellen (Whitmore), Feb. 22, 1857, P.R.60.
Mary Jane, ch. Thomas and Elizabeth, Mar. 16, 1811.
Thomas, h. Elizabeth, Aug. 28, 1777.
Thomas, ch. Thomas and Elizabeth, Oct. 7, 1816, in Bristol.
W[illia]m M., ———, 1847, G.R.1. [William Whitmore Stewart, s. John Nelson and Sarah Ellen (Whitmore), Apr. 26, P.R.60.]

STICKNEY, Sarah Maria, ch. Dudly and Anna, July 8, 1824.
Thomas, ch. Dudly and Anna, Apr. 18, 1812.

STIMPSON, Amanda M. [———], w. S. G., Sept. 3, 1825, G.R.1.
Grace L., Dec. 26, 1873, G.R.1.
Herbert P., Dec. 28, 1863, G.R.1.

STODDARD, Amy Ellura, d. Augustine Oliver and Martha Esther (Smart), Sept. 19, 1883, in Athol, Mass., P.R.55.
Ann Francis, ch. W[illia]m and Mary D., Feb. 21, 1844.
Augustine Oliver, h. Martha Esther (Smart), Nov. 17, 1841, in Brunswick, P.R.55.
Edith May, w. Alfred M. Ferguson, d. Augustine Oliver and Martha Esther (Smart), June 1, 1874, in Lincoln, R. I., P.R.55.
Helen Edith, d. Geo[rge] W. and Amanda M., Aug. 21, 1872, G.R.1.

STONE, Edith Lydia, d. Martin and Electa B. (Pitcher), Mar. 9, 1868, P.R.173.
Ernest Joseph, s. Martin and Electa B. (Pitcher), July 12, 1862, P.R.173.
George Martin, s. Martin and Electa B. (Pitcher), Aug. 4, 1856, P.R.173.

STOVER, Alice G., w. John L. Dunnells, d. Jeremiah and Hannah, ——, 1859, G.R.1.
Hannah [————], w. Jeremiah, ——, 1825, G.R.1.
Jeremiah, Capt., h. Hannah, ——, 1823, G.R.1.
Luella L., d. Jeremiah and Hannah L., ——, 1848, G.R.1. [Nov. 26, P.R.123.]
Mildred H., d. Carrie M., Mar. 24, 1887, G.R.1.

STROUT, Anna, inf., bp. July 12, 1863, C.R.3.
Maria M. [————], w. Parish L., ——, 1840, G.R.1.
Parish L., h. Maria M., ——, 1838, G.R.1.

STUART (see Stewart), Lelia, ch. Horace M. and Diantha A., July 18, 1857.

STUBBE, Isabell J. [? m.], ——, 1847, G.R.13.

SULLIVAN, Eliza R. [————], w. Jere, Mar. 5, 1845, G.R.1.
James, June 10, 1822, G.R.1.
John H., s. Daniel, shoemaker (b. Kinsale, Ire.), and Margaret (Finnegan) (b. Glynn, Ire.), Dec. 25, 1850, P.R.171.

SUMNER, Cha[rle]s H., ch. J. G. and Harriet, Feb. 3, 1845.
Sarah L., ch. J. G. and Harriet, Jan. 27, 1843.

SWAN, Annabella Sarah, ch. Nathan and Annabella B. [dup. Annabellah Sarah Poor, ch. B'enj[amin]], Mar. 14, 1821.
Benj[amin] Poor, ch. Nathan and Annabella B. [dup. Benj[amin] Poor Jr., ch. Benj[amin]], Jan. 28, 1813.
Benj[amin] Poor, ch. Nathan and Annabella B. [dup. Benj[amin] Poor, ch. Benj[amin]], Dec. 2, 1816.
Dolly Joanna, ch. Nathan and Annabella B. [dup. Dolly Joanna Poor, ch. Benj[amin]], Dec. 8, 1818.
Francis M., ch. Nathan and Annabella B., Sept. 10, 1833.
Lydia Tyler Poor, ch. Nathan and Annabella B. [dup. Lydia Tyler Poor, ch. Benj[amin]], Sept. 25, 1814. [w. Ezra Bickford, G.R.1.]
William B., ch. Nathan and Annabella B., May 2, 1825.

SWEENEY, ——, d. Patrick, May 30, 1847, P.R.123.
——, s. John, Dec. 26, 1847, P.R.123.
——, s. John, Apr. 6, 1849, P.R.123.

SWEETSER, Charles Webb, ch. Samuel L. and Susannah H., Aug. 20, 1842. [h. Louisa Walton of Hull, Eng., s. Samuel L. and Susannah H. (Stephenson), Aug. 16, P.R.125.]
Geo[rge], ——, 1822, G.R.1.

SWEETSER, George R., ch. Samuel L. and Susannah H., Nov. 16, 1851. [h. Annie McBride of Blue Hill, s. Samuel L. and Susannah H. (Stephenson), P.R.125.]
Josephine Turner, ch. Samuel L. and Susannah H., Feb. 16, 1844. [w. Lucius P. Walton, d. Samuel L. and Susannah H. (Stephenson), P.R.125.]
Richard, ———, 1782, G.R.1.
S. E. L., ———, 1815, G.R.1.
Samuel L., ———, 1811, G.R.1. [h. Susannah H. (Stephenson), Apr. 20, in Waterville, P.R.125.]
Sarah D. [? m.], ———, 1790, G.R.1.
William Henry Harrison, ch. Samuel L. and Susannah H., Sept. 10, 1840. [h. Mary Foot of Salem, Mass., s. Samuel L. and Susannah H. (Stephenson), P.R.125.]

SWETT, Ann, ch. Ephriam and Asenath, Oct. 15, 1836.
Aves [———], w. Eph[rai]m, ———, 1820, G.R.1.
Ephraim, h. Aves, ———, 1804, G.R.1.
Francis, ch. Ephriam and Asenath, Apr. 21, 1838.
Francis Ann, ch. Ephriam and Asenath, July 2, 1840.
Franklin, ch. Ephriam and Asenath, Sept. 26, 1832.
George, s. Robert R. and Mary (Rowe), Dec. 30, 1845, P.R.130.
Mary Elizabeth, d. Robert R. and Mary (Rowe), Feb. 22, 1848, P.R.130. [Lizzie M., w. James H. Cunningham, P.R.131.]
Robert R., h. Mary (Rowe), Mar. 27, 1807, in Standish, P.R.130.
Roscoe, ch. Ephriam and Asenath, Feb. 16, 1831.
Sarah A., d. Robert R. and Mary (Rowe), Jan. 28, 1832, P.R.130.
———, s. Ephraim, May 23, 1848, P.R.123.

SWIFT, Charles Albert, s. Geo[rge] W. and M. M., Sept. 7, 1872, G.R.1.
Cha[rle]s F., ch. William A. and Rebecca, Oct. 12, 1843.
Elizabeth R., ch. William A. and Rebecca, Oct. 11, 1839.
Franklin B., h. Roseltha J., Aug. 27, 1843, G.R.1.
George W., ch. William A. and Rebecca, June 2, 1845. [h. Melvina M., G.R.1.]
Melvina M. [———], w. George W., Dec. 11, 1845, G.R.1.
Roseltha J. [———], w. F. B., Sept. 4, 1842, G.R.1.
W[illia]m A. Jr., ch. William A. and Rebecca, Nov. 18, 1840.
W[illia]m Oliver, ch. William A. and Rebecca, Nov. 6, 1837.

SYLVESTER, Elizabeth Jane, ch. Daniel and Jane, Nov. 17, 1839.

SYLVESTER, Eugene, ch. Daniel and Jane, Dec. 11, 1840.
Geo[rge] W., ch. George and Mary, June 18, 1835.
Gilmore, h. Olive, ——, 1808, G.R.I.
Nancy, ch. George and Mary, Aug. 5, 1830.
Olive [———], w. Gilmore, ——, 1811, G.R.I.
Rhoda, ch. George and Mary, Sept. 4, 1828.

TAGGART, Emile (Taggert), ch. David and Anna, Jan. 2, 1805.

TALBOT, Ezra Leonard, Oct. 5, 1861, G.R.I.
Roy Seth, Aug. 27, 1889, G.R.I.

TAPLEY, Polly W. [———], Jan. 31, 1797, G.R.I.
Thomas, Mar. 15, 1794, G.R.I.

TASKER, Lydia, w. James Pattee, Apr. 30, 1844, G.R.I.

TAYLOR, Dolphin D., ch. Samuel G. and Huldah, June 1, 1817, in Augusta.
Frances Caroline, ch. Samuel G. and Huldah, Oct. 5, 1828.
George Greenleaf, ch. Samuel G. and Huldah, July 25, 1821, in Hallowell.
Harry W., ch. Samuel G. and Huldah, Jan. 15, 1824, in Hallowell.
John F., ch. Samuel G. and Huldah, July 20, 1815, in Augusta.
Justus Hurd, ch. Samuel G. and Huldah, Apr. 3, 1834.
Sanford Kingsbury, ch. Samuel G. and Huldah, June 30, 1819, in Hallowell.
Sanford M., ch. George G. and Juliann, Dec. 30, 1845.
Thomas, h. Annie M. (Carter) (formerly w. Philip T. Eastman), s. Thomas and Annie, Apr. 16, 1825, in Lyth, Eng., G.R.I.
Wilson Prescett, ch. Samuel G. and Huldah, July 15, 1826.

THAXTER, Betsey, w. William Colburn, w. Samuel Spring, Apr. 30, 1791, P.R.19. [Betsy, in Wiscassett, P.R.20.]

THAYER, Ethel May, July 17, 1882, G.R.I.

THOMAS, Ann Eliza, ch. Charles G. and Mary Elizabeth [Elizabeth *crossed out*], Nov. 18, 1846.
Charles Frederick, ch. Charles G. and Mary Elizabeth [Elizabeth *crossed out*], Oct. 16, 1840.
Charles G. Jr., ch. Charles G. and Mary Elizabeth [Elizabeth *crossed out*], Nov. 18, 1844.
Charles W., s. Charles G. and Ella J., ——, 1871, G.R.I.
Ella J. [———], w. Charles G., Sept. 8, 1852, G.R.I.

THOMAS, Mary Elizabeth, ch. Charles G. and Mary Elizabeth [Elizabeth *crossed out*], Sept. 15, 1838.
William Henry, ch. Charles G. and Mary Elizabeth [Elizabeth *crossed out*], Aug. 26, 1842.

THOMBS, Charlie E., Apr. 13, 1862, G.R.1. [Charlie Eddy Thombs, s. Jos[eph] S. and Ella N. (Osborn), in China, Me., P.R.9.]
John B., h. Mary A., Apr. 4, 1839, G.R.1.
Joseph S. [h. Ella N.], Aug. 27, 1834, G.R.1.
Mary A. [———], w. John B., Feb. 4, 1838, G.R.1.

THOMPSON (see Tompson), Agnes M., May 31, 1860, G.R.1.
Albert Wooster, h. Elizabeth M. (Winston), h. Alice (Woodworth), s. Horatio Palmer and Mary Elizabeth (Parker), May 17, 1864, P.R.165.
Edward P., s. H. P. and Delia W., Nov. 18, 1875, G.R.1. [Edward Parker Thompson, s. Horatio Palmer and Delia Wood (Parker), P.R.165.]
Edward P. H., May 31, 1835, G.R.1.
Hattie C. [———], w. W. P., May 15, 1841, G.R.1.
Horatio Palmer, Jan. 3, 1837, G.R.1. [h. Mary Elizabeth (Parker), h. Delia Wood (Parker), s. John and Mary (Palmer), in Frankfort (now Winterport), P.R.165.]
Mary E., Aug. 20, 1845, G.R.1.
Mary Hellen, ch. Moses W. and Lucinda, June 5, 1845.
Rebecca [———], w. Timothy, ———, 1829, G.R.1.
Timothy, h. Rebecca, ———, 1826, G.R.1.

THORNDIKE, Clara, w. Edward Sibley, ———, 1845, G.R.1.
Edward Octavius, ———, 1857, G.R.1.
Sarah Frances, w. John Peirce, Mar. 10, 1821, P.R.112.
Timothy, ———, 1817, G.R.1.

THURLOW, Charles Albert, s. Samuel Greenleaf and Anne Whittier (Hutchinson), May 6, 1839, P.R.159.
Charles Edward, ch. Samuel G. and Ann W. [Samuel Greenleaf and Anne Whittier (Hutchinson), P.R.159.], Mar. 20, 1852.
Eliza M., ch. Samuel G. and Ann W., Sept. 10, 1853. [Eliza Myra, w. I. H. Harmon, d. Samuel Greenleaf and Anne Whittier (Hutchinson), Sept. 10, 1854, P.R.159.]
Horace M., ch. Samuel G. and Ann W., July 9, 1856. [Horace Moody Thurlow, h. Etta May (Mathews), s. Samuel Greenleaf and Anne Whittier (Hutchinson), P.R.159.]

THURLOW, Marianna, ch. Samuel G. and Ann W., Jan. 1, 1846. [Marianne, w. Hiram Pitcher Farrow, d. Samuel Greenleaf and Anne Whittier (Hutchinson), P.R.159.]
Samuel Greenleaf, h. Anne Whittier (Hutchinson), Oct. 4, 1816, P.R.159.

THURSTON (see Thusten), Blanche, ch. Stephen and Mary E., Nov. 15, 1883.
Jane H. [———], Mar. 4, 1828, G.R.1.
Lillian M., ch. Stephen and Mary E., Dec. 28, 1886.
———, [? twin] ch. Jona[than], Aug. —, 1808, C.R.2.
———, s. Stephen, Jan. 19, 1847, P.R.123.

THUSTEN (see Thurston), Granillo, [? twin] ch. Jonathan and Polly, Aug. 6, 1808.
John, ch. Jonathan and Polly, Oct. 30, 1803.
Mary Jane, ch. Jonathan and Polly, May 6, 1811.

TIBBETTS, Ada Frances [———], w. Fred A., Jan. 2, 1872, G.R.1.

TILDEN, Adriann, inf. Capt. Thomas and w., bp. Sept. 6, 1835, C.R.2.
Alphonso Fitch, inf. Capt. Thomas and w., bp. May 3, 1835, C.R.2.
Charles K., ch. Charles W. and Juliet M. (Osborne), July 5, 1856, in Castine, P.R.9.
Deborah [———], w. William, ——, 1802, G.R.1.
Isabella, w. Alonzo Osborne, Feb. 8, 1802, P.R.9.
Mary Helen, ch. Thomas and Mary Ann, ———. [bp. Apr. 8, 1832, C.R.2.]
Ruth [———], w. William, ——, 1801, G.R.1.
William, h. Deborah, h. Ruth, July —, 1796, G.R.1.
William R., ch. Charles W. and Juliet M. (Osborne), Feb. 19, 1859, in Castine, P.R.9.

TINKHAM, Jane Maria, ch. Franklin and Jane, Mar. 2, 1823.

TITCOMB, Sarah D., w. Hiram Chase, Sept. 24, 1822, in Anson, P.R.75.

TODD, Charles G., ch. Alexander C. and Olive, Oct. 27, 1819.
Elisabeth, ch. Alexander C. and Olive, Dec. 22, 1807.
James, ch. Alexander C. and Olive, Jan. 11, 1812.
Mary, ch. Alexander C. and Olive, Nov. 15, 1809.
Samuel W., ch. Alexander C. and Olive, Apr. 3, 1823. [Samuel Worcester Todd, C.R.2.]

TOLMAN, Waitie S. [———], w. J. T., Sept. 24, 1845, G.R.1.

TOMPSON (see Thompson), ———, s. Joseph B., Mar. 31, 1847, P.R.123.

TOOTHAKER, Daniel C., Apr. 8, 1836, G.R.1.
John, Capt., Mar. 17, 1830, G.R.1.

TORREY, Albert S., s. Elijah and Hannah (Brown), Apr. 5, 1824, P.R.139.
Catherine Amanda, twin ch. Elijah and Hannah [(Brown) P.R.139.], Apr. 19, 1816.
Elijah B., s. Elijah dec'd and Hannah (Brown), Nov. 21, 1825, P.R.139.
Emeline G., Dec. 20, 1808, G.R.1. [Emmeline C., d. Elijah and Hannah (Brown), P.R.139.]
Erastus N., s. Elijah and Hannah (Brown), July 2, 1813, P.R.139.
Hannah [———], w. Elijah, Feb. 23, 1789, G.R.1. [Hannah (Brown), P.R.139.]
James M., s. Elijah and Hannah (Brown), Jan. 29, 1811, P.R.139.
Leander L., s. Elijah and Hannah (Brown), Oct. 17, 1807, P.R.139.
Mary Amelia, twin ch. Elijah and Hannah, Apr. 19, 1816. [w. Humphrey N. Lancaster, Apr. 19, 1811, P.R.108. twin d. Elijah and Hannah (Brown), Apr. 19, 1816, P.R.139.]
Sarah Elizabeth, ch. Elijah and Hannah, July 8, 1821. [w. William H. Dutton, G.R.1. d. Elijah and Hannah (Brown), P.R.139.]
William Lazier (Torey), ch. Elijah and Hannah, Jan. 25, 1819. [Torrey, h. Lucy T. Lancaster [*q.v.*], G.R.1. Torrey, s. Elijah and Hannah (Brown), P.R.139.]

TOWLE, Asenath O., ch. Joshua and Dorcas, July 1, 1839.
Calvin S., ch. Joshua and Dorcas, Oct. 24, 1830.
Joshua W., ch. Joshua and Dorcas, Nov. 15, 1832.
Mary D., ch. Joshua and Dorcas, Aug. 18, 1845.

TOWN (see Towne), Eben Davis, ch. Thomas and Mary B., Jan. 9, 1831.
Mary Frances, ch. Thomas and Mary B., June 15, 1832.

TOWNE (see Town), Albert Burgess, s. Eben D. and Harriet A. (Burgess), May 4, 1873, P.R.169.
Mary B. [———], w. Thomas, Jan. 11, 1805, G.R.1.

TOWNE, Thomas, Jan. 19, 1806, G.R.I.
William Roush, s. Eben D. and Harriet A. (Burgess), Feb. 4, 1860, P.R.169.

TOWNSEND, Arexine, [triplet] ch. Capt. Jessee and Jannette, Mar. 10, 1845. [Arexene H., G.R.I.]
Clara B. [———], w. Walter C., Aug. 18, 1875, G.R.I.
Eliza Jane, ch. Capt. Jessee and Jannette, Nov. 23, 1842.
Jesse, Capt., h. Jennette L. [(Hinds)], ——, 1807, G.R.I.
Joseph Curtis, ch. Capt. Jessee and Jannette, Nov. 3, 1840.
Josephine, [triplet] ch. Capt. Jessee and Jannette, Mar. 10, 1845. [Josephene H., G.R.I.]
Sarah Hepsebeth, ch. Capt. Jessee and Jannette, Dec. 15, 1838.
Victorine, [triplet] ch. Capt. Jessee and Jannette, Mar. 10, 1845. [Victorene H., G.R.I.]

TREADWELL, Charles, h. Isabella B. (Durham), Apr. 10, 1803, in Portsmouth, N. H. [Apr. 12, 1802, G.R.I.]
Isabella Josephene [dup. *crossed out*, Josaphine], ch. Charles and Isabella B. (Durham), May 12 [dup. *crossed out*, May 10], 1831. [Isabella Josephine, C.R.2.]
Mary Garafelia Mohalby [dup. *crossed out*, Mary Garofelin], ch. Charles and Isabella B. (Durham), Apr. 17, 1835. [Mary Garrafelia, C.R.2. M. Garafelia [w. ——— Stockham], Apr. 11, G.R.I.]
Robert Earl, ch. Charles and Isabella B. (Durham), Mar. 31, 1845.
William Cutter, ch. Charles and Isabella B. (Durham), Apr. 27, 1837. [Apr. 29, G.R.I.]

TREAT, Betsy, ch. Hulda, wid., bp. June 27, 1802, C.R.2.
George W., ch. Joseph and w., Mar. 22, 1822.
Jane E., ch. Joseph and w., Mar. 10, 1820.
John, ch. Hulda, wid., bp. June 27, 1802, C.R.2.
Joseph, s. Hulda, wid., bp. Jan. 5, 1802, C.R.2.
Mary A., ch. Joseph and w., Dec. 10, 1817.
Polly, ch. Hulda, wid., bp. June 27, 1802, C.R.2.
Richard Stimson, s. Hulda, wid., bp. July 31, 1803, C.R.2.
William A., ch. Joseph and w., Feb. 28, 1829.

TRIGGS, Georgie Annie, w. John L. Dow, d. William Franklin and Augusta Jael (Emerton), Mar. 11, 1884, P.R.50.
Holmes Franklin, s. William Franklin and Augusta Jael (Emerton), Mar. 13, 1878, P.R.50.
William Franklin, h. Augusta Jael (Emerton), Jan. 9, 1836, in Hermon, P.R.50.

TRIPP, Alice M., w. Edward W. Woods, Sept. 3, 1842, G.R.1.

TRUE, Abigail, ch. Henry and Martha, Aug. 24, 1787.
Aroline, ch. Samuel and Grace, Jan. 1, 1816.
Betsy, ch. Samuel and Grace, July 7, 1809.
Charlotte, ch. Henry and Martha, Nov. 29, 1797.
Charlotte, ch. Martha, wid., bp. ―――― [*rec. between* Oct. 6, 1805 *and* June ―, 1817], C.R.2.
Fanny, ch. Henry and Martha, Jan. 3, 1794.
Harriet, twin ch. Samuel and Grace, Jan. 19, 1813.
Harriot, ch. Henry and Sally, May 20, 1804.
Henry, ch. Samuel and Grace, Oct. 30, 1807.
Jane, twin ch. Samuel and Grace, Jan. 19, 1813.
Jenney, ch. Henry and Martha, Dec. 17, 1789.
Joseph, ch. Henry and Martha, Dec. 29, 1795.
Martha, ch. Henry and Martha, Jan. 14, 1800.
Martha, ch. Martha, wid., bp. ―――― [*rec. between* Oct. 6, 1805 *and* June ―, 1817], C.R.2.
Nancy, ch. Samuel and Grace, May 10, 1824.
Rosanna, ch. Samuel and Grace, Nov. 10, 1819.
Sally, ch. Henry and Martha, Jan. 1, 1792.
Samuel [dup. h. Grace], ch. Henry and Martha, Oct. 14, 1785 [dup. 1786].
Samuel, ch. Samuel and Grace, Feb. 22, 1822.
Thomas, ch. Samuel and Grace, Apr. 1, 1806.

TRUSSELL, Anson W., "Co. A. 4th Regt. Me. Vol.," ――, 1824, G.R.1.
Elizabeth J. [? m.], June 28, 1830, G.R.1.
Joseph, ch. Daniel and Mary, Apr. 23, 1839.
Sarah B. [――――], w. J. H., Oct. 22, 1837, G.R.1.
Willie, s. Joseph H. and Sarah B., Oct. 30, 1871, G.R.1.

TUFFTS (see Tufts), George Freeman, ch. William and Rhoda, Mar. 26, 1844.

TUFTS (see Tuffts), Bela Whitten, ch. Freeman and Harriet Jane, Mar. 16, 1835.
Freeman, h. Harriet J. (Hartshorn), ――, 1807, G.R.1.
Harret, ch. Thomas and Dorothy, Dec. 10, 1802.
John, ch. William and Amelia, Feb. 2, 1803.
John, ch. Thomas and Dorothy, July 6, 1804.
Jonathan, ch. John and Mary, Mar. 24, 1776.
Jonathan, ch. William and Amelia, Feb. 10, 1799.
Mary, ch. Joseph and Sally, July 11, 1794.
Mary, ch. Thomas and Dorothy, Nov. 17, 1800.

TUFTS, Permelia Abigail, ch. Freeman and Harriet Jane, Dec. 8, 1837.
Sally, d. Joseph and Sally, Feb. 3, 1796.
Sarah Jane, ch. Freeman and Harriet Jane, May 1, 1841.
Susanna, ch. John and Mary, Apr. 17, 1778.
William, ch. William and Amelia, Nov. 21, 1800.
William, ch. Freeman and Harriet Jane, Sept. 17, 1833.
TURNBULL, Jane, w. Dennis Emery, Aug. 6, 1797, in Digby, N. S. [Aug. 6, 1796, G.R.I.]
TURNER, Ann E. [———], w. Capt. James, June 5, 1812, G.R.I.
James, Capt., h. Ann E., Nov. 1, 1815, G.R.I.
TUTTLE, Adrian C., inf., bp. Mar. 1, 1874, C.R.3. [h. Minnie M. (Wentworth), h. Grace L. (Goodale) of Bucksport, s. W[illia]m C. and Georgiana (Conant), b. Oct. 27, 1869, in Appleton, P.R.137.]
Frank A., Aug. 26, 1877, G.R.I. [h. Clemmie (Rowell) of Castine, s. W[illia]m C. and Georgiana (Conant), P.R.137.]
Percy C., Sept. —, 1873, C.R.3. [s. W[illia]m C. and Georgiana (Conant), Sept. 6, P.R.137.]
William C., July 27, 1835, G.R.I.
TWOMBLY, Abby Caroline, June 3, 1859, P.R.47.
Benjamin, s. William, of Paris, and Mary (Wentworth), of Fryeburg, Feb. 27, 1856, P.R.154.
Charles, s. William, of Paris, and Mary (Wentworth), of Fryeburg, Nov. 10, 1853, P.R.154.
Ella M. [———], w. C. H., ———, 1856, G.R.I. [w. Charles H., d. Joshua Eustis Partridge and Mary Abbie (Arnold), Aug. 27, 1855, in Stockton, P.R.129.]
Elmer Wesley, s. William, of Paris, and Mary (Wentworth), of Fryeburg, Aug. 20, 1862, P.R.154.
Frederick William, s. William, of Paris, and Mary (Wentworth), of Fryeburg, Aug. 27, 1860, P.R.154.
Mary Ellen, d. William, of Paris, and Mary (Wentworth), of Fryeburg, Mar. 21, 1865, P.R.154.
Sarah, d. William, of Paris, and Mary (Wentworth), of Fryeburg, Sept. 17, 1867, in Searsmont, P.R.154.
William, ———, 1825, G.R.I.
TYLER, Enna J., Jan. 6, 1887, G.R.I.
ULMER, Fannie Nelson, ch. Lewis and Melissa Auburn (Holt), grand ch. William Holt and Hannah P. (Shute), Aug. 2, 1872, P.R.29.

ULMER, Frank Marion, ch. Lewis and Melissa Auburn (Holt), grand ch. William Holt and Hannah P. (Shute), Apr. 5, 1861, P.R.29.

UNDERWOOD, Almira, ch. Joseph and Selvia, Nov. 4, 1802.

VARNUM, Dora J. [———], w. Walter L., ———, 1869, G.R.1.
Joseph B., h. Julia A., ———, 1826, G.R.1.
Julia A. [———], w. Joseph B., ———, 1848, G.R.1.
Raymond K., ch. Joseph B. and Julia A., May 27, 1876.

VEAZIE, Charlotte N. [———], w. Capt. W[illia]m G., ———, 1817, G.R.1.
Vesta, w. ——— Hurlbert, ———, 1849, G.R.1.
——— (Vezie), d. Capt. William, Aug. 20, 1847, P.R.123.

WADLIN, Alice M., w. Oscar W. Gould, Aug. 17, 1859, G.R.1.
Daniel A., h. Eliza[beth] J., Apr. 29, 1830, G.R.1.
Eliza[beth] J. [———], w. Daniel A., Feb. 18, 1837, G.R.1.
John B., Mar. 12, 1822, G.R.3.

WAKEFIELD, Helen Augusta, ch. P. P. and w., Mar. 7, 1843.
Jane N. [———] [w. Paul P.], Dec. 20, 1817, G.R.1.
Mary S. [? m.], Apr. 7, 1780, G.R.1.
Mary Sargeant, ch. P. P. and w., Feb. 1, 1841.
Paul P. [h. Jane N.], July 11, 1813, G.R.1.
Roscoe Alden, ch. P. P. and w., Nov. 3, 1844.

WALES, Alexander, [twin] ch. John and Sarah, Nov. 29, 1826.
Betsy White, ch. John and Sarah, Aug. 20, 1831.
Catherine, [twin] ch. John and Sarah, Nov. 29, 1826.
Daniel Quimby, ch. John and Sarah, Oct. 14, 1830.
Elizabeth Frances, ch. Rev. Nathaniel and Sarah, Aug. 29, 1827.
Geo[rge] White, ch. John and Sarah, Feb. 22, 1824.
John Jr., ch. John and Sarah, July 19, 1814.
Julia Maria Antoinette [dup. w. Joseph Wheeler], ch. John and Sarah, Dec. 19, 1818.
Peter Thacher, ch. John and Sarah, Sept. 8, 1825.
Sarah E., ch. John Jr. and Lucy D., Nov. 14, 1845.
Sarah Elizabeth, ch. John and Sarah, Dec. 25, 1816.
Susan, ch. John and Sarah, Dec. 19, 1821.
Theodore Oscar, ch. John and Sarah, Jan. 30, 1834.
W[illia]m Atherton, ch. John and Sarah [dup. Sally], Aug. 23, 1812.
W[illia]m Atherton, ch. John and Sarah, Sept. 23, 1828.

WALKER, Benson [h. Catherine], June 30, 1824, G.R.1.
Catherine [———] [w. Benson], Dec. 15, 1832, G.R.1.
Celeste Ann, w. Henry Lunt Lord, Nov. 11, 1839, in Northport, P.R.174.
Elizabeth, ch. Jeremiah and Sally, Apr. 8, 1812.
Hannah, ch. Jeremiah and Sally, May 23, 1810.
Mary Elinor [? m.], ———, 1829, G.R.1.
Nancy, ch. Jeremiah and Sally, Aug. 8, 1814.

WALTON, Albert, ch. John and Mary, Nov. 9, 1826. [h. Sarah D. (Winslow), s. John and Mary (Whalen), P.R.126.]
Alice B., Apr. 13, 1870, G.R.1.
Charles H., s. Lucius P. and Josephine T. (Sweetser), ———, P.R.126.
Elizabeth H. [———], w. Willard, Jan. 25, 1811, G.R.2.
Ernest, s. John B. and Jennie (Benner) (first w.), ———, P.R.126.
Grace Ellen, d. Lucius P. and Josephine T. (Sweetser), ———, P.R.126.
Harry B., s. John B., ———, P.R.126.
Isa M., ch. John B. and Jennie (Benner) (first w.), ———, P.R.126.
Jennie M. [———], w. John B., ———, 1851, G.R.1.
John, h. Mary (Whalen), Mar. 15, 1802, in Wayne, P.R.126.
John B., h. Jennie M., h. Lizzie E., ———, 1844, G.R.1. [h. Jennie (Benner), h. Lizzie E. (Springer) of Northport, h. Emma B. (Leathers) of Brooks, s. John and Mary (Whalen), Jan. 28, P.R.126.]
John F., s. John B. and Jennie (Benner) (first w.), ———, P.R.126.
Lizzie E. [———], w. John B., ———, 1863, G.R.1.
Lucias, ch. John and Mary, Aug. 10, 1835. [Lucius P., h. Josephine T. (Sweetser), s. John and Mary (Whalen), P.R.126.]
Lucius A., s. John B., ———, P.R.126.
Lucy E., w. Jeremiah J. Hennessy of Fredericton, N. B., d. John and Mary (Whalen), Jan. 17, 1846, P.R.126.
Mary Addie, d. Salathiel F. and Susan (Watts), ———, P.R.126.
Mary Jane, ch. John and Mary, Dec. 21, 1830. [w. Everett S. Carter, d. John and Mary (Whalen), P.R.126.]
Sadie E., ———, 1888, G.R.1. [Sadie Emma, d. John B., P.R.126.]
Salatheal, ch. John and Mary, Sept. 16, 1828. [Salathiel F., h. Susan (Watts) of Knox, s. John and Mary (Whalen), P.R.126.]

WALTON, Salathiel Roscoe, s. Salathiel F. and Susan (Watts), ———, P.R.126.
Sarah Ann, ch. John and Mary, Apr. 22, 1833. [w. Enoch Hilton, d. John and Mary (Whalen), P.R.126.]
Willard, Nov. 2, 1797, G.R.2.
Willis Blackwell, s. John B. and Jennie (Benner) (first w.), ———, P.R.126.

WARDWELL, Lizzie Maria, d. Esther C., bp. Sept. 14, 1857, C.R.2.

WARREN, Dallas H. [ch. Thomas and Hannah], Mar. 18, 1855, G.R.I.
George, ch. Napoleon B. and Julia A., Oct. 30, 1874.
Hannah [———], w. Thomas, Aug. 31, 1812, G.R.I.
John A., ch. Napoleon B. and Julia A., Aug. 24, 1877.
Lenda P. [———], w. Royal A., Oct. 8, 1840, G.R.I.
Maria L. [ch. Thomas and Hannah], May 18, 1844, G.R.I.
Mary E., ———, 1871, G.R.I.
Phebe P., w. Stephen E. Phipps, w. James Bucklin, Sept. 3, 1815, in Thorndike, P.R.39.
Thomas, h. Hannah, May 12, 1815, G.R.I.
Zilica H. [ch. Thomas and Hannah], Oct. 12, 1846, G.R.I.
———, d. Silvanus, Nov. 30, 1847, P.R.123.
———, s. Capt. Porter, Mar. 28, 1849, P.R.123.
———, d. Thomas, Nov. 18, 1849, P.R.123.

WASHBURN, Adelaide, ch. Oliver A. and Jane, ——— [rec. after ch. b. Sept. 19, 1828].
Ann Maria, ch. Oliver A. and Jane, Jan. 13, 1821, in Bridgwater, Mass.
Eugene L., ch. H. G. O. and Hannah E., Feb. 7, 1839.
Frances Augusta, ch. Oliver A. and Jane, Mar. 12, 1825.
Jane Amanda, ch. Oliver A. and Jane, Apr. 19, 1815, in Bridgwater, Mass.
Julia Elizabeth, ch. Oliver A. and Jane, Sept. 19, 1828.
Mary Kinsley, ch. Oliver A. and Jane, Aug. 20, 1817, in Bridgwater, Mass.
Newell, ch. Zebah and Susan, Sept. 18, 1828.
Olive, w. Luther Gannett, Feb. 25, 1785, in E. Bridgwater.
Oliver Alden, ch. Oliver A. and Jane, Nov. 20, 1819, in Bridgwater, Mass.
Susan, ch. Zebah and Susan, Dec. 26, 1825.
———, ch. H. G. O. and Charlotte F. (second w.), Mar. 2, 1846.
———, ch. H. G. O., Dec. 4, 1848, P.R.123.

WATERMAN, Abigail, ch. Robert and Abigail, Aug. 17, 1842.
Alfred, ch. Robert and Abigail, June 14, 1832.
Alfred, ch. Joseph M. and Rachael, Sept. 10, 1844. [Alfred P., G.R.I.]
Charles, ch. Joseph and Mary, Feb. 20, 1828.
Joseph Jr. [h. Mary Hinds], ———, 1787, G.R.I.
Joseph M. [h. Rachel P.], ———, 1811, G.R.I.
Joseph T., ch. Joseph M. and Rachael, Oct. 31, 1840.
Louisa C., ch. Joseph M. and Rachael, Aug. 3, 1843.
Mary Hinds [———] [w. Joseph Jr.], ———, 1792, G.R.I.
Rachel P. [———] [w. Joseph M.], ———, 1820, G.R.I.
Robert Jr., ch. Robert and Abigail, July 30, 1837.
———, ch. Richard, Mar. 29, 1848, P.R.123.

WATKINS, Mamie [———], w. Charles B., Oct. 15, 1872, G.R.I.

WATSON, Apha [w. William Quimby], Aug. 15, 1799, G.R.I.
Caroline Lucretia, ch. George and Eliza, May 1, 1808.
Deborah, ch. Simon and Lucy, Jan. 18, 1816.
Elisha K., ch. Simon and Lucy, Apr. 17, 1823.
Ellen Jane, ch. George and Eliza, Dec. 15, 1806.
George, ch. George and Eliza, Dec. 24, 1811.
George I., May 27, 1856, G.R.10.
Isaac, ch. Simon and Lucy, May 13, 1814.
John G., ch. Simon and Lucy, Dec. 16, 1827.
Lucy, ch. Simon and Lucy, Oct. 2, 1820.
Nancy, ch. Simon and Lucy, Feb. 17, 1817.
Sarah Brimmer, ch. George and Eliza, Sept. 10, 1809.

WATTS, Susan F., w. Salathiel F. Walton, May 8, 1831, G.R.I.

WEBB, Mary Hellen, ch. Albert and Susan, Apr. 26, 1846.
———, s. ——— ("John Wiggin's wife's father"), Feb. 28, 1847, P.R.123.

WEBBER, Eliza Ann, ch. William and Mary, bp. June 18, 1826, C.R.2.
Elizabeth M. [———], w. Henry W., Mar. 11, 1861, G.R.I.

WEBSTER, Ann Louisa, ch. James W. and Mary Elizabeth, May 12, 1832.
Annie H. [? m.], Dec. 15, 1864, G.R.I.
Caroline Elizabeth, ch. James W. and Mary Elizabeth, June 8, 1830.
David Wilson, ch. David and Mary, Oct. 5, 1817.

WEBSTER, Joseph Thomas, ch. Washington and Abigal, Sept. 21, 1810.
Mary R., ch. Geo[rge] and Martha A., July 24, 1861.
Octavius R., June 8, 1849, G.R.I.
Paulina Moody, ch. James W. and Mary Elizabeth, Sept. 11, 1828.
Stephen Wheeler, ch. David and Mary, July 12, 1819.

WEEKS, Elizabeth, ch. Lemuel and Elizabeth, Dec. 5, 1790.
Martha [w. Cyrus Hall], Apr. 7, 1801, G.R.I.

WELCH (see Welsh), Ann Caroline [dup. *crossed out omits* Caroline], ch. Peter and Anna, June 28, 1834.
Bridget Myric, ch. Peter and Anna, May 19, 1844.
Caro F., d. Mark and F. E. (Mahoney), Jan. 23, 1851, P.R.96.
Cha[rle]s A., s. Mark and F. E. (Mahoney), Aug. 20, 1857, P.R.96.
Clara A., d. Mark and F. E. (Mahoney), Oct. 23, 1854, P.R.96.
Clary J., w. James H. Stinson, d. Mark and F. E. (Mahoney), June 27, 1860, P.R.96.
Edward, ch. Peter and Anna, Nov. 11, 1840 [*sic*, see Sarah Elizabeth].
Eleanor [dup. *crossed out adds* Jane], ch. Peter and Anna, Jan. 30, 1839.
Geo[rge] A., s. Mark and F. E. (Mahoney), Sept. 20, 1859, P.R.96.
Hattie A., d. Mark and F. E. (Mahoney), July 1, 1869, P.R.96.
Helen S., d. Mark and F. E. (Mahoney), Sept. 28, 1852, P.R.96.
Horatio M., s. Mark and F. E. (Mahoney), Oct. 24, 1855, P.R.96.
James, ch. Peter and Anna, July 24, 1837.
Lottie D., d. Mark and F. E. (Mahoney), Sept. 26, 1865, P.R.96.
Mark, h. F. E. (Mahoney), Oct. 31, 1815, P.R.96.
Mark H., s. Mark and F. E. (Mahoney), Nov. 28, 1853, P.R.96.
Martha H. [? m.], Mar. 24, 1849, G.R.I.
Mary E., d. Mark and F. E. (Mahoney), Oct. 29, 1861, P.R.96.
Matthew W., July 16, 1847, G.R.I.
Peter F., ch. Peter and Anna, Dec. 4, 1835.
Sarah Elizabeth, ch. Peter and Anna, Feb. 7, 1841 [*sic*, see Edward].
William F., s. Mark and F. E. (Mahoney), Nov. 5, 1848, P.R.96.

WELLMAN, Eben, h. Nancy J., Mar. 10, 1816, G.R.I.
Grace L. [————], w. Alger F., Dec. 23, 1874, G.R.I.
Leonora E., w. [William] McCabe, ———, 1853, G.R.I.

WELLMAN, Nancy J. [———], w. Eben, Feb. 20, 1825, G.R.I.
Viola M., w. Henry W. Ames, July 1, 1853, G.R.I.
WELLS, Abigail Ingram, d. Nathaniel and Mary (Clark), July 11, 1824, in Thomaston, P.R.140.
Augusta A., Sept. 19, 1828, G.R.I. [d. Nathaniel and Mary (Clark), in Thomaston, P.R.140.]
Benjamin Franklin, Jan. 9, 1838, G.R.I. [s. Nathaniel and Mary (Clark), Jan. 9, 1837, P.R.140.]
Edward R., Oct. 26, 1834, G.R.I. [Edward Ruggles Wells, s. Nathaniel and Mary (Clark), P.R.140.]
Emma, d. Nathaniel and Mary (Clark), Jan. 5, 1843, P.R.140.
George Godding, s. Nathaniel and Mary (Clark), Mar. 27, 1840, P.R.140.
Jane Elizabeth, twin d. Nathaniel and Mary (Clark), Oct. 14, 1832, P.R.140.
Julia Abigail, twin d. Nathaniel and Mary (Clark), Oct. 14, 1832, P.R.140.
Lucy, d. Nathaniel and Mary (Clark), Feb. 5, 1827, in Thomaston, P.R.140.
Lucy Ann, d. Capt. W[illia]m and Sarah, bp. Sept. 14, 1857, C.R.2.
Martha, d. Nathaniel and Mary (Clark), July 23, 1822, in Thomaston, P.R.140.
Mary Ada, inf. William and Sarah, bp. Aug. 22, 1852, C.R.2.
Mary Ann, d. Nathaniel and Mary (Clark), Sept. 2, 1820, in Gardiner, P.R.140.
Nathaniel, h. Mary (Clark) (b. Little Compton, R. I.), Jan. 7, 1793, in Gardiner, P.R.140.
Nathaniel Harris, s. Nathaniel and Mary (Clark), Oct. 13, 1818, in Gardiner, P.R.140.
Sarah Ellen, inf. William and Sarah, bp. Sept. 13, 1847, C.R.2.
William, s. Nathaniel and Mary (Clark), Feb. 6, 1817, in Gardiner, P.R.140.
William Edwin, s. William and Sarah, bp. Mar. 16, 1851, C.R.2.
WELSH (see Welch), Caddie A., ———, 1865, G.R.I.
Eleanor B. [? m.], May 25, 1833, G.R.I.
James E., Apr. 16, 1851, G.R.I.
Peter Jr., ———, 1867, G.R.I.
WENTWORTH, Albion K., ch. Hezekiah and Betsy, Jan. 11, 1825.
Daniel, ch. John and Diantha, July 1, 1834.
Delinda, ch. John and Diantha, Mar. 17, 1823.

WENTWORTH, Diantha, ch. John and Diantha, Mar. 18, 1829.
Diantha, ch. John and Diantha, Aug. 5, 1831.
Ezekiel, ch. John and Diantha, Apr. 10, 1836.
Franklin A., ch. Hezekiah and Betsy, June 6, 1836.
Freelan, ch. Hezekiah and Betsy, Apr. 1, 1827.
Hezekiah 2d, ch. John and Diantha, June 7, 1821.
John, ch. John and Diantha, July 13, 1827.
Lydia C., ch. John and Diantha, May 28, 1825.
Mary E., ch. Hezekiah and Betsy, Sept. 21, 1840.
Nancy, w. Isaac Conant, Dec. 29, 1794, P.R.68.
Nicholas C., ch. John and Diantha, Dec. 13, 1818.
Noyes K., ch. Hezekiah and Betsy, Mar. 2, 1834.
Olive Enora, ch. Hezekiah 2d and Louisa, Aug. 31, 1846.
Sophia W., ch. Hezekiah and Betsy, Jan. 2, 1844.
Susan E., ch. Hezekiah and Betsy, Apr. 10, 1838.
Thomas T., ch. Hezekiah and Betsy, Oct. 2, 1831.
William J., ch. Hezekiah and Betsy, Aug. 15, 1822.
———, d. Almond, Apr. 30, 1848, P.R.123.
———, d. Jonah, July 29, 1848, P.R.123.
———, d. Hezekiah, June 29, 1849, P.R.123.

WEST, Aaron Hadley, ch. Stetson and Margret, Nov. 1, 1807. [s. Stetson and Margaret (Gibson), P.R.100.]
Abigail, ch. William and Abigail, Aug. 2, 1802.
Asa, ch. Stutson and Margaret, bp. ——— [rec. between Oct. 6, 1805 and June —, 1817], C.R.2. [h. Nancy, b. Feb. 18, 1794, G.R.1. s. Stetson and Margaret (Gibson), b. Feb. 18, 1794, P.R.100.]
Asenath, ch. William and Abigail, Nov. 26, 1812.
Betey, ch. Stetson and Margret, Oct. 17, 1800. [Betsey, ch. Stutson and Margaret, C.R.2. Betsey, d. Stetson and Margaret (Gibson), P.R.100.]
Charles Francis, ch. Asa and Nancy, Apr. 21, 1835.
Dorcas, ch. William and Abigail, Jan. 29, 1811.
Elijah, s. Stetson and Margaret (Gibson), June 17, 1811, P.R.100.
Ellen Paulina, ch. Asa and Nancy, Mar. 25, 1838.
Eva Annette, ch. William W. and Martha, July 1, 1845.
Fanny, ch. Stetson and Margret, May 24, 1805. [Fancy, ch. Stutson and Margaret, C.R.2. Frances, d. Stetson and Margaret (Gibson), P.R.100.]
Frances Augusta, ch. Asa and Nancy, July 25, 1831.
Fred, eldest s. Amos W. and Emily F., May 6, 1869, G.R.1.
Geo[rge] W., ch. John and Harriet, Aug. 20, 1845.
Hannah J. [———], w. Walter H., June 5, 1859, G.R.1.

WEST, Harriet E., ch. John and Harriet, May 30, 1840.
Isabella M. [———], w. S. A., ———, 1843, G.R.1.
James Gorden, ch. Asa and Nancy, Sept. 12, 1829.
John, ch. Stutson and Margaret, bp. ——— [rec. between Oct. 6, 1805 and June —, 1817], C.R.2. [s. Stetson and Margaret (Gibson), b. May 24, 1796, P.R.100.]
John, ch. William and Abigail, Jan. 26, 1816.
John Bemis, ch. Asa and Nancy, Sept. 28, 1825.
Joseph T., ch. John and Harriet, Oct. 31, 1840. [*This entry crossed out.*]
Laifey, ch. Stetson and Margret, Sept. 10, 1802. [Lefy, ch. Stutson and Margaret, C.R.2. Relief, d. Stetson and Margaret (Gibson), P.R.100.]
Lettie Emma, Sept. 22, 1874, G.R.2.
Louisa C., ch. John and Harriet, Aug. 3, 1[*sic,* ? 1841, *rec. after* ch. b. Oct. 31, 1840]. [*This entry crossed out.*]
Margaret (see Peggy).
Martha, ch. Eneas and Ann, July 27, 1802.
Mary H., ch. William and Abigail, Nov. 17, 1804.
Mary Hartshorn, ch. William, bp. ——— [*rec. between* Oct. 5, 1805 *and* June —, 1817], C.R.2.
Moschel, s. Stetson and Margaret (Gibson), Aug. 10, 1809, P.R.100.
Myra A., d. Amos W. and Emily F., May 18, 1871, G.R.1.
Nancy [———], w. Asa, Jan. 20, 1801, G.R.1.
Nancy Jane, ch. Asa and Nancy, Jan. 2, 1824.
Peggy, ch. Stetson and Margret, Oct. 27, 1798. [ch. Stutson and Margaret, C.R.2. Margaret, w. Samuel Bullen, d. Stetson and Margaret (Gibson), P.R.100.]
Peter, ch. Stutson and Margaret, bp. ——— [*rec. between* Oct. 6, 1805 *and* June —, 1817], C.R.2. [s. Stetson and Margaret (Gibson), b. May 28, 1790, P.R.100.]
Relief (see Laifey).
Rosina A., ch. John and Harriet, Feb. 22, 1843.
Samuel, ch. Eneas and Ann, June 20, 1798.
Sarah, ch. Eneas and Ann, Aug. 21, 1800.
Sarah E., ch. George W. and Ella E., Jan. 25, 1882.
Stetson, h. Margaret (Gibson), Oct. 25, 1768, P.R.100.
Stetson, ch. Stutson and Margaret, bp. ——— [*rec. between* Oct. 6, 1805 *and* June —, 1817], C.R.2. [s. Stetson and Margaret (Gibson), b. Feb. 11, 1792, P.R.100.]
Walter H., h. Hannah J., Feb. 18, 1853, G.R.1.
William Watson, ch. Asa and Nancy, Feb. 29, 1820.
William Wiseman, ch. William and Abigail, Nov. 4, 1807.
———, ch. William and Abagigal, bp. Aug. 26, 1821, C.R.2.

WEST, ———, d. Elijah, July 23, 1848, P.R.123.
——, s. S. A. and I. M., ——, 1882, G.R.I.

WHALEN (see Whaling), Mary, w. John Walton, Dec. 10, 1808, in Sedgwick, P.R.126.

WHALING (see Whalen), Melissa Jane, ch. James and Rhoda, May 5, 1846.

WHEELER, Emma Atherton, ——, 1847, G.R.1. [d. Joseph, P.R.123.]
Hawthorn G., ch. Joseph and Julia Maria Antoinett (Wales), Apr. 14, 1851.
John Theodore, ch. Joseph and Julia Maria Antoinett (Wales), Jan. 28, 1854.
Joseph, h. Julia Maria Antoinett (Wales), May 14, 1816, in Bowdoinham.
Joseph Wales, ch. Joseph and Julia Maria Antoinett (Wales), Mar. 11, 1845.
Julia Ella, ch. Joseph and Julia Maria Antoinett (Wales), Mar. [March *written above* June *crossed out*] 17, 1843.
Lydia A. [———], w. Fred[eric]k L., Apr. 9, 1844, G.R.1.
Nathan C. F., ch. Joseph and Julia Maria Antoinett (Wales), Dec. 17, 1848. [Dec. 17, 1849, P.R.123.]
Parkhurst W[illia]m, ch. Joseph and Julia Maria Antoinett (Wales), Sept. 24, 1857.

WHITAKER (see Whittaker, Whitiker).

WHITE, Albert Starrett, ch. James P. and Mary Ann, Dec. 15, 1839.
Annette Wilson, ch. James Esq. and Lydia Shaw, Jan. 3, 1837.
Ansel Lothrop, ch. Robert Jr. and Lois, June —, 1835. [h. Mary A., June 26, G.R.1.]
Asa, ch. William and Easter, bp. ——— [*rec. between* Oct. 6, 1805 *and* June —, 1817], C.R.2.
Augustus Starret, ch. Robert Jr. and Lois, Sept. 14, 1833.
Betsey [———], w. Job, Dec. 25, 1797, G.R.2.
Camilla Augusta, ch. James Esq. and Lydia Shaw, Mar. 31, 1842.
Caroline E., ch. William B. and Elcey, May 30, 1845.
Charles Tolman [*sic*, Tallman], ch. James P. and Mary Ann, Sept. 23, 1835.
Clifton H., ch. Wallace B. and Harriet E., Aug. 4, 1862.
Dorothy, ch. William and Easter, bp. ——— [*rec. between* Oct. 6, 1805 *and* June —, 1817], C.R.2.

WHITE, Eliza A. [———], w. Robert Jr., Feb. 11, 1821, G.R.1.
Eliza Jane [———], w. George U., Jan. 1, 1832, G.R.2.
Elizabeth Maria, ch. William and Lydia A., Feb. 11, 1821.
Ernest H., s. Ernest L. and Nellie F., Feb. 17, 1885, G.R.2.
Ernest Lucius, ch. George U. and Eliza Jane, Aug. 29, 1859.
Eugene Llewellyn, ch. James Esq. and Lydia Shaw, Jan. 31, 1833.
Eunice M., ch. William and Mary, Jan. 17, 1829.
Frances Ann, ch. William and Lydia A., Apr. 5, 1822.
Francis Eleanor [dup. Frances Elinor], ch. James P. and Mary Ann, Oct. 27, 1825.
Fred A., Capt., h. Jennie V., ———, 1852, G.R.1.
Fred G., Feb. 13, 1864, G.R.1.
G. W. V., ch. Job and Grace, Feb. 5, 1832. [George U., h. Eliza Jane, h. Katie J., G.R.2.]
George Franklin, ch. Robert and Susanna, Jan. 18, 1821. [Jan. 18, 1822, P.R.148.]
Grace U. [———], w. Job, June 5, 1797, G.R.2.
Grace Ulmer, ch. George U. and Eliza Jane, Feb. 20, 1861. [w. Willis S. Hatch, G.R.2.]
Harriot, ch. Jonathan and Jenney, Mar. 14, 1797.
Heber Milton, ch. James Esq. and Lydia Shaw, Jan. 29, 1844.
Hortense Eugenia, ch. James Esq. and Lydia Shaw, Sept. 15, 1834.
Ida M., ch. Wallace B. and Harriet E., Jan. 21, 1861.
Ida May, ch. George U. and Eliza Jane, Sept. 30, 1857.
James, ch. William and Mary, Apr. 8, 1823.
James A., ch. William and Mary, May 10, 1834.
James Clark, ch. James P. and Mary Ann, July 7, 1833.
James P., ch. Robert and Susanna, Sept. 2, 1800.
Jennie V. [———], w. Capt. Fred A., ———, 1856, G.R.1.
Job, h. Betsey, h. Grace U., Aug. 26, 1785, G.R.2.
John, ch. William and Easter, bp. ——— [*rec. between* Oct. 6, 1805 *and* June —, 1817], C.R.2.
John Alvin, ch. William and Mary, Nov. 8, 1842.
John Warren, ch. Robert and Susanna, Aug. 9, 1809.
Jonathan, ch. Jonathan and Jenney, Jan. 7, 1805.
Julia Anna, ch. William and Mary, Aug. 14, 1838. [w. ——— Warren, ———, 1840, G.R.1.]
Julia Elizabeth, ch. James P. and Mary Ann, Aug. 19, 1827.
Katie J. [———], w. George U., Oct. 24, 1843, G.R.2.
Lefy, ch. William and Easter, bp. ——— [*rec. between* Oct. 6, 1805 *and* June —, 1817], C.R.2.
Lucy E., ch. William and Mary, May 19, 1831.

WHITE, Lydia Gordon, ch. William and Lydia A., July 31, 1819.
Margaret, ch. William and Easter, bp. ——— [*rec. between* Oct. 6, 1805 *and* June —, 1817], C.R.2.
Maria Antonette, ch. Robert and Susanna, Aug. 18, 1818. [w. ——— Bean, P.R.148.]
Marietta [? m.], June 10, 1854, G.R.1.
Martin P., ch. Jonathan and Jenney, Feb. 7, 1802.
Mary A. [———], w. Ansel Lothrop, July 17, 1843, G.R.1.
Mary Ann, ch. Robert and Susanna, July 12, 1815. [w. Daniel Faunce, P.R.147.]
Mary Ann, ch. James P. and Mary Ann, Apr. 19, 1829.
Mary E., ch. William and Mary, Feb. 21, 1827.
Mary E., ch. William and Lydia A., ———.
Mary Jane, ch. Jonathan and Jenney, Oct. 27, 1807. [w. ——— Lothrop, G.R.1.]
Oliver Gordon, ch. William and Lydia A., ——— [*rec. after* ch. b. Oct. 5, 1823].
Orville S., ch. James Esq. and Lydia Shaw, May 31, 1838.
Peggy P., ch. Jonathan and Jenney, Aug. 26, 1799.
Percy L., ch. George O. and Martha J., Feb. 15, 1878.
Relief (see Lefy).
Robert, h. Susannah [(Patterson)], June 11, 1770, P.R.148.
Robert, ch. Robert and Susanna, Mar. 18, 1807. [Robert Jr., Mar. 14, P.R.148.]
Roscoe James, ch. James Esq. and Lydia Shaw, Sept. 16, 1835.
Russell Homer, ch. James Esq. and Lydia Shaw, Oct. 27, 1839.
Sarah Isabella, ch. William and Lydia A., Oct. 5, 1823.
Sarah Russell [———], w. L. O., June 9, 1856, G.R.1.
Starret, ch. Robert and Susanna, Jan. 3, 1803. [Starrett P., P.R.148.]
Susan Jane, ch. Robert and Susanna, June 7, 1812.
Susan Jane, ch. James P. and Mary Ann, May 30 [dup. Apr. 29], 1831.
Susanna, ch. William and Easter, bp. ——— [*rec. between* Oct. 6, 1805 *and* June —, 1817], C.R.2.
William, ch. Jonathan and Jenney, Oct. 29, 1794.
William, ch. William and Easter, bp. ——— [*rec. between* Oct. 6, 1805 *and* June —, 1817], C.R.2.
William, ch. William and Lydia A., June 1, 1818.
W[illia]m A., ch. William and Mary, Feb. 14, 1825.
William Bloomfield, ch. Robert and Susanna, Dec. 29, 1804.
Willis Tracy, ch. James Esq. and Lydia Shaw, Nov. 1, 1845.
———, d. William and Maria Antoinette, Jan. 5, 1815.
———, s. Robert, July 29, 1847, P.R.123.
———, d. J. Warren, May 13, 1848, P.R.123.

WHITIKER (see Whittaker), Hannah, [? twin] ch. Moses and Betey, Mar. 20, 1808.
James, [? twin] ch. Moses and Betey, Mar. 21, ——— [? 1808].
Lucindy, ch. Moses and Betey, Feb. 20, 1813.
Samuel, ch. Moses and Betey, June 24, 1805.

WHITING, George F., ch. John R. and Dolly W., Oct. 14, 1843.
Helen A., w. James R. Farnsworth, ———, 1850, G.R.1.
Isabella A., ch. John R. and Dolly W., May 19, 1845.
———, d. John R., Dec. 7, 1848, P.R.123.

WHITMORE (see Whittemore), Augusta Ann, ch. John and Hannah, July 21, 1838.
Francis, Feb. 18, 1823, G.R.1.
Francis W., ———, 1856, G.R.1.
Hannah [? m.], ———, 1796, G.R.1.
Hannah E., ch. John and Hannah, Aug. 13, 1828.
John, ———, 1800, G.R.1.
John E., ch. John and Hannah, Oct. 14, 1823.
Linville Francis, s. Francis W. and Mary Hannah (Stewart), June 17, 1890, P.R.60.
Lucy E., ch. John and Hannah, Jan. 28, 1831.
Mary G., ch. John and Hannah, July 29, 1833.
Rebecca Isabel, ch. John and Hannah, Jan. 11, 1836.
Sarah E., ch. John and Hannah, Feb. 23, 1826. [Sarah Ellen, w. John Nelson Stewart, P.R.60.]

WHITNEY, William, m., Mar. 16, 1819, G.R.1.

WHITTAKER (see Whitiker), Benjamin Brown, ch. David S. (Whitaker) and Elisabeth, Sept. 22, 1842.
Caroline Josephene (Whitaker), ch. David S. and Elisabeth, Aug. 6, 1840.
Mary Griffin, ch. David S. (Whitaker) and Elizabeth, Aug. 1, 1845.
———, d. John, Jan. 11, 1847, P.R.123.

WHITTEMORE (see Whitmore), Angelina, ch. Edmund and w., bp. Oct. 7, 1838, C.R.2.
George Washington, ch. Edmund and w., bp. Oct. 7, 1838, C.R.2.
James, ch. Edmund and w., bp. Oct. 7, 1838, C.R.2.
Nancy, ch. Edmund and w., bp. Oct. 7, 1838, C.R.2.

WHITTEN, Nathan, ———, 1828, G.R.13.

WHITTIER, Benja[min] Franklin, ch. Benja[min] Esq. and Ann, Jan. 9, 1812.
Charles Thomas, ch. Benja[min] Esq. and Ann, Dec. 24, 1821.
Eliza (see Eliza Pitcher).
Elizabeth Allice, ch. Benja[min] Esq. and Ann, Apr. 28, 1814.
Hannah Maria, ch. Daniel and Betsy, Jan. [dup. June] 8, 1821.
Joannah, ch. William F. and Mary C., Jan. —, 1840.
Joseph Hathaway, ch. Benja[min] Esq. and Ann, Mar. 16, 1820.
Julia Maria, ch. Benja[min] Esq. and Ann, Nov. 17, 1815.
Lois (see Lois Lothrop).
Lois Melissa, ch. William F. and Mary C., ——— [*rec. between ch. b.* Jan. —, 1833 *and ch. b.* Aug. 12, 1838].
Mary Elizabeth, ch. Daniel and Betsy, June 23, 1819.
Thomas Francis, ch. William F. and Mary C., Aug. 12, 1838.
William Wallace, ch. William F. and Mary C., Jan. —, 1833.

WIGGIN, George W., ch. Nathaniel and Sarah A., Feb. 22, 1837.
Juliette Augusta, ch. Nathaniel and Sarah A., Dec. 5, 1839.
Sarah Catharine, ch. Nathaniel and Sarah A., May 30, 1835.

WIGHT, Abigail, ch. Edward, June 27, 1799, P.R.2.
Abigail, ch. Capt. Samuel and Hannah, Aug. 15, 1831.
Ann, ch. Capt. Samuel and Hannah, Feb. 1, 1834.
Annie Burgess, ch. George E. and Lucy Ann, June 10, 1858.
Caroline, ch. Capt. Samuel and Hannah, Nov. 1, 1838.
Edward, h. Hannah, ———, 1776, G.R.13.
Edward, s. Edward, July 22, 1797, P.R.2.
Edward, ch. Capt. Samuel and Hannah, Nov. 1, 1836.
Edward N., ch. George E. and Lucy Ann, June 3, 1862.
Eliza Helen, ch. Nathan and Pamela, Aug. 15, 1840.
Eliza M. [———], w. Samuel, ———, 1833, G.R.13.
Elizabeth, ch. Capt. Samuel and Hannah, May 8, 1825.
Fred A., ———, 1850, G.R.13.
George Edward, ch. Joseph and Sarah, Nov. 26, 1827. [Nov. 24, G.R.1. h. Lucy A. (Nash), s. Joseph and Sarah (Burgess), Nov. 26, P.R.3.]
Hannah [———], w. Edward, ———, 1776, G.R.13.
Hannah, d. Edward, Jan. 1, 1805, P.R.2.
Hannah Matilda, ch. Nathan and Pamela, May 1, 1845.
Harriet E. (see Herriet E.).
Harriet Newhall, ch. Nathan and Pamela, Apr. 3, 1832.
Haskell [dup. Haskel], Nov. 3, 1807 [dup. 1809], G.R.13. [Haskil, s. Edward, Nov. 3, 1807, P.R.2.]
Herriet E., d. Joseph and Sarah (Burgess), Aug. 26, 1849, P.R.3.

WIGHT, Hezekiah, ch. Nathan and Pamela, Apr. 16, 1830.
James Haskall, ch. Joseph and Sarah [(Burgess) P.R.3.], Aug. 13, 1838.
James P., ch. John and Caroline (Paul), June 27, 1838. [June 28, G.R.1.]
Joanna (see Joanna Perkins).
John, h. Caroline (Paul), Aug. 25, 1809. [s. Edward, Aug. 26, P.R.2.]
John Warren, ch. Joseph and Sarah, Feb. 6, 1835. [h. Julia A. (Burgess), s. Joseph and Sarah (Burgess), P.R.3.]
Joseph, h. Sarah, Apr. 1, 1801, in Penobscot. [s. Edward, P.R.2. h. Sarah (Burgess), P.R.3.]
Joseph Franklin, ch. Joseph and Sarah, Oct. 24, 1832. [Joseph T., s. Joseph and Sarah (Burgess), P.R.3.]
Lucy, d. Edward, Nov. 2, 1814, P.R.2.
Lucy, ——, 1819, G.R.13. [d. Edward, Apr. 30, P.R.2.]
Lucy A., ch. John and Caroline (Paul), Aug. 19, 1836.
Lucy Ann, ch. Joseph and Sarah [(Burgess) P.R.3.], Sept. 24, 1830.
Lucy Ann [———], w. Geo[rge] E., Mar. 14, 1834, G.R.1.
Lunette [? m.], ——, 1858, G.R.13.
Mary E., ch. Capt. Samuel and Hannah, Oct. 1, 1841.
Matilda Miller (see Matilda M. Robbins).
Nathan, h. Pamelia O., July 14, 1795, G.R.13. [Nathen, s. Edward, P.R.2.]
Pamelia O. [———], w. Nathan, Mar. 11, 1805, G.R.13.
Ralph Holbrook, ——, 1867, G.R.1.
Samuel, h. Eliza M., ——, 1811, G.R.13. [s. Edward, Oct. 3, P.R.2.]
Samuel, ch. Capt. Samuel and Hannah, Mar. 25, 1827.
Sarah [———], w. Joseph, Nov. 24, 1804, in Penobscot. [Sarah (Burgess), P.R.3.]
Sarah Eleanor, ch. Joseph and Sarah, July 29, 1836. [w. ——— Durham, G.R.1. w. Frank H. Durham, d. Joseph and Sarah (Burgess), P.R.3. Sarah Ellen, w. Franklin H. Durham, P.R.4.]
Sarah Elizabeth, ch. Nathan and Pamela, Feb. 5, 1835. [Sarah L., Feb. 5, 1836, G.R.13.]
Sarah Ellen (see Sarah Eleanor).
Sarah Ellen, ch. George E. and Lucy Ann, Apr. 6, 1856.
William, ch. Capt. Samuel and Hannah, May 17, 1829.
William H., May 15, 1872, G.R.1.

WILDER, Albert L., ch. Cornelius and Susan, July 29, 1845.
Benjamin Lewis, s. John, bp. June 22, 1834, C.R.2.

WILDER, John Emery, ch. John W., bp. Nov. 2, 1828, C.R.2.
Jonas Brooks, ch. John W. and Betsey, July 4, 1827.
Jonas Brooks, ch. John W., bp. Nov. 2, 1828, C.R.2.
Joseph Warren, ch. John W., bp. Nov. 2, 1828, C.R.2.
Sarah Elizabeth, ch. John W. and Betsey [Betsey W., C.R.2.], July 21, 1830.
William Otis, ch. John W. and Betsey, Dec. 27, 1824.
William Otis, ch. John W., bp. Nov. 2, 1828, C.R.2.

WILEY, Elisha W., ch. Elisha and Pricilla, Jan. 9, 1835.
Ephriam H., ch. Elisha and Pricilla, Apr. 22, 1837.
Mercy Jane, ch. Elisha and Pricilla, Dec. 28, 1829.
Susanna A., ch. Elisha and Pricilla, Aug. 31, 1831.
William A., Sept. 26, 1863, G.R.1.

WILLIAMS, Hannah, w. Timo[th]y Thorndike, ———, 1824, G.R.1.
Harriet H., ch. John and Sally, Apr. 17, 1823.
John Parker, ch. John and Sally, July 19, 1817.
Mighill Parker, ch. John and Sally, Feb. 24, 1826.
Nelson, ch. John and Sally, Mar. 12, 1820.
Robie Frye, ch. John and Sally, June 8, 1829.
Sarah Maria, ch. John and Sally, Mar. 12, 1815, in Ilesboro[ugh].

WILLIAMSON, Ada Caroline, ch. Joseph and Ada H., Sept. 14, 1858.
Caroline, ch. Joseph and Caroline (Cross), ——— [rec. after ch. b. Apr. 13, 1836].
Frances, ch. Joseph and Ada H., Oct. 6, 1860.
George Ralph, ch. Joseph and Caroline (Cross), Apr. 13, 1836.
Joseph, ch. Joseph and Caroline (Cross), Oct. 5, 1828.
Joseph, ch. Joseph and Ada H., Feb. 14, 1869.
Mary, ch. Joseph and Caroline (Cross), Aug. 31, 1826.
William Cross, ch. Joseph and Caroline (Cross), Jan. 31, 1831.

WILSON, Allice, ch. Jonathan and Eleanor, Mar. 22, 1785.
Ann Maria (see Annie W. Ellis).
Caroline, ch. Jonathan and Eleanor, Sept. 6, 1804.
Caroline Augustine, ch. George U. and Sarah, Mar. 2, 1838.
Charles Austin, ch. George U. and Sarah, Apr. 3, 1843.
Charles F., ch. John Sheen and Nancy, Mar. 8, 1830.
Eliza Ann [———], w. John, Dec. 29, 1809, in Taunton, Mass., P.R.94.
Eliza Jane, ch. John Esq. and Hannah, Dec. 17, 1821.

WILSON, Elizabeth M., ch. Jonathan and Eleanor, Feb. 10, 1793.
Ellen D. [———], w. Everard A., Mar. 18, 1863, G.R.1.
Frank P., s. Jefferson F. and Lizzie F. (Davis), Oct. 3, 1878, P.R.93. P.R.110.
George Flowers, ch. Sarah Brown Wilson, wid., bp. Mar. 3, 1839, C.R.2.
George Franklin, ch. John Sheen and Nancy, Aug. 1, 1834.
George W., ch. Jonathan and Eleanor, June 24, 1802.
Hannah [———], w. Hon. John, Dec. 23, 1788, in Middleboro, Mass., G.R.1.
Hannah, ch. John Esq. and Hannah, Sept. 24, 1808.
Harriet Elizabeth, ch. George U. and Sarah, Nov. 7, 1839.
Hellen, ch. George U. and Sarah, Oct. 3, 1841.
Henry K., ch. Jonathan and Eleanor, Oct. 27, 1799.
Henry O., ch. William Faulkner and Sarah, May 17, 1843.
Ida Albertine, w. George D. Mahoney, d. James Albert and Hannah Augusta (Herrick), Nov. 15, 1859, P.R.95.
James Albert, ch. John Jr. and Eliza A., Apr. 14, 1833 [sic, see John Oscar]. [———, 1833, G.R.1. h. Hannah A., s. John and Eliza Ann, Apr. 14, 1833, P.R.94. h. Hannah Augusta (Herrick), Apr. 14, 1833, P.R.95.]
Jane, ch. Jonathan and Eleanor, June 9, 1788.
Jefferson Franklin, ch. John Jr. and Eliza A., July 26, 1839. [h. Lizzie F. (Davis), P.R.93. P.R.110. s. John and Eliza Ann, P.R.94.]
Jesse E., h. Edna B. Carscadden, s. Jefferson F. and Lizzie F. (Davis), Jan. 24, 1870, P.R.93.
Jessee Alden, ch. John Jr. and Eliza A., Apr. 2, 1843. [Jesse Alden Wilson, s. John and Eliza Ann, P.R.94.]
Joanna Amelia, ch. Sarah Brown Wilson, wid., bp. Mar. 3, 1839, C.R.2.
John, Hon., Apr. 23, 1777, in Peterboro, N. H., G.R.1.
John Jr., ch. John Esq. and Hannah, Mar. 17, 1810. [h. Eliza Ann, Mar. 7, P.R.94.]
John M., ch. Jonathan and Eleanor, May 29, 1797.
John Oscar, ch. John Jr. and Eliza A., May 9, 1833 [sic, see James Albert]. [s. John and Eliza Ann, May 9, 1835, P.R.94.]
John S. Jr., ch. John Sheen and Nancy, Sept. 22, 1833.
Jona[than] Dayton, ch. Jonathan and Eleanor, July 1, 1807.
Jones Everett, s. John and Eliza Ann, Dec. 5, 1846, P.R.94.
Joseph Biron, ch. John Jr. and Eliza A., Apr. 19, 1837. ["Co. K. 4th Me. Regt.," G.R.1. Joseph Byron Wilson, h. Austina G., s. John and Eliza Ann, P.R.94.]

WILSON, Joseph G., ch. John Sheen and Nancy, Nov. 18, 1839.
Joseph Henry, ch. John Esq. and Mary Frances (second w.), May 9, 1830.
Julius Augustus, ch. John Jr. and Eliza A. [Ann, P.R.95.], Aug. 20, 1841.
Justus Martin, ch. John Jr. and Eliza A. [Ann, P.R.94.], Oct. 10, 1844.
Lovisa E., ch. John Sheen and Nancy, July 6, 1831.
Lucy A., ch. William Faulkner and Sarah, May 4, 1845.
Mabel Lennie, w. Leslie P. Miller, d. James Albert and Hannah Augusta (Herrick), Aug. 25, 1867, P.R.95.
Mary, ch. John Esq. and Hannah, Jan. 4, 1812.
Mary Frances [———], w. Hon. John, Sept. 12, 1795, in Wiscassett, G.R.1.
Mary Rebecca, ch. George U. and Sarah, Feb. 15, 1846.
Nancy, ch. Jonathan and Eleanor, May 14, 1795.
Nathaniel, ch. Jonathan and Eleanor, Dec. 26, 1790.
Rubie J., ———, 1877, G.R.1. [Ruby Jennie, d. James Albert and Hannah Augusta (Herrick), Jan. 15, P.R.95.]
Sally, ch. John Esq. and Hannah, June 11, 1815.
Sarah C., ch. John Sheen and Nancy, Apr. 22, 1843.
Sarah Elizabeth, ch. John Jr. and Eliza A., June 19, 1831. [w. David L. Hatch, d. John and Eliza Ann, P.R.94.]
Sarah Jane, ch. George U. and Sarah, Aug. 15, 1835.
Susan Elizabeth, ch. Sarah Brown Wilson, wid., bp. Mar. 3, 1839, C.R.2.
William Henry, ch. John Sheen and Nancy, Oct. 2, 1837.

WING, Clarence J., ch. James E. and Lizzie A., July 8, 1880.

WINSLOW, Benjamin, ch. Peter and Sally, Sept. 24, 1809, in Vassalboro[ugh].
Elijah, ch. Peter and Sally, Apr. 16, 1823.
John Clark, ch. Peter and Sally, May 12, 1806, in Portland.
Lydia, ch. Peter and Sally, Mar. 12, 1819.
Martha, ch. Peter and Sally, Nov. 23, 1827.
Martin, ch. Peter and Sally, Oct. 22, 1825.
Peter Jr., ch. Peter and Sally, Apr. 5, 1821.
Phebe Pope, ch. Peter and Sally, Dec. 10, 1816.
Sally, ch. Peter and Sally, Oct. 20, 1811, in Vassalboro[ugh]. [Sarah, w. William Pitcher, G.R.1.]
Sarah [———], w. Peter, Jan. 8, 1785, G.R.1.
Urana F., ch. William and Ann, Feb. 3, 1845. [Urania F., Feb. 3, 1844, G.R.1.]

WINSLOW, William, ch. Peter and Sally, Dec. 11, 1807, in Portland. [h. Anna C. [(Smith)], G.R.I.]
William H., ch. William and Ann, Aug. 15, 1840.

WISE, Elizabeth [———], w. J. A., Apr. 24, 1841, G.R.I.
Freddie A., s. J. A. and E., May 1, 1866, G.R.I.
George W., ———, 1835, G.R.I.
Malvie, s. J. A. and L. P., Sept. 21, 1873, G.R.I.

WOOD (see Woods), Alonzo Isaac, ch. James and Deborah, Sept. 30, 1841.
Caroline A., ch. James and Deborah, Mar. 17, 1832.
Charles Albert, ch. Josiah and Susan, July 2, 1841.
Charles Albert, ch. Josiah and Susan, Feb. 13, 1844.
Deborah Jane, ch. James and Deborah, Dec. 24, 1827.
Edgar W., ch. J. W. and J. A., ———, 1860, G.R.13.
Elcy Jane, ch. Josiah and Susan, July 2, 1838.
Isaac, ch. Isaac and w., Sept. 4, 1841.
James M., ch. James and Deborah, Mar. 26, 1835.
Joanna A. [———], w. J. W., ———, 1835, G.R.13.
Joseph Mark, ch. Joseph Jr. and Lydia, Nov. 29, 1835.
Josiah, ch. James and Deborah, Feb. 26, 1844.
Julianna, ch. James and Deborah, May 15, 1839.
Keziah, ch. Isaac and w., Mar. 15, 1843.
Lavinia [———], w. John M., July 23, 1813, G.R.13.
Lewis H., ch. J. W. and J. A., ———, 1872, G.R.13.
Lydia Eleanor, ch. Joseph Jr. and Lydia, Dec. 7, 1831.
Mary S. [? m.], Oct. 9, 1836, G.R.I.
Rosina, ch. Josiah and Susan, Nov. 13, 1842.
Sarah Alvira, ch. Joseph Jr. and Lydia, Mar. 23, 1830.
Sarah E., ch. Isaac and w., May 4, 1839.
Wealthy Jane, ch. Joseph Jr. and Lydia, Aug. 8, 1825.
———, inf. J. W. and Joanna A., ———, 1857, G.R.13.
———, inf. J. W. and Joanna A., ———, 1862, G.R.13.
———, inf. J. W. and Joanna A., ———, 1866, G.R.13.
———, inf. J. W. and Joanna A., ———, 1867, G.R.13.
———, inf. J. W. and Joanna A., ———, 1868, G.R.13.

WOODCOCK, Daniel Faunce, s. Hartwell L. and Alice W. (Faunce), Apr. 30, 1885, P.R.147.
Lucy Anna [———], w. Marlboro P., Sept. 26, 1828, G.R.I.
Marlboro P., Sept. 11, 1823, G.R.I.

WOODS (see Wood), Edward W., h. Alice M. (Tripp), June 7, 1840, G.R.I.
Emily P., w. L. T. Shales, July 20, 1852, G.R.I. [d. William M. and Celia J. (Frye), P.R.151. w. Lendal T. Shales, P.R.152.]

WOODS, George W., ch. Edward W. and Alice M. (Tripp), Jan. 26, 1877, G.R.1.
Ida E., ch. Edward W. and Alice M. (Tripp), Sept. 10, 1867, G.R.1.
Mary J., w. Samuel G. Ellis, Aug. 15, 1833, G.R.1.
Sarah, w. Daniel A. McManus, Oct. 5, 1820, G.R.1.
William M., h. Celia J. (Frye), Nov. 9, 1821, G.R.1.   P.R.151.

WOOSTER, Lucy, ch. John and Fanny, Jan. 12, 1813.

WORTHAN (see Worthing), John S., ch. Isaac Newton and Mary, Dec. 5, 1843.
Pheobe J., ch. Isaac Newton and Mary, Sept. 16, 1837.
Thomas O., ch. Isaac Newton and Mary, July 30, 1841.
William A., ch. Isaac Newton and Mary, Jan. 25, 1834.

WORTHING (see Worthan), ———, d. Isaac N., Dec. 15, 1848, P.R.123.

WRIGHT, Edward Patterson, ch. Solomon and Sarah L., Jan. 1, 1830.
Sarah Louisa, ch. Solomon and Sarah L., Apr. 15, 1827, in Castine.
Sarah Louise, d. Solomon, bp. Apr. 3, 1831, C.R.2.

YATES, Jennie M., w. Merle H. Martin, June 22, 1880, G.R.1.

YORK, Ann, ch. Daniel, Mar. 6, 1802.
Fanny Eliza, ch. Archibald and Fanny, Dec. 9, 1814.
Harriot, ch. Daniel, Nov. 7, 1809.
Henery, ch. Daniel, May 16, 1813.
Maria, ch. Archibald and Fanny, Dec. 26, 1816.

YOUNG, Amanda M. [———], w. William L., ———, 1825, G.R.4.
Aurelia E., ch. Moses H. and Rosina, Sept. 20, 1828. [Sept. 20, 1830, G.R.1.]
Benjamin, ch. Benjamin and Dinah, Sept. 9, 1804.
Carrie J., ———, 1871, G.R.1.
Cha[rle]s W[illia]m, ch. Capt. James and Sarah J., Jan. 14, 1833.
Ellen F. [? m.], ———, 1848, G.R.1.
Elve Jane, ch. Amaziah and Charlotte, Mar. 29, 1851.
Emma N., ch. Capt. James and Sarah J., June 24, 1835.
Frances Sarah, ch. Benjamin Jr. and Ruth, June 22, 1844.
Franklin G., ch. Moses H. and Rosina, June 18, 1824. [June 18, 1825, G.R.1.]

YOUNG, Franklin G., May 4, 1871, G.R.1.
George A., ch. Moses H. and Rosina, Aug. 7, 1840.
George S., ch. Capt. James and Sarah J., June 5, 1841.
Hannah, ch. Benjamin and Dinah, Oct. 19, 1820.
Hellen P., ch. Capt. James and Sarah J., Feb. 4, 1843. [Helen P., w. Capt. N. B. Foss, G.R.1.]
Henry, ch. Benjamin and Dinah, Aug. 24, 1806.
James, ch. Benjamin and Dinah, May 14, 1799.
James H., ch. Capt. James and Sarah J., Aug. 27, 1829.
Jane S., ch. Capt. James and Sarah J., Jan. 31, 1828.
John B., ch. Capt. James and Sarah J., Sept. 9, 1838.
Joseph, ———, 1770, G.R.1.
Margaret, ch. Benjamin and Dinah, Mar. 8, 18[*illegible, rec. between ch. b. Dec. 5, 1809 and ch. b. Oct. 19, 1820*].
Margaret A. R., ch. Moses H. and Rosina, Aug. 21, 1830.
Mary Ann, ch. Benjamin and Dinah, Dec. 5, 1809.
Moses H. [h. Rosannah], Dec. 25, 1802, G.R.1.
Pheobe S., ch. Moses H. and Rosina, Nov. 19, 1826.
Rachel [? m.], ———, 1773, G.R.1.
Reuel S. (see Ruel S.).
Rosannah [————] [w. Moses H.], Mar. 13, 1804, G.R.1.
Ruel S., ch. Moses H. and Rosina, June 24, 1836.
Samuel, ch. Benjamin and Dinah, Aug. 17, 1811.
Seth William, ch. Benjamin Jr. and Ruth, Mar. 28, 1843.
William, ch. Benjamin and Dinah, Nov. 23, 1802.
William L., h. Amanda M., ———, 1821, G.R.4.

UNIDENTIFIED

———, ———, ch. ——— (Frenchman), Feb. 27, 1849, P.R.123.